Dr. Kleponis' groundbreaking bc ____ ___ loneliness, selfishness, and weakness in confidence from childhood and adult life that drive pornography use. This important book then offers an excellent, comprehensive treatment plan for recovery that includes Catholic spirituality. While twelve step programs can be helpful, they need to be completed by the deep understanding and wisdom offered in this book.

Rick Fitzgibbons, MD
Director of the Institute for Marital Healing

The pornography epidemic in America requires straight-forward well-researched analysis, as well as adherence to moral standards. Dr. Kleponis' work is the most comprehensive plan for victory. He doesn't ignore the problem of pornography with women or priests and seminarians. This is the most helpful attempt to understand the problem of pornography and then to take action against it.

Al Kresta
Host of "Kresta in the Afternoon" on Ave Maria Radio

The world says pornography is all about sexual freedom and pleasure. The widespread fallout, including among practicing Catholics, tells us something quite the opposite. Pornography at its core is all about bondage and misery. But there is an answer for those who struggle, and as Dr. Kleponis explains, it begins with a closer look at the teachings of Jesus and His Church. *Integrity Restored* is an important book with the potential to provide hope and healing for men, women, and families who are hurting because the plague of pornography has swept into their lives.

Teresa Tomeo
Motivational speaker, best-selling author,
syndicated Catholic talk show host

Dr. Kleponis has provided a comprehensive, practical response to those who struggle with pornography. As a seminary rector, this resource will help me and the faculty to assist our seminarians who themselves may struggle with pornography while also preparing them to minister to people of all ages who are affected by the problem of pornography.

Reverend James A. Wehner
Rector of Notre Dame Seminary in New Orleans

Finally, a resource for those caught in the trap of compulsive pornography use, and for those who love them. *Integrity Restored* by Dr. Peter Kleponis gives us a practical, psychologically and biblically sound approach to a disturbingly common problem. Avoiding the two extremes of moralizing and passive acceptance of the dangers of porn, Kleponis offers the golden mean: the hard work of recovery and the abundant grace God gives to those who stay in the fight. Highly recommended.

Patrick Coffin
National radio host and author of *Sex Au Naturel*

Few cover the scope of the pornography tsunami in this country like Dr. Kleponis does in this book. With both the academic understanding and practical application through his clinic, he has helped and continues to help scores of individuals and marriages. He communicates with both the clinical precision important to real recovery and with a Catholic compassion that together make him a true source of encouragement to the many victims of this cultural blight. I recommend his book to anyone looking to understand what all too many Catholics are dealing with in their lives.

Dan Spencer
Executive Director of the National Fellowship of Catholic Men

I strongly recommend that you read Dr. Kleponis' book if you or someone close to you is struggling with pornography addiction. Dr. Kleponis guides you through the necessary steps not only to bring you back on the ROAD TO RECOVERY, but also to instill in you a SENSE OF HOPE for a new life—freedom from addiction. Of course, with God's help.

Danny Abramowicz
National Catholic speaker and former NFL player and coach

Integrity Restored is the most comprehensive work I have read on one of the most pressing problems in the world—and in the Church—today. With wisdom and grace, Dr. Kleponis gives insight and real life answers to deal with today's elephant in the room. This book will help so many understand that there is healing available through Christ and His Church. A must-read for men and women, especially parents and members of the clergy.

Gus Lloyd
Host of "Seize the Day" on Sirius XM's
The Catholic Channel and author

The pornography addiction epidemic is tearing apart families and the lives of those afflicted in ever increasing numbers. In this book, Peter Kleponis, PhD, illustrates the reasons why he is one of our most knowledgeable and powerful Catholic voices, leading men and women past this affliction to the healing and mercy found only in the Cross.

Wendy Wiese
Host of "On Call" on Relevant Radio

This is a truly important book in the discussion of pornography addiction. It embeds this difficult topic within a full context so that every reader gains a common sense understanding of how pornography can lead to tragic consequences, even in the lives of good and ordinary people. At the same time, Dr. Kleponis masterfully explains why Catholics need to retrieve and safeguard the Church's foundational teachings on human sexuality and restore the value we have always placed on healthy relationships. Dr. Kleponis approaches his topic from a sound pastoral perspective which makes his book a "must" in the library of not only individuals looking for personal guidance in this area of behavior, but also for every Catholic leader responsible for the formative development of others. The things he writes about speak to our Catholicity but can be helpful to anyone that wants to know what can be done about pornography addiction. I applaud Dr. Kleponis for being gentle but unafraid about refuting an old notion that these matters are meant only for the Confessional. Expanding his conversation and openly addressing this topic again in a scholarly but pastoral way will be a blessing for so many Catholics in every walk of life. Dr. Kleponis' case studies that include practical recommendations for recovery and new life show us again that there is always hope when we face the truth and step into the light with faith in Christ.

Reverend Joseph M. Mele, PhD
Secretary for Leadership Development and Director for
Post-Ordination Formation in the Diocese of Pittsburgh

Finally! A book I can recommend wholeheartedly to all those affected by pornography. It is a comprehensive, clear, and compassionate guide towards restoring the integrity porn erodes. Thank you Peter Kleponis!

Matt Fradd
Author of *Delivered: True Stories of Men and*
Women who Turned from Porn to Purity

Integrity Restored: Helping Catholic Families Win the Battle Against Pornography is a fundamental resource for the New Evangelization. Pornography and the pornified culture are the greatest obstacles our Church faces when proclaiming the love of Christ to the modern world. Dr Kleponis' seven point plan provides clear framework for pastors, counselors, and lay people to find a path to a collaborative effort which can bring hope and healing to the countless members of the Church who suffer in silence due to sexual addiction in their own lives, in their families, and in their communities. His combination of clinical expertise and personal vignettes open the door for us to approach people who suffer from pornography addiction with the compassion and love of Christ. Pope Francis says that the Church is a "field hospital," and if that is the case, *Integrity Restored* is the fundamental field manual for bringing hope and healing to an over-sexualized culture.

Rev. Sean P. Kilcawley, STL
Director of Family Life and Evangelization, Diocese of Lincoln

If you want insight, understanding, and direction on how to deal with and overcome one of the most threatening challenges of our day, than *Integrity Restored* is an absolute must read. In a time when pornography has become a global epidemic, this is your best defense!

Drew Mariani
Award-winning journalist, writer, and
nationally syndicated talk show host

INTEGRITY RESTORED

HELPING CATHOLIC FAMILIES WIN
THE BATTLE AGAINST PORNOGRAPHY

INTEGRITY RESTORED

HELPING CATHOLIC FAMILIES WIN
THE BATTLE AGAINST PORNOGRAPHY

PETER C. KLEPONIS, PH.D.

EMMAUS
ROAD
PUBLISHING

Steubenville, Ohio
www.emmausroad.org

Emmaus Road Publishing
1468 Parkview Circle
Steubenville, Ohio 43952

Library of Congress Control Number: 2014946698
ISBN: 978-1-940329-91-8

Front cover design by Theodore Schluenderfritz
Layout and design by Theresa Westling

To Maria, Jack, and Matthew, who inspire
me to be the man God created me to be.

Table of Contents

Introduction

People often ask me, "Why write a book on pornography addiction for Catholics?" The answer is simple. "There's a great need for one!" Pornography addiction is an epidemic in America, and millions of men, women, and youth are becoming addicted. It's ruining individual lives, marriages, families, and careers, and more importantly, it's damaging peoples' relationships with God. No one is immune to this epidemic. Unfortunately, few people are talking about it.

Most people are unaware of the tragic impact that pornography is having on our culture. For example, Family Safe Media and Covenant Eyes report:

- Pornography plays a significant role in 56% of all divorces.
- The largest single population of Internet pornography users is teenagers between the ages of twelve and seventeen.
- It's reported that 20% of men admit to accessing pornography at work, and many are losing their jobs because of this.
- Most sexual predators began with an addiction to pornography.
- While pornography addiction is mainly a men's issue, it's growing among women.

In personal conversations, hundreds of priests have acknowledged that pornography use is one of the most common sins heard in Confession today. This epidemic can no longer be ignored. As Catholics, we need to take action. Fortunately, there are resources available to help protect families from pornography, and programs designed to help those trapped in pornography addiction find freedom.

Because of the tremendous amount of unhealthy shame associated with pornography addiction, few people seek treatment. Many are also afraid to seek help from our Lord because they believe their sins are so terrible that God could never forgive them. These people need to know how much God loves them and wants to heal them. The Catholic Church has many great resources for this, starting with the Sacrament of Reconciliation. The Church is a great source of love and compassion, and can help struggling men and women on the path of recovery.

In my first book, *The Pornography Epidemic: A Catholic Approach*, I presented a ninety-five-page overview of the pornography epidemic in America, its addictiveness, and how it affects men, women, marriages, families, teens, and children. I also presented an overview of my *Integrity Restored Recovery Program*, which has been highly effective in helping people recover from pornography addiction. The book was very popular, selling almost four thousand copies in one year, but there was much more to be said about pornography addiction and recovery. So I wrote this second, more comprehensive book addressing the pornography epidemic in more detail and providing more information on overcoming pornography addiction, protecting youth, and restoring marriages.

This book is divided into two parts. In Part One I discuss the pornography epidemic in America and present my current research findings, along with my professional experience. I portray the true scope of the epidemic, who it affects, and how widespread it is. I examine pornography's effect on men, women, marriages, children, teens, and clergy. I also explain the Church's teaching on pornography.

In Part Two I discuss how to help those struggling with pornography addiction and how to protect families from this scourge. I present the *Integrity Restored Recovery Program* first. In following chapters I offer road maps to healing for individuals, couples, and clergy, and show how the Church can help. I also encourage a model of healthy sexuality based on John Paul II's *The Theology of the Body* and *Love and Responsibility*. Finally, I provide practical strategies to protect families from pornography along with an extensive list of resources for individuals, couples, and families.

Throughout this book I present stories of real people, both men and women, who have struggled with and suffered from pornography and went on to find healing and freedom. Many are people I have worked with. Others are amalgamations of people. All illustrate the painful effects of pornography addiction, as well as the freedom and restoration that come with recovery. I hope these anecdotes inspire all my readers.

For those struggling with pornography addiction, I hope this book inspires you to seek help. There is no need to suffer in silence. There is hope for a life without pornography! For spouses, there is hope for healing and restoration of your marriage. For those who want to protect their families from pornography's reach, this book provides proven strategies and resources to keep the cancer away. Here is where an ounce of prevention is worth a pound of cure. For all readers of this book, I pray that God will bless you and inspire you to join the fight against pornography. With His help, we can fight porn in our culture and win!

God bless,
Peter C. Kleponis, PhD

INTEGRITY RESTORED

HELPING CATHOLIC FAMILIES WIN
THE BATTLE AGAINST PORNOGRAPHY

PART I
UNDERSTANDING THE PROBLEM OF PORNOGRAPHY

1

The Pornography Epidemic in America

Tom and Janet were both visibly distraught when they came into my office. I could easily see that Tom was filled with shame. He slumped in his chair and said little at first. He obviously did not want to be here. Janet was very angry. When I asked them why they came to me, Janet immediately said it was because of Tom's pornography use.

Tom and Janet had been married for fifteen years, had four children, and this wasn't the first time Janet had caught him viewing pornography. She found Tom viewing Internet pornography late at night on several other occasions. At first, he tried to dismiss it as pop-ups on the computer screen. Janet knew, deep down, that Tom was lying, but she wanted to give him the benefit of the doubt. She knew he was a good person who loved her and their children very much. But the pornography use continued. She even tried to justify it by telling herself, "All men do it," but this didn't alleviate the pain. Janet felt hurt and betrayed. For her, Tom's pornography use was no different than an extramarital affair. She finally had had enough and gave Tom an ultimatum: either he gets help to end his pornography use or she would leave him.

Tom knew his pornography use was a problem. He tried to stop many times, but kept going back. Sometimes the compulsion to use pornography was so great that he couldn't help himself. It was as if the pornography controlled him. His life was out of control. Tom was addicted.

Tom's pornography use began early in life. He and his friends found *Playboy* magazine at a local construction site when he was ten years old. They took the magazine and hid it in the woods. He and his friends would go into the woods to look at it frequently. Tom had not yet entered puberty, but he still found looking at the magazine exciting. Two years later, when he did enter puberty, the desire to look at pornography and to masturbate grew. When he was attending high school, he would frequently go to a friend's house and view pornography on cable television. During his college years, he was renting pornographic videos and DVDs from a local video rental store. Tom's use of pornography grew as the accessibility to pornography grew. His use of pornography and masturbation really escalated after he graduated from college and got his own apartment. Now, no one could stop him from viewing pornography. He began to go on binges and spend entire weekends viewing it. He also engaged in phone sex and went to strip clubs and massage parlors.

Tom was raised in a strong Catholic home and attended Catholic schools. His family attended Mass on Sundays. Tom knew that viewing pornography was wrong, but the compulsion to use it was too strong. He justified it by telling himself that it was "harmless adult entertainment." The fact that many of his friends also viewed pornography made it seem more acceptable.

Tom's pornography use decreased when he met Janet. He had little time to view it between his career and spending time with her, and he also did not want to bring it into his marriage. He wanted Janet to be the only woman in his life. However, soon after they were married, the Internet took off and Tom fell back into viewing pornography. The Internet made it too easy. Most of his pornography use was late at night after Janet and the kids were in bed. At first, he would occasionally spend a few minutes online viewing pornography, but eventually he ended up viewing it almost every night. He was back into his addiction. Tom admitted that on a deeper level he wanted to get caught. His life was spinning out of control. The pornography had taken over, and the guilt and shame he felt were unbearable. As difficult as it was to sit in my office and talk about his addiction, he was relieved to finally have it out in the open. Now he was ready for recovery.

Stories such as this are not uncommon to me. Pornography addiction is an epidemic in America, and sadly, few people are talking about it. This has left many to suffer in silence. Fortunately, there is hope. People can find freedom from pornography addiction. Lives can be redeemed and marriages restored, but we first have to start talking about it. To begin, we need to understand the impact of pornography on our culture and how serious the epidemic is.

It's no secret that we live in a pornified culture. Sexualized images abound. They're in movies, television, advertisements, magazines, catalogs, video games, popular music, literature, and on the Internet. The reason for this is simple: sex sells. The advertising world figured this out decades ago. Men immediately notice sexualized images. When a product is sexualized, it gets their attention. Just watch the television commercials during a football game and you will see that exploited.

Many people object to the pornification of our culture because it degrades women and corrupts the innocent minds of children. However, many don't realize how addictive pornography is and how it is ruining lives.

Defining Pornography

To be able to discuss pornography, we must first define it. This can be difficult since its definition can be different for everyone. Debates over the definition of pornography go back decades. In 1964, during the trial of *Jacobellis vs. Ohio*, Supreme Court Justice Potter Stewart was asked to define hardcore pornography. In a second concurring opinion, he wrote: "I shall not today attempt further to define the kinds of material I understand to be embraced within that shorthand description ["hardcore pornography"]; and perhaps I could never succeed in intelligibly doing so. But *I know it when I see it*, and the motion picture involved in this case is not that" (378 U.S. 184, 197, regarding possible obscenity in *Les Amants* [The Lovers], emphasis added).

Many people would agree that defining pornography is difficult, but they *know it when they see it*. The term "pornography" comes from

the Greek, *pornografia* (pornoi="fornicators"; graphia="pictures").
While there are many definitions of pornography, here I present two
working definitions: my clinical definition of pornography and the
definition presented by the Catechism of the Catholic Church. Both
definitions complement each other.

Clinical Definition of Pornography
- Pornography is any image that leads a person to use
  another person for his or her own sexual pleasure. It is
  devoid of love, intimacy, relationship or responsibility.
  It can be highly addictive. (Kleponis, 2008)

The key word in this definition is "use." Because of this, an image can
be pornographic and show no nudity at all. What matters is that the
individual is using the person in the image for his own sexual pleasure.
In *The Theology of the Body* and *Love and Responsibility* Pope St. John
Paul II wrote that the opposite of love is not hate, but "use." God never
created his children to use one another (Love and Responsibility Foundation, 2002).

Based on this definition, pornography does not simply consist of
naked images of people, or people engaging in sexual activity, it can
come in many forms: women at the beach, lingerie catalogs, beer commercials, etc.

Catechism of the Catholic Church Definition of Pornography
- Pornography consists of removing real or simulated
  sexual acts from the intimacy of the partners, in order
  to display them deliberately to third parties. It offends
  against chastity because it perverts the conjugal act, the
  intimate giving of spouses to each other. It does grave
  injury to the dignity of its participants, since each one
  becomes an object of base pleasure and illicit profit for
  others. It immerses all who are involved in the illusion
  of a fantasy world. It is a grave offense. Civil authorities

should prevent the production and distribution of pornographic materials. (2354)

This definition focuses more on the damage caused by pornography
for both the consumer and the producers. Pornography has taken sex
from a holy expression of love between a husband and wife that is open
to new life and turned it into a recreational activity where people are
selfishly used.

In both definitions we can see how pornography leads people to
"use" others. When a man views pornography, he is not thinking that
the woman he is looking at is a person with thoughts and feelings.
He's not thinking that she is somebody's daughter, or about the terrible
circumstances that may have led her into a career in pornography. All
he knows is that she is there for his pleasure and he is going to use her.
He is only thinking of himself. He is simply using her instead of loving her. There is an extreme selfishness in this. In addition, he neither
is thinking of how addictive pornography can be to men nor how he
could become enslaved to it.

Adding to the Church's definition of pornography and the damage
it causes, bishops have written pastoral letters on pornography.

Paraphrasing Pope St. John Paul II, Bishop Robert Finn (2007)
wrote: "The problem with pornography is not that it reveals too much
of the person (exposed in the image), but that it reveals too little of the
person. The person in the image is reduced to their sexual organs and
sexual faculties and is thereby de-personalized."

Bishop Loverde (2006) wrote: "This plague stalks the souls of men,
women and children, ravages the bonds of marriage and victimizes
the most innocent among us. It obscures and destroys people's ability
to see one another as unique and beautiful expressions of God's creation, instead darkening their vision, causing them to view others as
objects to be used and manipulated. Those who engage in such activity
deprive themselves of sanctifying grace and destroy the life of Christ in
their souls."

Pornography's Effects on Individuals

The effects of pornography on individuals are numerous. First, it promotes a deep selfishness, leading a person to turn inward and pursue only what is pleasurable. This can extend beyond sexual pursuits to life in general. The belief that happiness in life only comes from selfish pursuits rather than self-giving ultimately leads to a life of loneliness and despair, which can be seen in those who spend hours viewing pornography online. They often will give up invitations to spend time with family and friends, and even neglect important responsibilities in order to view pornography.

Pornography presents the illusion of intimacy. The women in pornography promise men true love and happiness, but this is a false promise. They are like the Sirens, beckoning men to come to them only to meet with disaster. After a long session of viewing pornography and masturbating, the man feels empty and full of guilt and shame. Unfortunately, like the Sirens, the false promises of pornography lead men back to it over and over again.

Regrettably, the pornography industry has led many women to believe that in order to attract and keep a man, they must look and act like porn stars. This often leads them to engage in sexual acts that are degrading, such as anal and group sex. Despite the advances of women over the past fifty years, pornography continues to degrade and reduce them to sex objects (APA, 2007).

For many young people, including children, pornography warps their view of relationships and sexuality. It sends the message that sex is meant for personal pleasure and not an expression of love between a husband and wife. Pornography also promotes the "sexual utilitarian philosophy," a notion that says it is okay to use another person for one's own sexual pleasure (Fitzgibbons, 2010). Pornography also introduces young people to many deviant and even dangerous sexual practices. Verbal degradation, bondage, and rape scenes are common in pornography, and many now accept those things as normal because they are presented over and over again.

This will be addressed in detail in chapter two, but here we must mention the addictiveness of pornography. We now know that pornography is an addictive substance and its effects on the brain are similar to drugs and alcohol. Because men are visually stimulated, they can easily turn to pornography to self-medicate deep emotional wounds. Pornography's effects on brain chemistry, along with its ability to ease emotional pain, are what make it highly addictive (Struthers, 2009).

Research on the Effects of Pornography

Over the past thirty years, significant research has been conducted in the field of sexual addiction; much of it has been done by Dr. Patrick Carnes. In his book *Don't Call it Love,* Dr. Carnes presents the results of a groundbreaking longitudinal study with over one thousand individuals suffering with sex addiction (Carnes, 1991), which included people addicted to pornography. However, only in the past decade have people begun to realize the devastating effects of pornography addiction and the scope of the problem in America.

Statistics from Family Safe Media, 2010
➡ 4.2 million pornographic websites
➡ 420 million pornographic web pages
➡ 68 million daily search engine requests (Google) for pornography
➡ 25% of all search engine requests
➡ 4.5 billion average daily pornographic emails
➡ 100,000 child porn websites worldwide
➡ Men admitting to accessing pornography at work: 20%
➡ Adults in the United States who regularly visit Internet pornography websites: 40 million
➡ Promise Keeper men who viewed pornography in one week: 53%
➡ Christians who claim pornography is a major problem in the home: 47%
➡ Adults admitting to Internet pornography addiction: 10%
➡ Breakdown of male/female visitors to pornographic websites: 72% male, 28% female
➡ Breakdown of male/female persons addicted to pornography: 83% male, 17% female

As sobering as these statistics are, they are probably gross underestimates of how serious the problem is. Porn sites get more visitors each month than Netflix, Amazon, and Twitter combined, and 30% of all data transferred across the Internet is porn (Huffington Post, 2013). The fact is that there is no way to accurately measure this epidemic. We do know it is an epidemic, however, by the sheer number of lives damaged by it.

The Five A's

Internet pornography has been called the new drug of choice because of the "Five A's" of pornography. These consist of five principles of Internet pornography that have led many men and women into addiction: It's Affordable, Accessible, Anonymous, Accepted, and Aggressive.

1. *It's Affordable*. While many addicted persons eventually spend large sums of money on porn, much of it is free. Thousands of websites provide pornographic images and videos without cost, often making pornography preferable over drugs and alcohol. By offering their products for free, pornographers get more people addicted so that they eventually will spend thousands of dollars on it.

2. *It's Accessible*. In the past, if a person wanted to view pornography they had to go out and look for it, which usually meant going to a sleazy porn shop or convenience store and hoping no one they knew would see them entering or leaving the establishment. With the advent of the Internet and portable electronic devices, such as cell phones and tablets, pornography is just a click away—like the old Visa Card slogan, "It's everywhere you want to be."

3. *It's Anonymous*. Unlike drugs or alcohol where a person can become visibly impaired and cause bodily harm, few can tell if a person has been using pornography. It can be done in the

privacy of one's own home without anyone knowing, making the addiction easy to hide. Others don't find out about it until a family member discovers it, or the addicted person has spent thousands of dollars on it, or loses their job because of it.

4. *It's Accepted.* Pornography has been accepted as a part of our culture, especially among young people who freely admit they view porn. They even joke about it. The mass media and pornography industry have been very successful in making pornography more acceptable by recasting it as "adult entertainment" instead of pornography. This has given men license to view it without fear, guilt, or shame, and has led to many addictions.

5. *It's Aggressive.* Internet pornography is often referred to as "the new crack cocaine" because of how aggressively it takes over a person's life. Some become addicted after only a few encounters. Traditionally, people start out with "gateway" drugs and then move onto harder drugs as the addiction sets in. For example, a person may start out smoking cigarettes, then move on to marijuana, then heroin, and finally crack cocaine. However, with Internet pornography there is no gateway drug. A person can log onto the Internet and immediately encounter the most extreme form of hardcore pornography, which can have the same highly addictive effect on the brain as crack cocaine.

While the pornography industry would have people believe they are simply producing "harmless adult entertainment," it's having devastating effects on people's lives. This drug harms both men and women.

Pornography's Effects on Marriages and Families

Nowhere is the harm of pornography seen more vividly than in marriages and families. While this will be covered more thoroughly in chapters five and six, a brief discussion is needed here to understand the scope of the problem in America.

Research shows that when a woman discovers her husband's pornography use, she feels angry, hurt, and betrayed. To her, it's as serious as an extramarital affair. The effects of pornography use can be seen in the infidelity it can bring to marriages. A 2004 study found that those who had affairs were over three times more likely to have used Internet pornography than those who did not have an affair. In addition, those who had used the services of prostitutes were almost four times more likely to have used Internet pornography than those who did not engage in paid sex (Stack et al., 2004). Pornography use leads men to place less value on sexual fidelity and more value on casual sex (Carroll et al., 2008). In fact, pornography use has led many young men not to want to make a commitment to marriage. They believe that happiness can only come through sexual encounters with multiple partners. Here is where we see the sexual utilitarian philosophy at work (Fitzgibbons, 2010).

The effects of pornography use can also be seen in divorces. According to a 2003 study by the American Academy of Matrimonial Lawyers (a.k.a. divorce lawyers), 56% of divorce cases involved one spouse with an obsessive interest in Internet pornography (Paul, 2004). A married person who has viewed a pornographic movie in the past year is 25.6% more likely to be divorced. They are also 65.1% more likely to have had an extramarital affair and 13.1% less likely to report being "very happy" with life in general (Doran & Price, 2009).

Some men turn to pornography because of marital problems. They may feel lonely or unappreciated by their wives, or they may be angry with cold, critical, and demanding wives. Some men will openly blame their wives for their pornography use. This damages the marriage further because it only intensifies the hurt, anger, and betrayal a wife feels.

The discovery of a man's pornography use can be very traumatizing for a wife. For years, she thought she knew her husband, and now she learns that he has a secret life. To her, he now seems like a total stranger. Her ability to trust him has been shattered. She loses all respect for him and no longer sees him as a good role model for their children. The healing of the marriage can take years. Forgiving her husband may come quickly, but rebuilding trust can take a long time.

It's not only wives who are hurt by pornography use. Women are also becoming addicted to pornography and this is injuring their husbands. Approximately 17% of persons addicted to pornography are women, and many are addicted to online chatting where they engage in erotic conversations with men. When this activity is discovered, their husbands can also feel angry, hurt, and betrayed (Family Safe Media, 2010).

The detrimental effects of pornography extend well beyond marriages. Children are also affected. First, there is the possible breakup of the family due to divorce, which can happen if the person struggling with pornography addiction refuses to get help. Even if the family stays together, children can suffer due to the loss of time spent with the addicted parent. These parents often forgo family activities to spend time online. There is also the risk of children discovering the addicted parent's "stash" of pornography. Kids are often more technologically savvy than their parents, so even the most well-hidden pornography can be found. This is very traumatic for small children. Imagine the psychological damage to a six-year-old girl logging onto the computer and discovering a video portraying a woman being raped by several men! The relationship between the addicted person and his teenage children can also be damaged due to his pornography use. A teenage boy who finds pornography on his father's computer may take that as a sign that it's okay for him to view pornography too, which in turn can lead him into pornography addiction. A teenage girl who discovers her father's pornography can lose all respect for him, and the man she had always admired and looked up to is now viewed as a common pervert.

The research is clear. Pornography use is tearing apart marriages and harming families. God has called men to be leaders, providers, and protectors of their marriages and families. By using pornography they give up their ability to fulfill those roles, because they become enslaved to a drug that only hurts the people they love the most.

Pornography's Influence on Sex and Relationships

The mass media and the pornography industry have changed the way Americans view relationships. Gone are the days when it was expected that single people would remain chaste until marriage. Gone are the days when one's virginity was considered a precious gift to be given to one's spouse. Many of these changes in sexual standards came from the mass media.

Over the past fifty years, the media has steadily pushed the envelope on what was considered morally objectionable. It has taken sex from the marriage bedroom and brought it into everyone's living room. Prime time sitcoms have gone from making veiled references to sex to making blatant comments about it. It is not uncommon for unmarried characters in television shows to be openly having sex with one another. Characters talk about using pornography without any sense of guilt or shame. Shows, such as *Two and a Half Men* and *How I Met Your Mother,* are notorious for this. This has had a tremendous effect on how Americans view sex and relationships.

The media has also changed the way Americans view pornography. Using pornography is no longer considered a shameful activity to be hidden from the public. In many circles, especially among young people, it is perfectly acceptable to use pornography. The mass media helped secure this acceptance by successfully changing the image of pornography, sanitizing it to appear less objectionable. Pornography is simply referred to as "adult entertainment," and it has changed the way people view sex and relationships.

Because of pornography's acceptance and its easy access on the Internet, it is difficult to find a young person who has never seen pornography. Good, credible information and statistics are provided by moralityinmedia.org, Maryland Coalition Against Pornography, and Family Safe Media.

Sobering statistics from Family Safe Media, 2007
➡ Average age of a child's first exposure to pornography: 11
➡ 15–17 year olds who have had multiple exposures to hardcore porn: 80%
➡ 8–16 year olds who have viewed porn online: 90%
➡ 7–17 year olds who would freely give out their home address online: 29%

➡ 7–17 year olds who would freely give out their email address online: 14%

➡ Solicitations of youth in chat rooms that are sexual: 89%

➡ Two thirds of college men go online weekly to search for pornography

➡ The largest single population of Internet pornography users: 12–17 year olds

For many young people today, especially men, sex and pornography are considered necessary for a relationship. I have spoken to many teens and young adults who believe that if a couple has not had sex by the third date, there must be something wrong with the relationship. A lot of Internet pornography portrays one woman being sexually used, often in violent or aggressive ways, by one or more men. This is the type of sex many men are now expecting in a relationship. It's a sad fact that many young women feel they have to degrade themselves sexually to maintain a relationship (Dines, 2010). Aggressive acts occur in 88.2% of top-rated porn scenes with the aggression directed towards the woman 94% of the time. Only 9.9% of the top-selling scenes analyzed contained behaviors such as kissing, laughing, caressing, or verbal compliments (Bridges et al., 2010).

Pornography's influence on our culture has made it unnecessary to have an intimate relationship with someone in order to have sex with that person. It's not uncommon for people to develop relationships specifically for the purpose of having sex, or "friends with benefits." This is most prevalent among college students. There are now several websites designed to help people find sex partners using a cell phone GPS system.

Pornography has affected how both young and older people view sex and relationships. Most of the women in pornography are very young and beautiful, but due to plastic surgery, makeup, and digital enhancements, these women don't exist in real life. Unfortunately, this is the type of women men expect to date. It has hampered their ability to appreciate the true beauty of real women, and has left average middle-aged women feeling ugly, inadequate, and undesirable. They feel there is no way they can compete with the women in porn.

The most disturbing effect of pornography on relationships is that it has led men to believe that women are there for them to control sexually for their own pleasure. Women, in turn, believe they must look and act like a porn star to get a man and keep him. Pornography has removed love and respect from relationships. This is no foundation for a healthy relationship.

In 2013, Medical Daily reported a "disturbing new survey" that revealed an overwhelming majority of relationship therapists questioned by *Cosmopolitan* magazine found that 90% of the therapists had seen a growing number of relationship problems caused by the use of porn. Some likened it to a "ticking time bomb in relationships" that is "destroying confidence in the bedroom for both men and women." According to *Cosmopolitan*, more and more men are suffering from performance anxiety because of the "impressive" performance of the porn stars, and women are feeling insecure about their own bodies and under pressure to "perform" like porn stars. With an increasing number of young people learning about sex through pornography, psychosexual therapist Karen Lobb-Rossini said it is having a "devastating effect on their perception of themselves and their bodies." *Cosmopolitan* editor Louise Court added, "While some experts have claimed porn can help some relationships, many experts now believe it can have a devastating effect by skewing what is expected in the bedroom" (Medical Daily, 2013).

Pornography's Effects on Business and Careers

For over a decade, inappropriate use of the Internet in the workplace has been a problem. The result is billions of lost revenue due to decreased productivity. Vault.com estimates surfing costs companies $54 billion annually in lost productivity. For example, in the summer of 2000, Victoria's Secret posted a forty-four minute, daily weekday webcast. It had an estimated audience of two million viewers, costing employers as much as $120 million (Adschiew, 2000).

Time.com cited a survey of two hundred U.S.-based data security analysts from Threat Track Security that reveals 40% of them removed malware from a senior manager's computer or mobile device after the executive visited a porn site (Winograd, 2013).

Sex Tracker posted that 70% of all Internet porn traffic occurs during workdays from 9 a.m.–5 p.m. (2012). The Huffington Post reported that 66% of human resource professionals have found porn on employees' work computers (2013).

The Washington Times published an article in 2009 about the National Science Foundation (NSF) agency inspector having to place a great deal of his time into investigating government employees using government computers to view porn, rather than investigating grant fraud. Overall, the investigative recoveries exceeded $2 million for the year (Washington Times, 2009).

In a survey of 224 corporations by Websense, Inc., an electronic monitoring firm, 64% of the companies surveyed have disciplined and more than 30% have terminated employees for inappropriate use of the Internet. Specifically, 42% of disciplinary actions or terminations were due to accessing Internet pornography at work (Websense, 2000).

Today, many companies are monitoring their computers and have strict policies for Internet use at work. For example, The Vanguard Group of Investment Companies uses a "two strikes and you're out" policy. Employees receive a warning after their first offense and are fired after the second.

Xerox terminated forty employees for surfing pornographic and shopping websites at work (AP, 2000). Dow Chemical Company fired fifty employees and suspended another two hundred, some up to four weeks, without pay for accessing hardcore pornography and violent subject matter at work (Collins, 2000).

The cost to employers comes from lost productivity and the time and resources needed to hire and train new employees to replace those terminated. This can add up to millions of dollars.

Pornography also has indirect effects on employers. Pornography is known to play a significant role in over half of all divorces. In the year following a divorce, employees lose an average of forty-two days of work time. In addition, the high marital distress before or during a divorce can cause an employee to lose more than thirty-eight workdays. Thus, pornography use at home causes high marital stress, divorce, and can cost an employer up to eighty days of lost employee productivity (Mark, 2007).

Even if an employee never accesses pornography at work, having an addiction to it can affect his work. Many addicted persons have reported that without regular "fixes," they have difficulty functioning due to the withdrawal symptoms they experience. These can include depression, anxiety, difficulty with concentration, fatigue, and headaches. This problem is known as "presenteeism." The employee is present at work but unable to focus and give their best effort (Mark, 2007). The Harvard Business Review estimates that presenteeism costs American businesses $150 billion per year (Dixon, 2005).

The cost to employees is obvious. They can be fired or suspended without pay, which can be financially devastating for a person who is married with children and has a mortgage. Finding a new job may be difficult, especially for older people or minorities who often experience discrimination in the workplace. There is also the guilt and shame associated with being fired for pornography use, and in some instances the knowledge of a person's online activity at work has been made public. In September 2011 the Avalanche-Journal of Lubbock, Texas, published the names of six city officials who faced allegations of viewing pornography on city computers. All had been fired from their jobs (Pyle, 2011).

Companies are closely monitoring their computers and making it easier to identify crimes. If criminal activity is suspected, such as viewing child porn, the FBI and other law enforcement agencies can be called to investigate. The computer files of the accused employee are thoroughly searched, and if there is any question as to whether certain pornography could be classified as child porn, the Center for Exploited and Missing Children can also be called in to help. Ultimately, any discovery of child porn can lead to legal prosecution and being permanently listed as a sex offender.

Pornography addiction affects future careers. It is estimated that 64% of college men go online for sexual content at least once a week. This is also true for 18% of college women (Covenant Eyes, 2011). This is leading to addictions and lower grades. Some students fail out of college because of the hours spent online viewing porn, often causing them to miss classes and neglect homework. The easy access to sex partners on college campuses can also feed the addiction. Students end up spending a great amount of time pursuing pornography and sex.

Despite how seriously problematic pornography addiction is in the workplace, companies offer little help or protection for those addicted. If a person is an alcoholic and is willing to get help, a company cannot fire that employee because alcoholism is a recognized psychiatric disorder. Alcoholics are protected under the Americans with Disabilities Act. However, pornography addiction is still not recognized as a valid psychiatric disorder, and as a result there are no legal protections for persons addicted to pornography who are willing to get help. They can easily be fired from their jobs without recourse.

Big Money

It's well known that the pornography industry brings in high profits. Back in 2007, the industry was earning over $97 billion each year, of which over $13 billion came from the United States.

Family Safe Media, 2007

➡ Every second $3,075.64 is being spent on pornography.

➡ Pornography revenues exceed that of the top technology companies combined: Microsoft, Google, Amazon, eBay, Yahoo, Netflix and Apple.

➡ Pornography revenues exceed that of the three major television networks combined: ABC, NBC and CBS.

➡ Child pornography generates $3 billion each year.

Here is the breakdown of the $13 billion in pornography revenues in the U.S. for 2007:

- Adult Videos .... $3.62 bil
- Internet... $2.84 bil
- Cable TV/Pay-Per-View/ Phone Sex..................... $2.19 bil
- Strip Clubs... $2.00 bil
- Novelties .... $1.73 bil
- Magazines .... $.95 bil

Total .... $13.33 bil

There is no way to accurately measure just how much is spent on pornography today. We saw a peak in porn revenues in 2007 that dropped in subsequent years due to the increasing amounts of free porn available, but today it still remains a multibillion-dollar industry in the U.S. alone.

Because so much Internet pornography is free, one may wonder how this is possible. A person can spend hours online viewing porn and never spend a cent. As one of the Five A's of Internet pornography, I had mentioned that this makes pornography so "affordable." However, this has not prevented the pornography industry from amassing billions of dollars in profits, primarily due to two of the other Five A's of pornography: it's accessible and accepted.

Now that pornography is so accessible and accepted by many in our society, it is being used as a regular form of entertainment and is the reason many men have become fans of specific porn stars. They not only watch videos of their favorite porn stars online, but they also purchase their DVDs and magazines. Some men will travel hundreds of miles to attend porn conventions where they can meet their favorite porn stars in person (Dines, 2010). The accessibility and acceptance of pornography has also brought sex toys into the mainstream.

Much of the free pornography online is used to lure men into subscribing to websites where they eventually do pay for it. Here is where the pornographers really make a lot of money. The process is very simple. When a man logs onto a pornographic website, he is given a few free pages to view. These "teasers" offer some free pornographic images or a few free minutes of video. Their purpose is to entice the man to see more, and after viewing these pages the man is asked for credit card information to subscribe to the website, giving him full access to all the pornography on it. Although the monthly subscription fee can be fairly low, it can add up to huge revenues for pornographers. For example, if a pornographer charges $4.95 per month for a subscription and 50,000 people subscribe, that equals $247,500 per month or $2,970,000 per year. That amount can be multiplied if the pornographer operates several websites. These are not small websites operated out of someone's garage. They are operated by major media companies.

Pornographers know their product is addictive and their goal is to get as many men addicted as possible. A man who is addicted to pornography can spend thousands of dollars on it (Struthers, 2009), leaving him in financial straits. Married men have spent their mortgage money on pornography. College students have spent their tuition money on it.

For some, the addiction gets to the point where viewing pornography online is no longer stimulating. They want to experience it live. This can lead to frequenting strip clubs, massage parlors, and prostitutes where they spend even more money. Dr. Mark Laaser has worked with celebrities who are struggling with pornography addiction and who have spent millions on pornography and sex (Laaser, 2004).

To justify their work, many pornographers will claim that they are simply exercising their right to free speech or that they are creating "art." Some will assert they are providing a valuable service to society by making the claim that pornography can prevent rape; however, there are no studies that definitively prove that pornography use prevents rape or any other sexual crime The pornography industry is a business and its main goal it to turn as big a profit as possible. They are doing this on the backs of addicted people.

How We Got Here

Looking at how saturated our culture is with pornography, one may ask, How did we get here? America is traditionally a Christian country guided by Judeo-Christian values. If a woman showed as much as an ankle or a bare elbow one hundred years ago, she was considered scandalous. Being a person of virtue and strong moral character was highly valued. This all changed in less than seventy-five years. So what happened?

If we look at each decade since the 1940s, we can see how our cultural values have eroded and we were lulled into accepting pornography.

- **The 1940s:** "Pinup girls" became popular during this decade. These were pictures of girls, usually on calendars, dressed in bathing suits or bikinis. During World War II, service men would fold up these pictures, put them in their pockets, and take them onto the battlefields to encourage them to win the war. Whether this helped win the war is questionable; however, this did change the way Americans viewed women. The bathing suits and bikinis the pinup girls wore were very modest by today's standards, but it was the first time that we Americans became accustomed to seeing women who were not fully clothed. And we accepted it.

- **The 1950s:** Hugh Hefner first published *Playboy* magazine during this decade. He knew if he marketed *Playboy* as pornography it would never be accepted, so he marketed it as a men's lifestyle magazine. He hired some of the best journalists in the country to contribute articles on business, politics, sports, entertainment, and style. The magazine also happened to have photos of nude women. Because of the way Hefner marketed his magazine, we Americans accepted it. This opened the door to acceptance of other pornographic magazines that were much more graphic, such as *Penthouse* and *Hustler*.

- **The 1960s:** This was the decade of the sexual revolution and oral contraceptives, which together made sex available to everyone. No longer did two people need to be married to have sex. Having sex at any time and with anyone became a personal right. Instead of being an expression of love open to new life between a husband and wife, sex was reduced to nothing more than a recreational activity. Pornography promoted this activity and we accepted it.

- **The 1970s**: While the sexual revolution continued, this decade brought us cable television that piped pornography into people's homes. Though it would be considered soft porn by today's standards and shown late at night, we came to accept sexual content on television. Even the standards of prime time television began to change. It seemed like the network censors just gave up and went home.

- **The 1980s**: This decade is where pornography addiction began to take off. Many Americans purchased videocassette recorders (VCRs) for their homes. To meet the need for movies, video rental stores opened in most towns, and in the back of most of these stores was the "adult room" where one could find hardcore pornographic videos for rent. It was as if the sleazy porn shop from the seedy part of town moved into everyone's community. Although local obscenity laws kept minors from entering these rooms or renting pornographic videos, we accepted having such materials readily available in our communities.

- **The 1990s**: During this decade, pornography use became more widespread as videocassettes gave way to DVDs. Phone sex became popular and the Internet was invented. Pornographers realized how powerful this medium could be in selling their products, and they used it well. Now, a person could view pornography any time of day or night, and the types of pornography were unlimited. Any sexual fetish could be satisfied. Pornography profits skyrocketed and more men became addicted.

- **The 2000s**: As the Internet grew, more forms of pornography became available, including chat rooms, video chats, prostitution websites, and sex hookup websites. Strip clubs and pole dancing rose in popularity. The proliferation of pornography by this point resulted in the acceptance of most forms of sexuality, and with the exception of pedophilia, no form of sex was considered deviant or taboo. This has resulted in people engaging in extremely dangerous forms of sex.

- **The 2010s**: Today, there are few boundaries with pornography and sex. Love, commitment, relationship, and responsibility are no longer requirements. Sex is viewed as a personal right. Anyone who disagrees with an individual's sex life is labeled "judgmental" and "close-minded." There is no morality in sex anymore.

There's an old axiom that states, "If you put a frog in a pot of boiling water, it will jump out. If you put a frog in a pot of cold water and slowly turn up the heat, it will boil to death without even knowing it." We are like the frog that is boiling to death. Over the past seventy years, we have seen our country's moral values slowly erode away as the pornographers have taken over our media and our culture.

Women in Porn: The Real Victims

We couldn't have a discussion about pornography without talking about the women in porn. The pornography industry portrays these women as young, modern, liberated women who have made the conscious choice to be in that industry. In interviews and at porn conventions they are bright, bubbly, and appear to love their work. However, this image couldn't be farther from the truth.

First, one must ask, "What kind of woman would choose to be in the pornography industry?" and second, "What kind of a woman would allow herself be used and abused by men?" The answer is: a deeply wounded one. I don't know of any healthy young women who would say she wants to grow up to be a porn star. It's not uncommon for women in pornography to come from families plagued by abuse, addiction, rejection, abandonment, and neglect. Many porn stars themselves are runaways, alcoholics, and/or drug addicts (Dines,

2010). These women are desperate and pornographers prey on them. At first, they agree to go into porn for survival. It's the only thing that keeps them from being homeless. However, they are soon trapped in an industry that simply uses them and they become commodities that are simply thrown away when the pornographers are done with them.

Because of the abuse, addiction, rejection, abandonment, and neglect female porn stars experienced in their families, many suffer from trauma. They enter the pornography industry as a way of dealing with their own trauma. We will examine those trauma reactions in chapter four.

We should also mention the common misperception that women in pornography love men. In their videos they beg for sex and can't get enough of it, when in reality the opposite is true. Many of the women in pornography despise men and most of the abuse these women have suffered was at the hands of men. They have learned that men are abusive and can never be trusted (Dines, 2010).

To understand how women are sexually abused in porn, all one has to do is view it objectively. Pornography does not portray the gentle loving sex that occurs between a husband and wife. Much of the pornography offered today portrays a woman being sexually abused by one or more men. Women in porn are forced to engage in sexual acts that are degrading and physically dangerous: rape scenes, verbal degradation, group sex, bondage, and so on.

One clear piece of evidence that the pornography industry harms the women in it is their life expectancy. In one study, the deaths of 129 porn stars over a 20-year period were analyzed. It was found that the overwhelming majority died premature deaths due to drugs, suicide, murder, alcohol abuse, accidental death, and disease. The average life expectancy of a porn star is only 37.43 years (Jennings, 2013).

It's amazing how many men who view pornography regularly say they love women. Is this the way they show it? In her book *Pornland: How Porn Has Hijacked Our Sexuality* (2010), Gale Dines appropriately states that the men in porn don't make love to women, they make hate. It's obvious the women in porn are victims and the men who use porn support an industry that truly hurts women.

Hope for the Future

Pornography use and addiction is an epidemic in America. Millions of men are being drawn into it, damaging their marriages, families, and careers. Ultimately, it consumes a man's life. So what hope is there for our culture? Plenty, but we need to understand a few things about pornography.

First, pornography is not going away, and because of our First Amendment right to freedom of speech, it is unlikely to be outlawed. Legally speaking, pornographers have the right to publish their material. While we may not approve of the material they produce, and as wonderful as it might seem to ban pornography as morally objectionable material, we have to remember that "objectionable" is a relative term in today's society. Some people consider the Bible objectionable, and we wouldn't want them to ban it. As much as we might abhor pornography, the path to victory will not likely be through the courts. Rather, we must change hearts and minds to expose pornography for the destructive force that it is.

While we can't outlaw pornography, we can make every attempt to limit its access in society with obscenity laws. These laws help ensure that children and families are not constantly bombarded with pornographic images, especially by the mass media. Just as we have laws against child pornography, laws can also be passed to prevent the production of violent pornography that degrades and abuses women. MoralityinMedia.org is currently working hard to achieve this.

Parents need to protect young children from pornography. This requires parental vigilance in monitoring the media to ensure that their children never encounter it. Parents and teachers need to educate teenagers on the dangers of pornography, and teach them that pornography is an addictive substance similar to drugs and alcohol. They also need to educate teens about healthy relationships and sexuality so the teens can recognize false and harmful information they receive online about sex and relationships.

Internet accountability is a necessity. It deters those who might be curious about Internet pornography and keeps out pornographers who use every opportunity to sneak into people's lives. Fortunately, software such as CovenantEyes.com is now available to help families and individuals avoid pornography use.

Help is available for those struggling with pornography addiction. Effective recovery programs can help individuals break free from pornography use. This book offers the Integrity Restored Recovery Program, which has been found to be highly effective in helping those who struggle with addiction to break free.

Most people struggling with pornography addiction also struggle with deep shame, and they need to know that God and the Church love them and want to help them find freedom. The Church should be able to refer struggling individuals to the proper resources for recovery. We can never give up on those who want help. God never does.

People often ask me, "How long will it take before our society changes its view of pornography?" My answer is, "About fifty years." I say this because I compare pornography use to tobacco use. Fifty years ago, doctors knew that tobacco was a killer. They knew that smoking caused lung cancer, heart disease, emphysema, bronchitis, and death. However, no one could say anything negative about tobacco. It was politically incorrect. Smoking was a personal right. People were smoking in restaurants, airplanes, and office buildings. Lucy and Ricky, and many other actresses, and actors were smoking on television. Smoking was portrayed as sexy and sophisticated. Tobacco producers claimed that tobacco was harmless, similar to what pornographers are saying today about their products. It took over fifty years of intensive education and millions of people dying before our society got the message that tobacco was harmful. Now, almost every place you go is smoke-free. Most young people today wouldn't even consider smoking. They know the dangers. I believe the same effort is necessary with pornography. We all must work hard to educate consumers about the dangers of pornography. People need to see how it ruins lives so that they can make the conscious choice to avoid pornography at all costs. The purpose of this book is to help begin this process.

In the following chapters you will learn more about the dangers of pornography and how it affects individuals, marriages, families, and careers. You will discover the addictiveness of pornography and how it ensnares the lives of good people. You will also understand the recovery process through the Integrity Restored Recovery Program and how Catholic spirituality plays a crucial role in it. God's plan for healthy sexuality will be presented in Pope St. John Paul II's *The Theology of the Body* and *Love and Responsibility*. Finally, you will learn how to protect yourself and your loved ones from the new drug of choice: pornography.

2

The Addictiveness of Pornography

Phil first came into my office appearing very sad and depressed. He could barely look me in the eye. When I asked him what was wrong, he could scarcely whisper that he had a problem with pornography and masturbation. He had been struggling with this problem for years and had often made the commitment to stop, but the longest he could go without viewing porn was two weeks. Phil was thirty-five years old and single. He eventually wanted to marry and have a family, but believed that no woman could ever love him. He viewed himself as a "sick pervert." Certainly he felt that God could never love him, which is a common belief of many who are addicted to pornography.

Phil's first encounter with pornography occurred when he was nine. He found one of his older brother's *Playboy* magazines and felt both shocked and excited by what he saw. During his middle school years, he would often sneak into his brother's room to look at the magazines. While in high school, Phil would occasionally go to a friend's house on Friday nights to watch porn. His friend's father had a large collection of pornographic videos. The Internet was taking off when Phil entered college, and suddenly every kind of porn imaginable was at his fingertips and he loved every minute of it!

Phil had been raised in a devoutly Catholic family. He knew that viewing pornography was wrong, but it seemed like most of the men in college were viewing it. It was accepted as harmless adult entertainment, which enabled Phil to justify his selfish behavior.

At first, Phil would go online and view pornography once a week for about twenty minutes. Soon it increased to over an hour a day, and the type of pornography Phil viewed also changed. He found himself searching for more deviant forms of pornography, including bondage, lesbians, and even bestiality. It sometimes shocked Phil to see the kinds of porn he was viewing, but he kept going back. On a few occasions he stayed up so late viewing porn that he slept through his classes the next morning. This had a detrimental effect on his grades.

The pornography use continued after college. Living on his own, Phil could view as much pornography as he wanted, and his typical routine was to come home from work, have a quick dinner, and spend several hours online viewing pornography. Phil continued to justify using it, despite knowing it was wrong, by telling himself "all men view porn" and "it's just harmless adult entertainment."

His pornography use progressed and Phil became dependent on it. He couldn't go a few days without a "fix." He would become irritable and have difficulty concentrating at work if he didn't view it and masturbate. Sometimes he would even struggle with insomnia if he didn't get a fix. Phil was addicted.

The final wakeup call for Phil was losing his job. He knew his company was monitoring their computer system and had a zero-tolerance policy for viewing pornography, but the compulsion to use pornography had become so great that Phil was willing to take great risks to view it. One day, he decided to go online at work to view pornography for "just a few minutes," but ended up viewing it for over an hour. The next day he was called into his supervisor's office and immediately fired. This action convinced Phil that he needed help.

Understanding the Addiction

It is widely accepted today that sex and pornography can be addictive, but this acceptance was hard won. When researchers like Dr. Patrick Carnes first began studying sexual addiction thirty years ago, few believed them. Many medical and mental health professionals found it difficult to understand how a natural desire, like sex, could be addictive. They envisioned addiction as introducing a foreign chemical into the body, such as drugs or alcohol, and then becoming dependent on it. They could not see sex and pornography as addictive substances because those are not foreign chemicals. People struggling with pornography addiction knew better. They knew what it was like to crave pornography and take incredible risks to get a "fix." They knew how it could take over and ruin one's life. Through Dr. Carnes groundbreaking longitudinal study of over one thousand recovering addicts, he has shown that sex and pornography are addictive substances (Carnes, 1991, 2001, 2007).

Other noted researchers have continued to increase our knowledge of sexual addiction, and we now know, through new research in the field of brain chemistry, that pornography affects the brain just like many other drugs. In comparing brain scans of sex addicts with cocaine addicts, similarities can be seen in brain activity and impairment. Like cocaine, pornography affects the prefrontal cortex of the brain, overstimulating the pleasure center while impairing the impulse control center. Thus, pornography addiction is no different than drug addiction (Struthers, 2009; Hilton & Watts, 2011). Similarly, when comparing porn addiction to alcohol addiction, a 2013 Cambridge University study looked at nineteen compulsive pornography users' brain activity. Their brains' reward center had the same reaction when viewing pornography as an alcoholic's brain when seeing advertisements for alcohol (The Independent, 2013).

Dr. Mark Laaser (2009) lists eight characteristics of sexual addiction that can also be applied to pornography addiction.

1. *It is Unmanageable.* In 12-step groups such as Alcoholics Anonymous, the first step to recovery is admitting one has a problem and that one is powerless over it—that the addicted person's life has become unmanageable. They will confess that they feel like their addiction has taken over their minds, bodies, and free will. When they feel the "itch to use," they believe they cannot help themselves but to "scratch the itch." This leads to a life

that is out of control and unmanageable, and is also symptomatic of a lack of trust in God. Whether they realize it or not, addicted persons struggle to place their trust in God, especially when times are tough. They choose to self-medicate instead of turning to God for help. This constant self-medicating leads to the addiction and a life that is totally out of control, a life that is unmanageable. As pornography takes over their life, they will neglect family, friends, school, career, and other important responsibilities. Their whole life becomes a constant search for pornography and sexual gratification (Paul, 2010).

2. *It Creates a Neurochemical Tolerance.* Viewing pornography triggers the release of large amounts of dopamine in the brain. This produces a high feeling that is intensified with an orgasm. This dopamine high is also experienced when using drugs such as cocaine or heroin. As with any other drug, a tolerance soon develops. More is needed to get the same effect. Thus, a man will spend increasing amounts of time online viewing pornography, and the type of pornography will necessarily become more extreme.

3. *It is Degenerative and Progressive.* Over time the addiction gets worse. As tolerance and dependence grow, the need for pornography grows. Instead of viewing soft porn, such as the *Sports Illustrated* Swim Suit Issue or the Victoria's Secret Catalog, the man now needs to view more deviant, hardcore pornography that is often violent and sometimes illegal. Instead of spending a few minutes once a week viewing pornography, he might now be viewing it for several hours every day. Eventually, the pursuit and use of pornography consumes the man's life. More will be stated about tolerance and dependence below.

4. *It has Negative, Destructive Consequences.* The physical, emotional, spiritual, and financial consequences of pornography addiction can be extensive. Physical consequences can include loss of sleep, stress, fatigue, and genital injury if the man engages in sexual acts that are sadomasochistic. If the addiction has

gotten to the point where he is acting out with other people, he runs the risk of contracting a sexually transmitted disease or creating an unplanned pregnancy. The emotional consequences of pornography addiction include isolation, loneliness, fear, guilt, shame, anger, depression, anxiety, and low self-esteem. Many addicted persons experience the loss of family, friends, and careers. The financial consequences can amass huge amounts of debt from all the pornography they have purchased, but the most dangerous consequence of pornography addiction is the loss of one's relationship with God. As we've seen, most pornography users know they are doing something wrong and harmful to their relationship with God, yet they choose to use it anyway. This can lead to a deeper loneliness that even pornography cannot ease.

5. *It is Used to Escape Negative Feelings.* Here is where we most often use the term "self-medicating." Those struggling with pornography addiction often use pornography as a coping strategy to deal with deep emotional pain they don't even realize is there. All they know is that pornography makes them feel really good and that they must go back to it over and over again. The fact that they cannot feel good without pornography is an indication that there is a deep wound for which they are using pornography to anesthetize.

6. *It is Justified by the Concept of "Entitlement."* Many men who use pornography do so out of a sense of entitlement. This often stems from narcissism or anger, as more and more people are focusing on their own wants and needs with little regard to how their actions affect others. Thus, a man who had a rough day at work might come home and feel entitled to view porn as a way to relax, despite how it may hurt his wife. Anger with his wife, boss, friends, or God can move an addicted person to feel entitled to use pornography as a way to "cool off."

7. *It is Used as a Reward.* Persons addicted to pornography often justify their pornography use by viewing it as a reward.

Whether they have been working hard in their career or around the house, they justify their pornography use as a reward for "a job well done."

8. *It Provides a Feeling of Power.* Like all addicted persons, pornography addicts feel they have little control in life, and their deep need to be heard, loved, affirmed, and blessed are not being met. This results in a feeling of powerlessness. Using pornography and (more specifically) the people in porn, gives them a sense of power, albeit a false sense that is short-lived. To feel a sense of control in their lives, they don't realize they need to acknowledge their powerlessness and turn to God as the one true source of power.

To understand the dynamics of pornography addiction, we have to look at it as two sides of a coin. On one side we have the physical addictiveness and on the other side the emotional addictiveness. Both sides work together to create one powerful addiction.

The Physical Side

We must know something about men's brain physiology to understand the physical side of the addiction. Due to hormonal levels in the womb and at puberty, and from various life experiences, men's brains are very different than women's brains. Men are physically wired to be visually stimulated. When a man encounters an erotic image, he automatically looks (Struthers, 2009)! Imagine the man who gets into an auto accident while driving because he is distracted by a pretty woman walking down the street. A more comical example is in cartoons. When Bugs Bunny or Elmer Fudd sees a beautiful woman, their eyes pop out of their heads, their hearts pound wildly, and their tongues roll out and onto the ground.

A structure in the man's brain, the thalamus, is responsible for picking out erotic images. Thus, if a man is viewing a hundred different images and one of them is erotic, the thalamus is going to single it out and the man will immediately pay attention to the erotic image. Once this happens, a chemical reaction occurs in the brain. The ventral tegmental area (VTA) of the midbrain releases dopamine into the brain in great quantities, which mixes with testosterone and creates a very powerful drug cocktail. The man will experience great excitement, and even a high, causing the brain to love this and want more. The VTA releases dopamine in response to nearly all drugs of addiction and is also associated with disorders of attention and motivation, such as attention deficit/hyperactivity disorder, obsessive compulsive disorder, gambling addiction, and compulsive shopping. In addition, dopamine suppresses serotonin in the brain, which can make a man impulsive and aggressive. This contributes to a man's susceptibility to addiction (Struthers, 2009).

On the subconscious level, the mind realizes how good this makes the man feel and how it eases deep emotional pain, and decides to return to pornography over and over again to keep emotional pain at bay. This is the emotional side of the addiction, which we will discuss shortly.

Many men claim that when they view an erotic image it gets "burned into their brains." A chemical is responsible for this, norepinephrine, which is also referred to as the "snapshot chemical." Norepinephrine is also responsible for a spike in testosterone, which adds to sexual excitement and aggressiveness. In addition, it sends a message to the autonomic nervous system so that the heart beats faster, breathing gets shallower, and some men even begin to sweat. A message is then sent down the spinal cord to the genitals for sexual arousal, an erection. With all this excitement and stimulation going on, a tension develops that is only relieved with an orgasm, so the man masturbates. With an orgasm, opiate chemicals, endorphins, are released into the brain, providing a sense of euphoria. This correlates with the euphoric states seen in heroin and cocaine use. After the orgasm the man experiences a great feeling of relaxation (Hilton & Watts, 2011; Struthers, 2009).

The entire process looks like this:

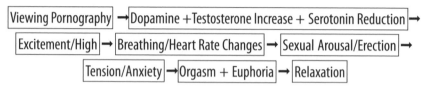

This is a very powerful drug that is highly addictive!

As with any other drug, a tolerance eventually develops. More of the drug is needed to get the same effect. When this happens, soft porn is no longer effective. The man needs to move onto stronger forms of pornography and needs more of it to get the desired effect. This is where a man can get in to hardcore pornography including violence, fetishes, and many other deviant forms of sexuality. The amount of time a man spends online can also increase. Instead of spending a few minutes online viewing pornography, he now spends several hours. The escalation of Phil's pornography use is a clear sign of the tolerance that develops.

For some men, viewing pornography eventually is not enough to stimulate them. They may desire to act out what they have seen in pornography with another person, possibly engage in extramarital affairs, or use prostitutes, escorts, one-night-stands, and even anonymous partners for sex. This can be very dangerous due to the risk of spreading sexually transmitted diseases. Men also may want to engage in the sadomasochistic forms of sex they have seen in pornography.

The reason why a tolerance develops is very simple. The brain is enjoying the effects from large amounts of dopamine, but the rest of the body realizes that this is not normal. The brain should not be releasing so much dopamine, so the body decides to shut off the dopamine. Because the brain loves the dopamine so much, the man must consume more extreme forms of pornography and in greater amounts to keep it coming. Thus, the tolerance is really the body's natural defense mechanism (Struthers, 2009).

Along with tolerance, the man will also develop a dependence on pornography. At this point, it isn't about the good feelings he gets from viewing pornography. Now he needs it just to get through daily life. The brain has become so accustomed to operating at such a high level of chemical stimulation that it needs to maintain that level just to function. If the man doesn't get his fix, he experiences withdrawal symptoms that may include depression, anxiety, insomnia, irritability, difficulty concentrating, headaches, stomachaches, and other symptoms. This accounts for the compulsion a man feels to use pornography regularly. He may desperately want to stop using pornography, but can't. Phil's willingness to risk losing his job by viewing pornography at work clearly shows his dependence on it.

The Emotional Side

Many men view Internet pornography and are eventually able to pass it up, but what is it about the men who need to return to it again and again? The real question is, "What are they self-medicating?" Any use of pornography is a search for intimacy; however, those who become addicted often use it to anesthetize a deep emotional wound. For these men it's more than just "harmless adult entertainment," and often they don't know the wound is there. All they know is that viewing pornography makes them feel really good, and since the effects are temporary, they need to go back to it incessantly. Thus, they become emotionally dependent on pornography to keep their pain at bay.

Below are some of the common emotional wounds that men use pornography to cope with, along with case studies to illustrate them.

1. *Narcissism:* This is becoming a big problem today, especially among young people. This extreme form of selfishness, beginning early in life with parents who overindulge their children, continues in school through self-esteem education and grade inflation, and in sports leagues where everyone wins a trophy. It's further reinforced by a society that encourages people to think only of their own wants and needs. "Me time." The result is an intense sense of entitlement (Twenge, 2003; Twenge & Campbell, 2003, 2009). Narcissism can lead to using pornography despite any negative consequences.

   After a long day at work Kyle would come home and view Internet pornography for about an hour. He justified it by saying to himself that he deserved a break. It didn't matter to Kyle that using pornography was hurtful to his girlfriend. His selfish sense of entitlement fueled his use of pornography. Men who regularly use pornography are often less likely to commit to marriage, believing true happiness comes from having multiple sexual encounters with women, both real and in porn, instead of making a lifelong commitment to one woman.

2. *Family-of-Origin Wounds*: Growing up, many men experience rejection and abandonment from their parents. Others experience abuse either physically, emotionally, or sexually. And still others experience neglect. In his research with one thousand sex addicts, Dr. Pat Carnes (1991) found that 97% were emotionally abused, 74% were physically abused, and 81% were sexually abused. Some men were introduced to pornography by their fathers as a rite of passage or to teach them about sexuality. Unfortunately, this only gave them an unhealthy, skewed view of sexuality.

   Randy grew up with a father who was an angry alcoholic. His father would often come home at night drunk and beat his mother, sisters, and Randy. Finally, when Randy was ten, his mother had had enough and moved out, leaving Randy and his sisters with their father. For the next eight years Randy's main focus was on protecting his sisters from their father. Randy moved out and joined the Navy when he was eighteen. Although he felt guilty for leaving his sisters, he couldn't take the violence and chaos at home any more. In the Navy, Randy became addicted to pornography as he medicated his deep emotional pain caused by his father's abuse and alcoholism and his mother's rejection and abandonment.

3. *Peer Rejection*: Some men who experienced peer rejection as a child, teen, or even an adult may turn to pornography for comfort. Peer acceptance is crucial for healthy development, especially among same-sex peers. When observing an elementary school playground, one normally finds boys playing with boys and girls playing with girls, with little intermixing. Boys bond through their rough and tumble play. This peer

acceptance helps them develop healthy confidence and self-esteem. Rejection from one's peers can be devastating. Rejection can start in elementary school with teasing. It can turn into bullying in middle school. It comes in the form of being ignored in high school. In the end, peer rejection can lead to feeling unwanted, inferior, and unworthy of being loved.

As a child, Tim was the "little guy on the block," the "runt." Instead of being athletic, he was artistically talented and very sensitive, and because of this, Tim was often picked on by his peers. He was teased and bullied. As a young adolescent he discovered Internet pornography, and the emotional high and physical pleasure he got from it provided an escape from the pain of peer rejection. Tim was addicted by the time he was seventeen. He would go online several times a day to view pornography and masturbate.

4. *Loneliness*: There are men who crave love, companionship, friendship, and parental love that they never received in childhood. Often people think that a person who uses porn to ease loneliness really wants a romantic or sexual relationship, but this often is not the case. Many people who turn to pornography do so to ease the pain of general loneliness, just as an alcoholic turns to drink. A man could simply be hungering for the intimacy of family or friendship.

David felt all alone in the world. His mother had been struggling with mental illness most of his life, and she committed suicide when he was a teenager. His father, who was also very cold and aloof, had recently died. While David had a few cousins, he did not come from a close-knit family. He worked the graveyard shift at a local hospital, which made it difficult for him to maintain friendships. He felt all alone in the world. Although he acknowledged his loneliness, David didn't know how to resolve it. In his pain he turned to pornography, logging onto the Internet after work each day and spending hours viewing porn. It provided some temporary relief from his loneliness, but it soon made him even more reclusive and only intensified his solitude.

Changes in modern society have also contributed to isolation. More emphasis is being placed today on the individual instead of being community oriented. This leads men to turn in on themselves and away from others, making it difficult to have a relationship with a woman and leaving them without any support system. Fifty years ago, men joined clubs, lodges, sports leagues, and civic organizations for the improvement of society. They attended church regularly and felt part of a parish community. Today, instead of interacting with others after work and on weekends, men isolate themselves at home and turn to the Internet for companionship. This easily leads to pornography use and addiction.

5. *Male Insecurity*: Some men don't have the confidence needed for a healthy relationship with a woman. Because they lacked the confidence to begin dating relationships earlier in their life, they now turn to pornography as a weak substitute for a romantic relationship. Often these men did not have healthy father-son relationships. Their fathers were not there for them either physically or emotionally. Thus, they did not have a good role model for developing healthy male confidence.

Paul had always been painfully shy. As a child, he would stay close to his mother and had only a small handful of friends. In high school he desperately wanted to date but couldn't muster up the courage to talk to girls, and the few times he tried, he became tongue-tied. He didn't think he had any special gifts or talents that a girl would be interested in, and envied the popular boys who seemed to have it all. These feelings continued throughout most of his teenage and young adult years. Paul discovered Internet pornography when he went to college. What attracted him most was the incredibly beautiful women—and they all seemed to want him! There was no threat of rejection from those women. They begged for him and couldn't get enough of him. As thrilling as this was for Paul, he knew, ultimately, that it was unfulfilling. However, his male insecurity coupled with his need for female love made it almost impossible for him to resist pornography.

6. *Poor Body Image*: Some men believe they are so unattractive that no woman could ever love them. Traditionally, body image disorders were considered young women's issues, but today more men are struggling with them. Men experience just as much pressure to have "the perfect body" as women. To be considered handsome, a man must be tall, athletic, muscular, and have "six pack abs." In fact, one third of those who struggle with eating disorders are men, and no matter how much weight they lose, they still, regrettably, view themselves as unattractive (Phillips, 2001). Not all men with body image disorders have an eating disorder. Men who are overweight and struggle to lose weight can also feel bad about their appearances, and this can lead them to pornography.

Steve had been overweight all his life. Growing up he was always "the fat kid" in school. He had never been on a date in his life and envied thinner men who seemed to have no problems attracting women. Every time Steve looked in a mirror, he felt disgusted by what he saw. He didn't think a woman could ever love him. To compensate for this, he turned to the women in pornography who would never reject him. He soon became addicted.

The struggle with body image is not limited to those who want to lose weight. About half of those who struggle with body image want to lose weight and the other half want to gain weight, and for some men, this turns into a body dysmorphic disorder (Phillips, 2001).

Joe is a perfect example of this. When he was a child, he was small, weak, not athletically gifted, rejected by his peers, and often picked on because of his size. When he entered college, Joe made a vow that he would never be pushed around again. He joined a gym and became a body builder, and by the end of college his body rippled with muscles. He looked better than most of his peers. However, when Joe looked in the mirror, he still saw that "ninety-eight pound weakling" that everyone picked on. All the weight lifting did nothing for his confidence with women. Joe had never had a date, and subconsciously he didn't believe any women could find him attractive, so he turned to the women in pornography.

Both Steve and Joe developed body image disorders because they thought they were ugly and unlovable. To compensate, they turned to pornography as a weak substitute for a real relationship, and in the process they became addicted to pornography.

7. *Anger:* Men can turn to pornography as a way of expressing unresolved anger, which is particularly true of men who view violent pornography, especially if the anger is toward a woman, such as a wife, girlfriend, or even one's mother. If a man is married to a woman who is cold, demanding, or critical, he may turn to pornography as a way of punishing her. He may even hope to be caught by her. A man might turn to pornography to cope with the anger of a failed relationship, such as a painful divorce or breakup. In addition, pornography can be used to self-medicate anger toward a mother who was cold, critical, or abusive.

Jason came into therapy with his wife BethAnn because of his pornography use. BethAnn was his second wife whom he loved dearly. He realized how much his pornography use hurt her and was committed to recovery and healing their marriage. Jason's first wife was cold and controlling, constantly criticizing him and never wanting sex. Jason's mother was also very cold and critical. Unaware of the deep anger he harbored toward his ex-wife and mother, Jason turned to pornography to self-medicate.

Anger toward women is not the only type of anger that men use pornography to self-medicate. Any kind of anger can lead a man to pornography, whether he's angry with his family, friends, boss, self, or life situation. As is true of most addictions, anger is often a trigger for using porn or for acting out.

Roger was angry and he knew it. His father had Alzheimer's disease. Roger cared for him the last two years of his father's life, but it became more than Roger could handle, especially during the last month of his life. None of his siblings offered to help, and they even objected and took Roger to court when he decided to place his father in a nursing home. They wanted their father at home under Roger's care, without their help. Fortunately, the judge sided with Roger and his father was placed in a nursing home, but this caused a huge rift between Roger and his siblings. To deal with his anger during the court battle, Roger turned to Internet pornography. Every night after he put his father to bed, he would go online to view pornography for two hours. This continued every night even after his father was in the nursing home. Roger became addicted to it.

8. *Mistrust of Woman*: Men who are deeply hurt in relationships may no longer feel safe enough to have a relationship with a real woman. This often is experienced by men coming out of painful divorces or breakups. Their ability to trust women has been severely damaged, and many swear off dating or ever having another relationship with a woman. Yet, they still crave love and intimacy. Pornography offers them the promise of intimacy without the risk of rejection or failure. But as we've shown, the promise of intimacy in pornography is a false promise, an illusion. While a man might feel good while using pornography, after it's all over he feels lonelier. Nonetheless, as an addicted person he keeps going back in the hope that the next time will be fulfilling.

Sean sought help for pornography addiction when his teenage daughter discovered his porn files on his computer. Sean's wife had divorced him two years earlier. The divorce was messy, and Sean felt betrayed by his ex-wife who had an extramarital affair and was now living with the other man. Sean swore he would never marry again, and although he claimed to be open to dating, he never sought a relationship. Instead, he turned to pornography. Little did he know that he was using pornography to compensate for his need for intimacy, and he eventually became addicted to pornography's allure of intimacy without risk of rejection, hurt, or betrayal.

9. *Excessive Pressures*: Often work, family, or financial stress lead men to use pornography for comfort or escape. Few would deny that life today can be very stressful, and making ends meet is a daily struggle for many. Due to corporate layoffs, many people are doing work that was once done by two or three people. Only a few complain for fear of losing their jobs. They plod along each day trying to keep up with demands, which can lead to anger, frustration, and burnout. To cope with this stress, a man might turn to pornography. It also seems like the perfect escape for those who are unemployed or underemployed. However, this escape can lead to more financial woes. As a man becomes physically and emotionally dependent on pornography, he ends up spending more time online, time that could be spent looking for a new job or training for a better one. Family stress is another reason why many men turn to porn. Raising a child with special needs, taking care of a sick or elderly parent, or just trying to keep up with the bills can be overwhelming for some.

Martin was laid off from a job he held for over ten years. To support his family, he worked two part-time jobs, but it wasn't enough to make ends meet. He felt awful that he couldn't give his family the things they wanted, but he knew he had to keep a roof over their heads and food on the table. Frustrated and discouraged with his situation, Martin turned to pornography instead of spending time with his family or looking for a better job when he got home from work. He isolated himself in the basement for hours viewing porn. Knowing how tired and irritated he was, his wife wouldn't disturb him when he was down there. She was, however, very hurt by his porn use. Martin soon became addicted. His wakeup call came when he was fired from one of his part-time jobs for coming in late too many times. He knew he was in trouble and sought help.

10. *Weak Spiritual Life*: A weak faith in God often results in a lack of moral virtues and an acute loneliness in the person. There is a deep hunger for God that one may not be aware of, and because they do not know the Lord, many people struggle with alienation and lack of purpose in life. Having a close relationship with God convinces a person that he was created for a specific purpose, that he has value and dignity, that he is "fearfully and wonderfully made." He knows that he is loved! Those who don't have a healthy relationship with God experience a deep emotional hunger that they attempt to satisfy with pornography's false promise of intimacy. While it feels pleasurable and fulfilling in the moment, it leaves one feeling emptier in the end.

Greg was raised in a home without any religion, although his family claimed to be Christian. The closest they got to any kind of religious practice was celebrating the commercialism of Christmas. Without any real practice of the faith, Greg lacked a moral compass and was left feeling lonely and empty inside. Not knowing where to turn, he accepted the false messages that society had told him about happiness coming from the pursuit of materialism, narcissism, and sexual gratification. This led him into pornography use. He came to believe that happiness could only come from multiple sexual encounters, not from a loving relationship with God or any human being. Greg became a person struggling with pornography addiction and fell into a deep depression. He had no sense of a greater purpose in life, no sense of his value and dignity, and no sense that he had a loving Father who cared for him.

Homosexual Pornography

There is just as much homosexual pornography on the Internet as heterosexual pornography, yet because those engaged in a homosexual lifestyle only make up about 3% of the total population (Sprigg

& Dailey, 2004), gay porn appears overrepresented in the population. The fact is that gay porn isn't something that only gay men view. Many heterosexual men view it because of weak male confidence, poor body image, or mistrust of women. Most of the men in gay porn are very muscular, athletic, and portrayed as strong and aggressive, traits that attract those who struggle with weak confidence or poor body image. When heterosexual men become addicted to gay porn, they don't necessarily want to have sex with men, but often they want to possess the traits of those men. Another reason straight men are attracted to gay porn is because they mistrust women and are unable to have a relationship with them. But they still crave love and intimacy. They feel safer with gay porn because there is no mystery with men as with women. They understand men and turn to gay porn for intimacy and sexual gratification that is safe for them.

For homosexual men who become addicted to gay pornography, all of the root causes listed above apply, but there may be two additional root causes.

1. Poor Father Relationship: Many of these men did not have a strong bond with their fathers growing up, and now they may search for this relationship through homosexual pornography. This is often seen in men who are attracted to older men in pornography.

2. Male Peer/Sibling Rejection: These men may have experienced much rejection from male peers or siblings while growing up. Their attraction to homosexual pornography is a weak attempt to gain male peer or sibling acceptance.

The type of pornography and sexual fantasies a man may be drawn to can tell us a lot about his deep emotional wounds. For example, a man who is drawn to violent pornography or fantasizes about dominating women sexually may be struggling with a deep anger or mistrust toward women. A man who is attracted to women in pornography who beg him for sex may be struggling with deep insecurity. He may fantasize about being the man in these sex scenes in order to boost his own ego.

Core Beliefs

The emotional wounds listed above don't necessarily themselves lead men to use pornography. Instead, they often feed five core beliefs (adapted from Carnes, 2001) that can lead men to use and become addicted to pornography.

1. I am unworthy of being loved.

2. If people really knew me, they would reject me.

3. I cannot trust anyone, including God, to meet my needs.

4. I must find something that I can control that will meet my needs.

5. Pornography/Sex is my greatest need and source of comfort.

In addition to the emotional wounds, the addiction itself can feed into the first core belief and can lead a man to continually cycle through all of the core beliefs. This can keep a man trapped in the addiction.

Triggers and Danger Zones

To understand the process of how a man falls into using pornography and acting out, we have to understand what triggers him to do so. There are countless triggers, but they fall into two basic categories: sexual triggers and nonsexual triggers.

Sexual triggers are easy to identify. For example, an afternoon at the beach surrounded by young women in bikinis can be a sexual trigger. Walking past a lingerie store in the mall or reading a sports magazine's swimsuit issue can be a sexual trigger.

Nonsexual triggers can be more difficult to identify, yet they can be more powerful. This following acronym helps understand the nonsexual triggers: BLAST (adapted from Gray, 2013). It stands for:

Bored or Burnt Out

Lonely

Angry, Apathetic, Afraid, or Alone

Sad, Stressed, or Selfish

Tired

Usually, when a man feels compelled to use pornography, it's not just due to one but a combination of triggers. For example, a man might feel bored, stressed, and tired at his job and be triggered to use pornography.

A danger zone is a time, place, or situation where a man is more prone to be triggered. A danger zone time could be late at night or just after a long day at work. A danger zone place could be a part of town where porn shops or strip clubs are located. A danger zone situation could be after a fight with one's wife, or receiving some bad news, or feeling lonely away from the family. Often all three triggers are combined. For example, a businessman might find himself in a danger zone while alone on a business trip and staying in a hotel near a strip club.

Putting It All Together

It's not the triggers *per se* that lead a man to use pornography. The triggers activate the pain from deep emotional wounds that feed the five core beliefs, and this can lead a man to use pornography to ease his pain. Most of the time, he is unaware of this process because it takes place in his subconscious. He simply has a strong urge to use pornography. Thus, for example, the boredom, stress, and fatigue a man experiences in his job might activate his emotional pain of being abused as a child by his parents. This reinforces his core beliefs. The emotional pain and core beliefs are what actually compel him to use pornography. Consistent use of pornography to keep this pain at bay can lead him to become emotionally dependent on it. The addiction process looks like this:

Addiction to pornography often begins with an emotional wound in which the person uses pornography to keep emotional pain at bay. However, with all of pornography's effects on brain chemistry, the more a man goes back to pornography, the more likely he will also become physically dependent on it. The physical side of the addiction works with the emotional side here and creates a strong addiction. What might seem like "harmless adult entertainment" is really the path to a life of misery.

The Five A's

The Five A's we discussed in chapter one also play a key role in addiction. Recall, it's Affordable, Accessible, Anonymous, Accepted, and Aggressive.

1. *It's Affordable.* By offering their products for free, pornographers get more men addicted so they eventually will spend thousands of dollars on it after they've been lured into it.

2. *It's Accessible.* With the advent of the Internet, men don't have to go out to a sleazy place to get their porn. There is no risk of being seen. It's only a click of a button away.

3. *It's Anonymous.* It's easy to hide in the privacy of his own devices. It's only found out after someone stumbles on a stash or a man loses his job or brings his family close to financial ruin.

4. *It's Accepted.* Its acceptance in our culture has given men permission to view it without any moral consequences of fear, guilt, or shame.

5. *It's Aggressive.* Men can easily go online and have the most extreme form of hardcore pornography on the screen, affecting their brain as seriously as crack cocaine.

The causes that lead a man to pornography addiction are many. Often there are a combination of root causes, and the Five A's only exacerbate the disease.

Evaluating Your Risk for Internet Pornography Addiction

Any use of Internet pornography is a problem, but if you are concerned that you might be addicted to it, please complete the following self-test created by Robert L. Delmonico (2000). While this test is fourteen years old, it is still the "gold standard" in evaluating one's risk for pornography addiction. It is highly valid and reliable. This instrument should only be used to assess one's risk for addiction. While it can help in evaluating one's risk to addiction, only a trained counselor can accurately diagnose an addiction to pornography.

Read each statement carefully in this *Internet Sex Screening Test*. If a statement is mostly TRUE, as it is applied to you, place a checkmark in the box next to the item number. If the statement is mostly FALSE, as applied to you, skip the item and place nothing in the box next to the item number.

1. ☐ I have some sexual sites bookmarked.
2. ☐ I spend more than five hours per week using my computer for sexual pursuits.
3. ☐ I have joined sexual sites to gain access to online sexual material.
4. ☐ I have purchased sexual products online.
5. ☐ I have searched for sexual material through an Internet search tool.
6. ☐ I have spent more money for online sexual material than I planned.
7. ☐ Internet sex has sometimes interfered with certain aspects of my life.
8. ☐ I have participated in sexually related chats.
9. ☐ I have a sexualized username or nickname that I use on the Internet.
10. ☐ I have masturbated while on the Internet.
11. ☐ I have access to sexual sites from computers in locations other than my home.
12. ☐ No one knows I use my computer for sexual purposes.

13. ☐ I have tried to hide what is on my computer or monitor so others cannot see it.

14. ☐ I have stayed up after midnight to access sexual material online.

15. ☐ I use the Internet to experiment with different aspects of sexuality, such as bondage, homosexuality, or anal sex.

16. ☐ I have my own website that contains some sexual material.

17. ☐ I have made promises to myself to stop using the Internet for sexual purposes.

18. ☐ I sometimes use cybersex as a reward for accomplishing something such as finishing a project or enduring a stressful day.

19. ☐ When I am unable to access sexual information online, I feel anxious, angry, or disappointed.

20. ☐ I have increased the risks I take online, such as giving out my name and phone number or meeting people offline.

21. ☐ I have punished myself when I use the Internet for sexual purposes, such as arranging a time-out from my computer or canceling Internet subscriptions.

22. ☐ I have met face-to-face with someone I met online for romantic purposes.

23. ☐ I use sexual humor and innuendo with others while online.

24. ☐ I have run across illegal sexual material while on the Internet.

25. ☐ I believe I am an Internet sex addict.

Now add up the number of items that you indicated were TRUE for you and record the total below.

Total: _____

Use the chart below to determine if Internet sex may be problematic for you.

1 to 8 items marked True = Low Risk:
You may or may not have a problem with your sexual behavior on the Internet. You are in the low-risk group, but if the Internet is causing problems in your life seek a professional who can conduct further assessments.

9 to 18 items marked True = Moderate Risk:
You are at risk for sexual behavior to interfere with significant areas of your life. If you are concerned about your sexual behavior online and have noticed consequences as a result of your online behavior, you should seek a professional who can further assess and help you with your concerns.

20 or more items marked True = High Risk:
You are at the highest risk for your online behavior to interfere with and jeopardize important areas of your life (for example, social, occupational, and educational). You should discuss your online sexual behaviors with a professional who can further assess and assist you.

Internet Sex Screening Test © 2000
David L. Delmonico, PhD, NCC
Duquesne University, Pittsburgh, PA

The Disease

It's important to view pornography addiction as a disease similar to any other addiction, and not simply a moral failing. No one wants to become an addict. The addiction silently creeps into a man's life and soon takes over. He becomes powerless over lust, his life becomes unmanageable, he hurts the ones he loves, and he puts everything he holds dear in jeopardy. Most men experience deep pain, guilt, and shame because they know what they are doing is wrong and they are trapped. Many don't know what to do or to whom to turn. We need to treat these men with love, mercy, and compassion. We need to refer them to professionals who can help them.

It is understandable that companies monitor their computer systems and have strict policies against viewing pornography at work, but they also need to view pornography addiction like any other addiction. Instead of firing such employees, they should assist these employees in finding help for recovery. Employee Assistance Programs could provide a great service and would save companies the cost of hiring and training new employees.

Hope

The good news is that freedom from pornography addiction is possible. Lives can be restored and marriages can be healed. It is rare that anyone is beyond hope. In chapter ten I present the Integrity Restored Recovery Program, which has helped countless men recover from pornography addiction.

3

How Pornography Affects Men

Kevin is a twenty-six-year-old man who sought counseling to help him with his relationships with women. In his entire life he had only dated two women and both of those relationships ended badly. Both women complained about how selfish and controlling Kevin was, how he lacked empathy and consideration for others, and that he seemed to believe that the world revolved around him. Looking deeper into his life, it was revealed that Kevin was a regular user of pornography. When it was suggested that this could be part of his problem, Kevin dismissed it. He couldn't believe that viewing pornography could harm his ability to relate to women. In fact, he believed it could actually help men. It took lot of work to convince him otherwise.

Kevin came from a nominal Catholic family. They attended Mass on most Sundays. Kevin attended religious education classes until he was confirmed. When he went off to college, he stopped attending Mass altogether. Kevin had no clue about God's plan for healthy relationships, but fortunately, he was open to learning about this. While he didn't consider himself a religious person, he realized his life lacked deeper meaning.

Kevin first began viewing pornography in 1998 late at night on cable television when he was twelve years old. His parents were unaware that they were getting late night "adult channels" for free. This continued until his parents got the Internet on their home computer. Being somewhat ignorant of this new technology, Kevin's parents were unaware of its dangers. They let him use it whenever he wanted without supervision. Soon he was viewing pornography every day. During high school, when his parents thought he was doing his homework, Kevin was actually viewing porn.

During his teenage years, Kevin wanted to date girls, but he was too shy to ask any out on a date. His parents, fearing an unwanted pregnancy, actually discouraged Kevin from dating. He also had a poor sexual education, and although his family never considered sex a dirty thing, it was never discussed at home. Most of what Kevin learned about sex and relationships, unfortunately, came from pornography.

Kevin's pornography use intensified at college. Equipped with his own laptop computer and dorm room Internet access, he could view it at will. His grades suffered because of this, but he did manage to graduate with a 3.0 GPA.

Kevin's first dating relationship was in college. He fell in love with Stacy, who shared the same major and many of Kevin's interests. At first, they really hit it off and enjoyed each other's company. Things began to get rough when, after a month of dating, Kevin began pressuring Stacy for sex. When she said no, he would get angry and more controlling because he believed that sex was necessary for a relationship. The type of sex he wanted was also shocking to Stacy. He shared with her some of his sexual fantasies, which included bondage and verbal humiliation. She broke up with him. Angry and hurt, Kevin's pornography use intensified.

His second relationship began two years after graduating from college. He met Jill through a dating website. Like his relationship with Stacy, Kevin and Jill were instantly attracted to each other, yet Kevin soon began demanding sex from Jill as well. This time, when she said no, he was even more angry and controlling. The relationship finally ended one night when he forced himself onto Jill, to the point where she threatened to have him arrested for date rape if he didn't leave. He left, begrudgingly, and they never spoke again.

Because of his constant use of pornography, Kevin came to believe that what he viewed online was normal, healthy sex. He came to think that sex is necessary in a dating relationship, that all women love sex, and that it's the man who controls the sex. Kevin bought the lie that women are there for his sexual pleasure. Ultimately, this instilled in him a deep selfishness. In his mind he didn't have to respect women or be considerate of their wants and needs. This paradigm, fortunately, doesn't exist in the real world. Kevin's solution when things didn't go his way was to get angry and become more controlling, and when this didn't work, he returned to pornography because it was something he *could* control.

In reality, if Kevin wanted to have a healthy relationship with a woman, he first needed to realize that everything he learned about sex and relationships on the Internet was wrong. He needed to overcome his selfishness and learn to put the needs of others ahead of his own. He needed to learn God's plan for healthy relationships.

Kevin's story is like many of the stories I've heard from young men and women affected by pornography. This chapter focuses on the many ways that pornography harms men and their ability to relate to others in healthy ways, and how men can change. I also discuss the true calling that God has for each man.

It's an Appetite, not a Need

The influence of narcissism, the sexual revolution, oral contraceptives, mass media, and pornography have all contributed to changing how sex is viewed. Those influences have led Americans to believe that sex is a need, and like all needs it must be met, and that it is okay to use other people for one's own sexual pleasure, whether it's a real person or an image of a person. This is the sexual utilitarian philosophy we referred to earlier. As we have already said, Pope St. John Paul II wrote that the opposite of love is "use." It's ironic how some men will call having sex "making love," when the opposite is true, and they are simply using women for their own selfish pleasure, and then justifying their actions by claiming they are meeting their needs.

An example of this is Dan, a sixty-year-old man who has been married for thirty years. Although he loved his wife Marilyn, she was not interested in having sex as often as he. (It was revealed later that

Marilyn did not want to have sex with Dan because she simply felt used by him.) Dan believed that sex is a need that all men share, and he used this belief to justify his use of pornography. As his use of pornography progressed, Dan became interested in more deviant forms of sex, particularly anal sex, and he wanted to engage in this with Marilyn. She refused. Feeling entitled to "get his needs met," Dan began seeing prostitutes, and this led him further into more deviant and dangerous forms of sex. Dan's activities came to light when Marilyn went to her gynecologist because of some discomfort she was having. Her doctor revealed to her that she had a sexually transmitted disease. She got it from Dan, who acquired it from prostitutes. Both Marilyn and Dan were devastated. Marilyn felt hurt and betrayed. To her, this was adultery. The Church also views this as adultery (CCC 2380). Dan felt horrible for what he had done to his wife, both physically and emotionally. It was Dan's belief that sex was a need he was entitled to meet that led to this disaster.

Sex is not a need. It's an appetite. A need is something that is required for life, such as food and water. A person would soon die without them. While the human race needs sex to procreate and continue our species, an individual person does not need sex to live. A man would not die if he was in an accident and his injuries resulted in him never being able to have sex for the rest of his life. That may be a heavy cross to bear, but he would go on living. Priests and religious are called to live chaste and celibate lives, and although it may be difficult at times, most live out this calling joyfully.

Sex is an appetite, and as with all appetites, it must be fed in the proper way. For example, I have an appetite for chocolate ice cream, but I would get sick if I ate it every day for breakfast, lunch, and dinner. If I reserve it for its proper use, namely, dessert on special occasions, it has more meaning and is more enjoyable. The same principle holds true for sex.

Sex is a holy gift from God. It is meant to be an expression of love between a husband and wife that is open to new life. It is an act of total self-giving. Every time a married couple engages in sexual intercourse, they renew their marital vows to love, honor, and cherish each other.

Many men are defiling God's holy plan for sex because our culture has convinced them that sex is a need they are entitled to meet. By using pornography, they are disrespecting their wives, their girlfriends, and God. There needs to be a paradigm shift in our culture towards one where men view sex as an appetite and strive to feed it properly, rather than indulging in gluttony. Traditionally, the Church has taught that it is more virtuous to control one's passions. By viewing pornography every time a man feels the urge, he is not truly in control of his passions or his life. The strong man is able to say no to a wrong, no matter how pleasurable it appears.

Using Women

To understand the effect that pornography is having on men today we must ask the question, "What are the messages they are receiving from porn?" The answer is this:

- It's okay for men to use women.
- Women can be controlled by men.
- Women are there for men's sexual pleasure.
- Women don't have thoughts or feelings.
- Women don't need to be respected.
- Women love sex and can't get enough of it.
- A relationship is not needed to have sex.
- If there is a relationship, sex and pornography should be part of it.

It's obvious these are false messages, yet many men buy into them. These messages fuel the sexual utilitarian philosophy or "hookup culture." Kevin, in the story at the beginning of this chapter, is an example of this. His use of pornography warped his view of sex and relationships.

He believed he could control his girlfriends for sex, and consequently he was unable to have a healthy and successful relationship.

While some men would agree that it is wrong to use women sexually, they justify their pornography use by claiming the women in porn independently decide to be in that industry. Thus, the producer and consumer are consenting adults. Regardless of how and why a woman enters the pornography industry, men need to realize that any use of another human, for whatever reason, is inherently wrong.

The hookup culture has become very popular today, especially among young adults. There are websites designed for this purpose. In 2011, students from the University of Chicago created a website where students could meet for casual sex, advertising that "chastity is curable if detected early." While the site received mixed reviews, students did use it for hookups (Huffington Post, 2011). Fortunately, the university was able to shut the site down, although numerous other websites have been created for the same purposes. One of the most popular sites for this is Craigslist.org. What started out as an "online yard sale" has expanded into a major hookup site as well.

Men enter the hookup culture for easy sex, using women to gratify their sexual desires without the responsibilities of a relationship. Women enter it for different reasons. Sarah, a college freshman, got into the hookup culture because she felt it was the only way to get a boyfriend. She believed that having sex with a man was the way to start and maintain a relationship. She ended up feeling hurt and used because none of the men she had sex with were interested in a relationship. Other women get into it as a reaction against men. Rachel became angry when she saw how men were using women for sex. If this is what men were doing to women, she thought, why shouldn't women do this to men? At first this gave her a sense of power over men; however, she soon tired of it because, deep down, she wanted a real relationship. But getting involved in the hookup culture only damaged her ability to trust men.

Sooner or later, pornography and the hookup culture only lead to disappointment. They present an unhealthy and unrealistic view of sex and relationships. There can be no healthy relationship if one is using another person. When these men try to enter into a real relationship, they are ill-equipped and don't know how to relate to a woman in a healthy way. They soon learn that women are not there for their sexual pleasure, that women expect respect, that women don't crave sex all the time, and certainly not the sex in pornography. These men must throw out everything they have ever learned from pornography, and start learning from scratch. Some men are not willing to change their paradigm and simply give up on relationships, and return to viewing pornography where they can control the women.

In teaching men to use women for their sexual pleasure, pornography and the hookup culture have robbed both men and women of the opportunity to have healthy relationships. It's ironic that the pornography industry promotes its products and aids to enhance relationships, but in the end, they destroy those relationships.

Violence toward Women

Instead of portraying sex as an exchange of love between a husband and wife, pornography presents sex as little more than a recreational activity to be enjoyed by all. Moreover, it presents all forms of deviant sex as "normal" and "healthy." A lot of pornography available online is violent toward women, including anal sex, group sex, bondage, rape scenes, bestiality, orgies, homosexuality, and lesbianism. Many of these practices are physically dangerous, but since they are widely presented in pornography, men have come to believe that women love this type of sex, and then they expect it from their wives and girlfriends.

Research shows that violent pornography impacts men's attitudes and behaviors toward women and sex. Reviews of current literature have shown that pornography use and acceptance of aggression and violence toward women are linked (Flood & Hamilton, 2003; Malamuth et al., 2000; Vega & Malamuth, 2007). In one study of 489 fraternity men at a midwestern university who regularly viewed pornography, it was found that such men would more likely commit sexual assault if they were assured of not being caught or punished. Those who viewed sadomasochistic pornography reported significantly less bystander efficacy to intervene in a rape situation (Foubert et al., 2011). For example, if such a man heard what sounded like a rape being committed, he would be less likely to intervene to save the woman, believing that she was simply engaging in "sexual role play" and really enjoying what was happening to her.

Erectile Dysfunction

For many men, long-term use of pornography can result in erectile dysfunction. With compulsive pornography use, a man's brain can become conditioned to only be stimulated by the constant parade of sexual images he encounters in pornography. Thus, when a man tries to be sexually intimate with one woman, his wife, he may find that he cannot achieve or maintain an erection. In order to be sexually aroused he needs the intense release of dopamine that comes from pornography, not the normal release that comes with a healthy sexual encounter with someone he loves and is committed to in marriage.

Psychology Today reports that when a man invests most of his sex life masturbating to online porn with "endless images of sexy, exciting, constantly changing partners," he is likely to find his one real-world partner less stimulating. There develops an "emotional disconnection that is manifesting physically as sexual dysfunction with real-world partners" (R. Weiss, 2014).

Allen experienced this condition. He became less able to perform sexually with his wife Theresa after months of viewing pornography every day. Initially, she thought it was her fault, that she wasn't pretty or sexually attractive any more. Theresa felt even worse when she caught Allen viewing pornography, because she thought that he was turning to pornography because he no longer found her sexually satisfying. Now, she felt completely rejected. He went to a urologist to discuss his erectile dysfunction, and the doctor was wise enough to ask Allen if he was a pornography user. When Allen admitted to this, the urologist explained how it was probably the cause of his problem and referred him to a therapist. Allen was relieved to learn that his erectile dysfunction was a temporary condition, but he still had a lot of work to do to restore his marriage. He had hurt Theresa deeply.

The False Promise

Most men who frequently view pornography will say they do it purely for entertainment purposes. But what is the real reason? There are many other forms of entertainment that don't use people selfishly. While narcissism is one of the main culprits, the need for intimacy is another. Indeed, pornography use has often been referred to as an "intimacy disorder."

Intimacy is a deep love and emotional connection between two people. Sex is one expression of this love between a husband and wife; however, love and intimacy do not equate sex. A deep love and intimacy between a parent and a child is nonsexual. The same is true for best friends. Lamentably, pornography has led people to equate intimacy with sex. In fact, pornography and the mass media often use the terms "sex" and "intimacy" interchangeably.

When a man views pornography on a regular basis, he is often subconsciously searching for intimacy. Wives and girlfriends are shocked to hear this. They wonder why they cannot fulfill their man's need for intimacy. This is because the intimacy the man craves often goes back to his family-of-origin.

These men grew up in homes where their need for intimacy was not met, and most are unaware of this because, as children, they simply took life one day at a time making the best of it. However, the need persisted throughout their life. This can be just one of many family-of-origin wounds that lead to pornography use. For example, Larry was seven when his father died. This was very hard on Larry. He loved his father dearly. He was his hero. Larry's mother, who also was deeply affected by the death of her husband, never fully recovered. She suffered many bouts of depression. The result was that this young boy, at the age of seven, lost his father physically and his mother emotionally. He was in many ways orphaned. Unknowingly, he craved his parents' intimacy.

As a teen, Larry discovered pornography as a way to self-medicate his need for parental intimacy. The women in pornography promised him all the intimacy he wanted, and then some. Initially, viewing porn was exciting, but it always left him feeling empty, because the promise of intimacy was a false promise. Like the Sirens, the draw of pornography was too great for Larry to resist, and he went back to it over and over again.

Larry was married to Linda and they loved each other very much. She couldn't understand why he sought intimacy from pornography and not from her. Looking at his family-of-origin wounds, we can see how Larry learned to use pornography as a substitute for parental intimacy while he was a teenager, and so by the time he got married he already had a way to self-medicate this need. He did not need Linda to meet it. Larry did acknowledge that he received plenty of spousal intimacy from his wife.

Other family-of-origin wounds can lead to using pornography for intimacy. These include divorce, abuse, neglect, and abandonment. In my practice, I have seen an especially high correlation between pornography use and adult children of divorce (ACODs). Non-family-of-origin wounds can also lead men to use pornography as a substitute for intimacy, such as marital problems, weak male confidence, and poor body image.

Even men who don't struggle with deep emotional wounds can get trapped in pornography's false promise of intimacy. It's easy for men to get caught up in the erotic scenes because the women in pornography are very beautiful. Men imagine themselves in the scenes where these women love them unconditionally. There is no risk of rejection. Furthermore, these women love sex, beg for it, only want it from these men, and can be controlled with the click of a mouse.

As long as men buy into pornography's false promise of intimacy, they will not be able to experience authentic, fulfilling intimacy that comes from a healthy relationship. They always end up disappointed. Those who use pornography as a substitute for their lack of intimacy need to be made aware of this. They need to experience true healing for their wounds and find healthy ways to meet their need for authentic intimacy.

Pornography has played the classic "bait and switch game" with men. First, it presents a false definition for intimacy (intimacy = sex). Then it promises to give men all the intimacy they want through sex. Finally, when it has men hooked, it leaves them feeling empty and unfulfilled. Pornography can never fulfill a man's true need for healthy intimacy.

Further Problems with Relationships

It is clearly evident that the narcissism and sexual utilitarian philosophy fostered by pornography have left many men unable to have healthy relationships with women. But pornography has created other problems for men in relating to women. Spending so much time online interacting with images has left men struggling with communication. While they can engage in online chatting, instant messaging, email, and texting, they have great difficulty talking with a real woman in person. They have very weak communication skills.

Real women cannot be easily controlled with the click of a mouse, and this has led to frustration for many men and women. Some men, like Kevin, get angry when they cannot control women. Others simply give up on relationships and focus solely on cybersex.

Although many men see nothing wrong with viewing pornography, there are those who, deep down, know it is wrong. They are ashamed of it and keep it a secret, and because of this secret life, they are unable to fully share their lives with women, which prevents them from having healthy relationships. They have divided hearts. Liam was one such man. He had been dating Kris for over a year and wanted to propose to her, but he knew his pornography use prevented him from having an honest and open relationship with her. He wanted nothing to come between him and Kris, so he sought therapy to help end his pornography use. As part of his recovery program, he confessed to Kris about using pornography, and although this was difficult for her to hear, she respected Liam's honesty. Fortunately, his honesty led to a deeper love and intimacy in their relationship, and Liam ended his pornography use and no longer had to hide anything from Kris.

Few women respect men who view pornography, and this is another reason why men who use pornography have difficulty with relationships. Men are visually stimulated. Women are relationally stimulated. When a man views pornography, he neither sees the porn stars as real people nor himself as having real relationships with them. Most women see porn stars as real people, even though they may not respect them. So when they catch their husband or boyfriend viewing pornography, to them, it's as serious as cheating. Pornography use damages a woman's trust in her husband or boyfriend. Most women don't see these men as trustworthy, mature, and worthy of respect. They see selfishness and immaturity. We'll talk a lot more about this in chapter five.

Although most men who view pornography may see it as "harmless adult entertainment," they must realize the damage it is causing in current and future relationships. Viewing pornography won't help a man with his love life. It won't make him irresistible to women. It will repel them.

Leaders, Providers, and Protectors

Men and women are equal, but God calls them to different roles and gives them unique gifts to fulfill those roles. He calls men to be leaders, providers, and protectors of marriages, families, parishes, communities, and society. This calling applies to all men whether they are single, married, a priest, or a religious. When men choose to live out these roles with virtue, they become the men God has called them to be. They are living to their fullest potential. A man cannot fulfill these roles if he is enslaved to anything. Pornography enslaves. Let's take a look at each of these roles and how they are affected by pornography.

- **Leader:** God calls men to be leaders in their actions and the example they set. A good leader understands what a great privilege and responsibility it is to guide others. He leads by living a virtuous life and avoiding vice. I am reminded of the Boy

Scout Law, which essentially is a list of virtues by which all scouts must live. It states, "A scout is trustworthy, loyal, helpful, friendly, courteous, kind, obedient, cheerful, thrifty, brave, clean, and reverent." There are many other virtues included, such as humility, honesty, and purity. A virtuous man can easily persuade others to follow him because they know he is trustworthy. A good leader avoids anything that would harm himself or others. He is not afraid to speak up for what is good and denounce what is harmful. One example of a great leader is Pope St. John Paul II. He strove to live a virtuous life to the point of going to Confession daily. He was merciful and forgave the man who shot him. He was also not afraid to denounce the "culture of death" and promote the "gospel of life." A man who uses pornography cannot be a good leader because he cannot be trusted. Who would want to follow a man who uses women for his own sexual pleasure or condones it in others?

- **Provider:** A man is a provider materially, morally, and spiritually. Through his example of living a virtuous life, he becomes a role model for his children, peers, and colleagues. He sets the standard for moral living. He deals with people with honesty and respect. In his career he offers an honest day's work and never cheats his employer. At school, he completes his assignments and never cheats. This example helps others to live virtuous lives. John Paul II was not only a great provider in the way he lived his life, but also in his work. Through encyclicals, pastoral letters, and writings, such as *The Theology of the Body* and *Love and Responsibility*, he provided tangible ways for people to live virtuous lives. The man who uses pornography cannot be a good provider because he is not a good role model for others, especially his children. He is a hypocrite. He also does not provide a loving and respectful relationship for his wife.

- **Protector:** A virtuous man knows the dangers of the world and strives to protect his wife, family, parish, community, and society. With regard to pornography, he is called to protect his marriage and family by ensuring that it never enters his home. He protects his wife's heart by ensuring that he never views it. He protects his family by monitoring all media that enters the home and removing anything that is offensive. He protects his parish by educating parishioners on the dangers of pornography and how they can protect themselves and their families. He protects society by making sure porn shops do not open in his community. Through his *The Theology of the Body* and *Love and Responsibility*, John Paul II protected the Church by offering a way to enjoy the holy gift of sexuality that protects people and honors God. The man who uses pornography is not protecting anyone and is offensive to his wife, children, parish, community, and society. He hurts women by supporting an industry that harms them. He hurts his wife by committing adultery through viewing pornography, and by allowing it into his home, he fails in protecting his children, who could discover it.

How Men Must Change

Since pornography prohibits men from having healthy relationships with women and prevents them from being the leaders, providers, and protectors that God has called them to be, the question becomes: How do we correct the damage caused by pornography?

For our society to heal from this damage, men must change their views on pornography, sex, and relationships. They need to realize how selfish pornography use is and how it only leads them to use women. Men must confront their own selfishness and work on growing in the virtue of humility. They will need to accept that sex is an appetite, not a need, and that they don't have the right to fulfill their sexual desires whenever they please, however they please. They will need to learn about healthy sex and relationships. They will need to strive to be the virtuous men that God has called them to be. Although daunting, this task is not impossible. Men can live happy and virtuous lives that respect God and women. This will be addressed in depth later in this book.

We began this chapter with Kevin. His process of change began by understanding the link between pornography and his failed relationships. It was difficult for him to accept, but he came to realize that he had bought into the lies of pornography and was using women rather than loving and respecting them. Kevin had to discard everything he had learned about sex and relationships from the Internet. He had to let go of his anger, pride, and narcissism. Through counseling, he learned about healthy sex and healthy relationships. With the help of a Catholic men's group, he began to live a more virtuous life. Trying to understand how hurt Stacy and Jill felt, Kevin also grew in empathy. Instead of feeling anger toward them, he now felt sorry for his actions and even grieved over the two lost relationships. Kevin enthusiastically embraced God's calling for him to be a leader, provider, and protector. He wanted women to see him as an excellent future husband and father. Kevin's situation was a bit extreme and his transformation process took several months, but it demonstrates how change is possible. Men don't have to be trapped in the lies and false promises of pornography.

4

How Pornography Affects Women

People often think of pornography use and addiction as a "men's issue." While the majority of pornography users and those addicted to it are men, this problem is growing among women. Regrettably, many women who struggle are afraid to come forward and seek help. Many feel immense shame that they are all alone and that no one else shares or even understands their struggle. Often their pornography use leads women to act out sexually with other people. This only adds to their shame, believing that because of their sin no one could ever love them, especially God. They also believe they would be rejected and labeled a slut or a whore if people found out about their struggle. So these women suffer in silence.

If you are a woman who struggles with pornography or sexual addiction, I'm here to tell you that you are not alone. Thousands of women struggle. Pornography and sex addiction affect women of all ages and backgrounds, including Catholic women who take their faith seriously. I also want you to know that you don't have to suffer. Help is available. There are many loving professionals, laypeople, and clergy who are there to help. Most of all, know that God still loves you! Nothing you could ever do could take His love away. He still sees you as a beautiful daughter. God has a wonderful plan for your life, starting with forgiveness and redemption. Sure, recovering from addiction takes work, but God will be with you every step of the way to love, encourage, affirm, and forgive you. Amy is one such woman who reached out for help. Along with healing and recovery, she discovered God's tremendous love for her. Here is her story.

Amy discovered pornography at the age of twelve. She and her family had just moved to a new town and she tried to make new friends in her new school. But interacting with peers was always difficult for Amy. Home life was also pretty lonely. Amy's mother worked long hours as a high school teacher, and her father was in sales and traveled most of the time. Her two brothers were preoccupied with sports and didn't have time for her. Amy usually came home from school every day to an empty house. She first experienced pornography when she found her brother's magazines in their shed. The pictures of men and women having sex mesmerized her. As a young adolescent, she wanted to know more about sex, but it was rarely talked about at home, and the sex education classes at school were weak. Amy was never taught about healthy love, sex, or relationships.

Amy's family wasn't very religious, but they attended Mass on Sundays and she had gone to Catholic schools. While Amy instinctively knew pornography was wrong, she wanted to see more. Her immense loneliness drew her back to pornography over and over again. Soon, she was also masturbating to it. The magazines gave way to searching for pornography on the Internet. Her parents did not have any filtering software on their home computer, so there was nothing stopping Amy from viewing pornography during the long hours when she was left alone at home. In desperate need for intimacy and affirmation, she often romanticized what she saw in pornography and dreamed of being with those men, and before long she was addicted. She spent every moment alone searching for porn. She came to equate love and intimacy with sexual activity.

As Amy's addiction progressed, she engaged in other forms of online sex, including erotic stories, chat rooms, and webcams. This sexual activity continued through high school and college. She never dated because her romantic relationships were with the men in porn, which was something she could control with no risk of rejection, and was always there for her.

Amy's wakeup call came when she was a junior in college. Cybersex was no longer satisfying. She wanted to act out all the sex scenes she viewed in pornography with a real man. She began cruising the sex hookup websites and emailing and chatting with men. After several weeks of searching, Amy thought she found a suitable partner, a gorgeous twenty-five-year-old single athlete. She suggested they meet for sex and they settled on a time and place, Friday night, 9:00 p.m. at a motel near her college campus.

That night Amy was both nervous and excited. She thought she was finally going to have the love and intimacy she craved. When the man showed up, however, he was nothing like his description or photo on the website. He was a husky fifty-year-old married man, and the thought of having sex with an older married man repulsed her. Although he tried to force himself on her, Amy was able to break free and run out of the hotel room to her car and speed out of the parking lot.

Amy ended up in her church parking lot that night. She sat in her car for over two hours crying. She couldn't believe how messed up her life was. To think that she was ready to have sex with a total stranger! She thought, "What kind of a horrible person am I? I am a slut, a real whore! Who could ever love me?" Amy's life was spinning out of control and she knew it. She was too ashamed to tell her parents about her addiction, and so the next day she called a close aunt who was very loving and compassionate. She put Amy in touch with a Christian therapist who worked with women. This was Amy's first step on the road to recovery. For the first time in her life, she didn't feel alone, and although she still felt shameful, she knew there were people who loved her and wanted to help her.

The Problem for Women

Amy's story is not uncommon. Unfortunately, treatment for pornography/sex addiction for women today is like alcoholism treatment eighty years ago—it's primarily considered a men's issue. Much of this was due to the stereotype of "the town drunk," and few people thought of women being alcoholics. Women hardly ever came forward seeking help for alcoholism because of the great shame that came with it. At that time, society still saw alcoholism as a moral failing, and women were supposed to live lives of high moral virtue. For a woman to admit that she struggled with alcoholism was to admit that she was a moral failure. Society's sanctions for this at that time were too much for many women to bear. They would face ridicule, humiliation, and ostracization. They would suffer in silence.

Fortunately, things have changed for alcoholic women. Thanks to the work of Alcoholics Anonymous, alcoholism is now viewed as a disease and not simply a moral failing. People also know that alcoholism does not discriminate. Anyone can become an alcoholic, including women. While there is always fear and shame associated with coming forward and admitting one's struggle with alcoholism, women no longer need to worry about how they will be treated by friends, family, colleagues, and society. Many find great support as they work through recovery.

But again, regrettably, this kind of progress has not yet occurred for women struggling with pornography/sex addiction. This still is mainly considered a men's issue. The books, articles, and treatment programs for pornography/sex addiction in men far outnumber those for women. While women like Amy are coming forward and seeking help, most females struggling with pornography addiction suffer in silence, often because of the shame they feel or the lack of resources for recovery for women.

For many women who do struggle with pornography/sex addiction, it began on the Internet. Here are some current statistics (Family Safe Media, 2007):

- Percentage of women visitors to adult websites: 33%.
- Persons addicted to pornography who are women: 17%.
- Women who keep their online activities a secret: 70%.
- Ratio of women to men who favor chat rooms: 2:1.
- Women accessing pornographic websites each month: 9.2 million.
- Women admitting to accessing pornography at work: 17%.

Those statistics have only gotten worse since 2007. For example, Nielsen/Net ratings indicate that thirteen million American women visit online porn once a month (Huffington Post, 2012).

Defining Pornography for Women

Women can become addicted to pornography just like men, but it's different because the definition of pornography for women is much broader than for men. In chapter one I defined pornography as "any image that leads a person to use another person for one's own sexual pleasure. It is devoid of love, intimacy, relationship, or responsibility. It can be highly addictive."

When we use the word "image" we usually think of a visual image, such as a picture or a video. However, women are not as visually stimulated as men. Women are more relationally stimulated. So how can women become addicted to pornography when they are not as visually stimulated? Images don't have to be visual. An image can be created with words, which is why many women are attracted to romance novels, soap operas, reality television, and "chick flicks." The promise of a romantic relationship gets the dopamine flowing in a woman's brain. That's why, along with visual pornography, women can become addicted to erotic literature, chat rooms, instant messaging, social media, video chats, etc.

A woman's age seems to play a role in the type of pornography she chooses. Younger women seem to prefer visual types of pornography over written types, an interesting phenomenon according to Dr. Mark Laaser (2009). It's as if our culture and pornography are rewiring women's brains to be more visually stimulated and aggressive. This is especially true for women under thirty. In a recent survey by Dirty Girls Ministries (an online support community for women who struggle with pornography addiction), 95% of the women surveyed said they started habitually and compulsively watching pornography or engaging in cybersex before the age of thirty. Even among the women who are over thirty, 84% said their compulsion started before the age of thirty (Gilkerson, 2012).

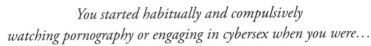

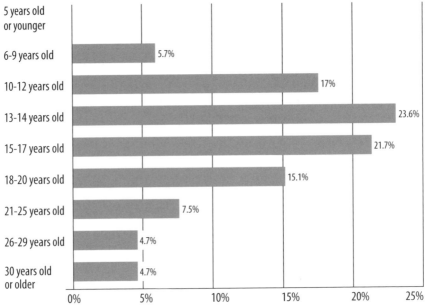

You started habitually and compulsively watching pornography or engaging in cybersex when you were...

- 5 years old or younger
- 6-9 years old — 5.7%
- 10-12 years old — 17%
- 13-14 years old — 23.6%
- 15-17 years old — 21.7%
- 18-20 years old — 15.1%
- 21-25 years old — 7.5%
- 26-29 years old — 4.7%
- 30 years old or older — 4.7%

Pornography's Effects on Women

As with men, pornography provides women with a whole host of lies and false promises, the greatest of which is intimacy. Many women turn to pornography craving intimacy. Pornography promises this intimacy in both visual and written forms, the latter including such things as erotic literature, chat rooms, and social media. It has also skewed how women view men and relationships. Love becomes equated with sex. According to neuropsychologist William Struthers, when a woman looks at porn, she comes to believe that this is what men want and this is how she should be (Gilkerson, 2012). She learns that to be considered beautiful, desirable, and loveable, she must look and act like a porn star, which can lead women to allow men to use them in degrading ways. Pornography has convinced many women that fantasy is better than reality. They give up on searching for a real relationship and instead focus on pornography. But as we have seen, all pornography use just leads to deeper loneliness, isolation, and unhealthy shame.

Pornography has also changed the way women view sex. It convinces them that the sex in pornography is normal and healthy, leads them to participate in degrading and dangerous sexual acts, and induces them to be more sexually aggressive. It rewires a woman's brain.

A while back there was a popular series of books entitled *Fifty Shades of Gray*. These books became international best sellers, even outselling the Harry Potter books. These books are considered "erotic literature." They are about an innocent young woman who gets involved with a severely disturbed man, who coerces her into engaging in dangerous sadomasochistic sex. The books are highly pornographic in the way they describe the sex scenes. In the end, the young woman becomes the man's savior. While the books may seem to have a happy ending, they have strongly influenced women's views of relationships and sex. They romanticize a relationship with a pathological man and normalize dangerous sex. Many women have become more interested in dangerous forms of sex, believing this will improve their relationships and their sexual experiences. It has led women to become more sexually aggressive and to seek out sexually domineering men.

This increase in aggressiveness, coupled with their deep need for intimacy, has led many women to take dangerous risks. Women are more likely to desire meeting the men they have bonded with online. It is well known that people often lie about themselves online, and so a woman might believe she is having a romantic rendezvous with a wonderful man at a local hotel when she could actually be meeting a dangerous predator.

Some women justify their pornography use by restricting its use to reading erotic literature. Whether the images are of real people in a video or mental images of fictitious characters in a book, using them for one's own sexual pleasure makes it a form of pornography. Most women would agree that visual images can be viewed as pornography, but many have difficulty understanding how this definition is applied to fictitious characters. Fictitious erotic "literature" is pornographic because they are images used to aid or induce "mental masturbation," and as we will see later, it's a very short leap from using fictitious characters to using real people. Such a person has taken the first step down a very dangerous slope.

From Pornography User to Sex Addiction

Pornography addiction is a type of sex addiction, but I make a distinction between the two. A person who struggles with pornography addiction is one whose addictive sexual activity is limited to the Internet, which includes visual pornography, chat rooms, erotic literature, and social media. A person struggling with sex addiction may participate in these activities, but they will also physically act out sexually, often with people they have met online. This is where men and women differ in their addictions. Men will often remain pornography addicts while women move on to becoming sex addicts.

Sexual addiction today often begins online with pornography. We discussed in chapter two how a person's tolerance grows as the addiction grows, that more of the substance is needed to achieve the same effect. As the soft porn becomes less stimulating, the addicted person turns to more extreme forms of pornography—hard core, violence, fetishes, verbal degradation, animals, children, etc. Recall that as the amount of time spent online engaging in cybersex increases, the need for greater stimulation grows, and the desire to act out with a real person emerges, which leads the addicted person to search for sex partners online, often through hookup websites, chat rooms, Craig's List, Facebook, and other forms of social media.

We discussed how both men and women who are searching for intimacy turn to pornography. Many men can limit their addictive behaviors to pornography use because they are primarily visually stimulated. Women, however, being more relationally stimulated, will often seek to develop relationships with men online. This is why women prefer chat rooms over men two to one, and it can lead to a series of cyber relationships, extramarital affairs, and anonymous sexual encounters. This is how women become addicted to sex. Amy was on her way to becoming a full blown sex addict, and had her encounter in the hotel room not been so traumatic, she may have had numerous similar sexual encounters.

Danger for Women

Because women are more apt to want to meet the men they've met online, they put themselves in tremendously dangerous situations, both physically and emotionally.

Women can become so wrapped up in the romance of an online relationship that they often overlook how dangerous meeting someone in person can be. People often lie about themselves online, as Amy learned when she discovered the man she planned to meet was not a handsome twenty-five-year-old athlete. Women often believe the men they meet online are wonderful, gentle, caring men who are also interested in a relationship. Often this is not the case. Women may believe they are having a romantic rendezvous with the man of her dreams when they really could be meeting a serial rapist or worse. Amy discovered this when the man she met tried to force himself on her. Fortunately, she was able to escape. Others haven't been so fortunate. One woman in Colorado became involved with a man through the Internet, and when she finally met him in person, he kidnapped her. He held her captive for six weeks before finally murdering her. Another woman traveled to Paris to meet her online lover, and he kicked her out after they had sex. She then committed suicide in the cold winter snow (Carnes, 2001). Like most addicts, these women suffered from a distortion of reality. They craved love and affirmation so badly that they were unable to see the danger in their actions. Additional physical risks to this behavior are sexually transmitted diseases and having a child out of wedlock.

Along with the physical risks of sexual addiction are the emotional risks. Consider the case of Dorie, a highly educated professional with a successful career in healthcare. She is married, has two children, and was also addicted to romance. This led her to become obsessed with a doctor at work. She constantly thought about him and fantasized about having an affair with him. The doctor had no idea she felt this way, and frustrated with this situation, Dorie turned to the Internet. This began a series of chat room and email romances. Because she traveled so much, Dorie was able to set up personal encounters with her online lovers.

When Dorie discovered the man she believed was her soul mate, she decided to surprise him. She arranged to fly to his city and showed up, unannounced, at his door at 10:00 p.m. He was startled to see her, but they soon were having sex. Afterward, he abruptly asked her to leave. Dorie found herself out in the dark far from a phone or taxi. She was shocked that he would simply use her sexually and then turn her out into the street. She thought she knew him. She believed they were soul mates. As she looked back toward his house, she saw a car pull into his driveway. A woman and several children got out. Dorie knew they were his wife and family, and the reality of her addiction finally set in (Carnes, 2001).

While every woman's story is different, they all share these common threads:

1. The search for love and affirmation
2. Becoming mesmerized by all the possible relationships the Internet proposes to offer
3. Romanticizing online relationships
4. Putting one's self in physical and emotional danger
5. Feelings of tremendous guilt and shame
6. Repeating the same behaviors over and over again despite the possible consequences
7. Feeling one's life is out of control

Root Causes

As with men, women's pornography and sex addiction is also both physical and emotional. Just as visual images trigger chemical reactions in a man's brain, the written images and promise of a relationship trigger similar reactions in a woman's brain. On the emotional side, the addictiveness is the same for both men and women. Both are searching for intimacy and trying to ease the pain of deep emotional wounds.

While the emotional wounds are similar, I want to point out a few that are particularly common for women who become addicted to pornography and sex.

1. *Family-of-Origin Wounds*: These wounds can include abuse, addiction, death, divorce, abandonment, and rejection. Abuse can include physical, emotional, and sexual abuse. Of these, sexual can be the most damaging. All children need to feel loved, affirmed, valued, and protected by adults. Abuse violates this and can lead children to feel that they are unlovable, that they are bad, dirty, and deserve to be abused. Children who live with an addicted parent often live in fear and chaos. They never know what to expect from one day to the next. Will their parent come home drunk? Will their parent be violent? Death and divorce are also painful for children, as they will often blame themselves for it. Associated with death and divorce are abandonment and rejection. Children who experience death often feel abandoned by the deceased spouse. Children whose parents divorce often feel rejected, especially by the parent who moves out. To deal with the pain, guilt, and loneliness of these wounds, children may turn to acting out sexually. Marnie Ferree is one such person.

   Marnie is a lovely woman and a Christian counselor who has been married for over twenty years and has two children. She is also a person recovering from sexual addiction. One would never think by looking at her that she had such a painful past; however, this is common of most women addicted to sex. Marnie's story is one of God's loving redemption. She now refers to herself as a "grateful addict" who helps other women struggling with this addiction.

Marnie's road to addiction began when she was just a small child. She had a loving family with a mother, father, and two older brothers. Her mother was diagnosed with cancer when Marnie was eighteen months old, and her mother died when Marnie was three. Although she felt hurt, lonely, and abandoned, no one in her family talked about the death. She wasn't allowed to properly grieve her loss. Marnie's father was a minister, college instructor, and college administrator, and very busy with his career. While her father was a good man whom she loved dearly, Marnie felt abandoned by him. She wondered why no one would love or care for her. She wondered if there was something wrong with her. Why was she so unlovable?

Because her father worked at a college, students were constantly visiting their home. As the only female in her house, Marnie was very comfortable around men. The sexual abuse began for Marnie when she was just five years old and lasted for fifteen years. Her abuser was twenty years older than she, a student at the college, and a longtime family friend. He showered her with love and attention. Every Saturday he would take her roller skating. She finally felt loved and affirmed by someone. Unfortunately, this came with a price: sexual abuse.

The abuse left Marnie confused about sex and relationships. She came to equate love and intimacy with sex. As a teen, she became very promiscuous, using her femininity to attract men and get the affirmation she so desperately needed. Deep down, however, she was craving the love, affirmation, and intimacy of her parents. She deeply missed her mother and was still grieving this loss. She also longed for her father's attention.

Growing up in a Christian home also left Marnie feeling conflicted. At first, she didn't see her relationship with her abuser as abusive. She loved him and enjoyed his attention. However, she knew that sex outside of marriage and her promiscuous lifestyle was sinful and her behavior violated her Christian values.

Marnie married her first husband when she was twenty, thinking this would solve her problems. She felt loved and affirmed by having someone who was readily available for sex, but she soon realized that he could not fill the deep emptiness in her wounded soul. Since her husband couldn't meet her needs, she decided to meet them on her own, which led to a series of extramarital affairs. As exciting as they were, the affairs only left her feeling emptier and eventually led to the demise of her marriage.

She married a second time and was determined not to make the same mistakes in this marriage. The first five years went well. She stayed faithful to her husband and had two beautiful children, but the stresses of life eventually led her back into her woundedness and sexual acting out. She again began another series of extramarital affairs.

The real wakeup call for Marnie came when she was diagnosed with cervical cancer as the result of a sexual transmitted disease she had contracted. She was addicted to sex and romance, and she felt her life was out of control. She didn't know who to turn to because of the incredible shame she felt. She thought God could never love her because of her past. In her mind she was a slut, a whore. Finally, out of desperation, she called a friend from church and, crying, she confessed all her sexual acting out to her friend. Fortunately, her friend responded with love and compassion and vowed to help Marnie, and introduced her to a therapist who helped her recover. Today, Marnie helps countless women find freedom from sexual addiction (Ferree, 2002).

Marnie didn't use pornography, but the end result was similar to women who do. She was looking for love and affirmation, and for many women this search begins by viewing pornography, which can lead to dangerous affairs. This is what is addictive for women. Ultimately, it leaves them feeling even more alone, dirty, and full of crippling shame.

2. *Trauma:* The experience of abuse, addiction, death, divorce, rejection, and abandonment can be very traumatic for women. Many use pornography and sex to deal with their trauma. Eight possible trauma reactions can lead women into porn (Laaser, 2009).

   a. *Trauma Pleasure.* One way a person can cope with trauma is to find pleasure in pain. For the woman who has been physically or sexually abused, being sexual becomes the only way to connect or find self-worth. When a parent has been sexual with a child, the child can conclude that the only way to have a relationship with someone is to be sexual.

   b. *Trauma Blocking.* The individual uses certain behaviors or substances to block their emotion pain. This can include drug and alcohol abuse and being hypersexual. It's no surprise that many women in porn struggle with addiction.

   c. *Trauma Shame.* The individual deals with the pain of trauma by owning negative self-beliefs. She comes to believe that because she was abused, she must be bad, stupid, and worthless, and that making porn is all she's good for. Trauma shame is also common among women in prostitution.

   d. *Trauma Repetition.* Many women who have been sexually abused will go into pornography to deal with their trauma. There is the belief that by repeating traumatic experiences, such as sexual abuse, they can achieve a different or better outcome. Unfortunately, this never happens. The trauma is only reinforced.

   e. *Trauma Splitting.* If the traumatic memory is too painful the survivor will disassociate. Her eyes will become blank and distant. She will retreat from consciousness and simply "tune out." Some will use unhealthy repetitive behaviors to help them block the pain, such as compulsive pornography viewing.

   f. *Trauma Reaction.* Here is where a survivor has mental and/ or emotional reactions to trauma including flashbacks, sudden and uncontrollable sobbing, anger outbursts, and nightmares. There can even be physical reactions such as high blood pressure, irritable bowel syndrome, fibromyalgia, chronic fatigue syndrome, headaches, backaches, etc. People with these symptoms are often diagnosed with Posttraumatic Stress Disorder (PTSD). Pornography can be used to cope with these symptoms.

g. *Trauma Abstinence.* To avoid triggering the pain, the survivor may avoid eating, communicating, certain relationships, driving, spending, etc. If a person has been sexually abused, she may avoid all sexual activity. This is also known as "sexual anorexia" or "acting-in."

h. *Trauma Bonding.* Some trauma survivors have a deep need to bond with their victimizer. They may develop relationships with those who can repeat the trauma. Their hope is that through this a true connection and bonding will occur and the pain will finally end.

It's important to note that men can also suffer from all of these reactions to trauma, which can lead them into pornography use and addiction.

3. *Loneliness:* Many women turn to the Internet for intimacy because of a deep loneliness they experience in their lives. This may have started when they were children and did not receive the love and affirmation they needed from their parents, especially their fathers. There is a special bond between fathers and daughters, which is why many women continue to refer to their fathers as "Daddy" well into their adult years. This bond can be observed at weddings, when a father walks his daughter down the aisle and dances with her at the reception. These are very emotional scenes for both father and daughter. Without this affirmation, a woman can grow up feeling lonely and unlovable. Loneliness can also result from peer rejection, especially male peers during the teenage and young adult years, leading

a woman to feel undesirable and unlovable. In either case, the lack of love, affirmation, and acceptance may lead a woman to the Internet for comfort. Cyber relationships may feel safer because there is no threat from face-to-face rejection. As the pornography use becomes an addiction, as we saw with Amy's situation, a woman can be more willing to make the dangerous move to meet the men she encountered online.

4. *The Five A's:* While not emotional wounds, these five principles of Internet pornography have also led many women into addiction.

   a. *It's Affordable.* By offering their products for free, pornographers can get more women addicted as easily as they do men. This is also includes chat rooms, which women are particularly drawn to.

   b. *It's Accessible.* Prior to the Internet, most pornography for women was in the form of racy romance novels. Most women would never dream of entering a porn shop. With the advent of the Internet, multiple forms of pornography are now available to women, including erotic literature, chat rooms, and social media as well as visual porn. Thanks to portable electronic devices, it is now just a click away.

   c. *It's Anonymous.* Since viewing pornography or visiting chat rooms can be done in the privacy of one's own home with no one ever knowing, women no longer have social stigmas to prevent them from obtaining pornography.

   d. *It's Accepted.* While few women would admit to using pornography, society's acceptance has made it easier for them to rationalize its use. The result is that many have become addicted.

   e. *It's Aggressive.* As with men, pornographers target women with hardcore pornography through visual, written or chat form. This can have the same effect on women's brains as men's, making it highly addictive.

These are just a few of the many reasons why women become addicted to pornography and sex. These wounds fuel the five core beliefs listed in chapter two (p. 51), which trap women in addiction. Whatever your reason may be, it's important to realize that help is available. You don't need to suffer in silence. You just need to reach out for help.

Guilt and Shame

Women struggling with pornography and sex addiction often find it difficult to reach out for help because they feel incredible guilt and shame. To understand this, we must first define guilt and shame. Many people use those terms interchangeably, but from a psychological perspective they refer to different things.

There are two senses of the term "guilt." The first sense is the objective state of knowing you have committed a wrong. The second sense is the knowledge that you've done something wrong and must fix it or make amends. This is good. In this book, we will be using the latter sense. When we experience guilt, it means our conscience is working properly. It requires apologizing to God and those we have hurt, and correcting our mistakes. Here is where the Sacrament of Reconciliation is so valuable. Many pornography users instinctively know it is wrong, but unfortunately, they often find ways to justify their behavior so as not to feel their guilt. Some people's consciences have become so desensitized and damaged by society and the media that they no longer feel any guilt when viewing pornography.

There are also two senses to the term "shame"—healthy and unhealthy shame. Healthy shame engenders compunction, sorrow, and remorse for one's sins and prompts them to seek help and forgiveness. This is good. However, unhealthy shame is the emotion that leads one to believe they are a terrible person, which leads them *not* to seek help or forgiveness. This is not good. Again, in this book, we will be referring to the latter sense, unhealthy shame.

We've all had experiences of shame. Think of a time when you did something humiliating and you just want to crawl under a rock whenever you think of it. Pornography use is a shameful thing for many people. This is especially true for women, which is primarily due to a double standard in our culture that accepts the premise that only men view pornography. It's a guy thing, and while many women don't approve of this, they do tolerate it. However, for women it's a different story. Women are supposed to be "pure," which means if a woman struggles with pornography or sex addiction, society labels her as a tramp. She faces judgment and condemnation. What is more, the unhealthy shame women face can lead them to believe that God could never love them. That is particularly painful.

If you are struggling with immense unhealthy shame due to your addiction, I'm here to tell you that you are not a bad person. You are not unlovable. God still loves you, and nothing you could ever do could take His love away from you. God wants to hold you in His arms and comfort you. You may not have had a loving protective father in your life, but God wants to be that father to you. As you reach out for help, you will come to know many people who want to help you instead of condemn you, especially God. Through your recovery, you will learn how incredibly special and lovable you are.

Crystal Renaud experienced this. She was raised in a good Christian home, but her mother struggled with depression and her father was busy with his career. This left her very lonely. She eased her loneliness with pornography, which led to a double life and an eight-year struggle with addiction. On the outside, Crystal presented the appearance of a faithful Christian woman. On the inside, she felt like a terrible hypocrite. What would people think of her if they discovered her "dirty little secret"? Like Amy, Crystal's pornography use went from magazines, to Internet porn, to chat rooms, to phone sex, and finally to arranging an encounter with a man she contacted online. Fortunately, she couldn't bring herself to go through with the rendezvous. Then one day God intervened. A woman at a Christian concert opened up to Crystal and shared about her struggle with pornography. This surprised Crystal because she believed she was the only Christian woman who struggled with pornography addiction. Crystal also admitted her struggle and both women became accountability partners, which was the beginning of Crystal's recovery. She came to realize God's great love for her and the love of the people He placed in her life. This allowed Crystal to let go of her shame (Renaud, 2011).

Like anyone in recovery, Crystal had her struggles, and yet she persevered. She now helps other women struggling with pornography addiction through her Dirty Girls Ministries. You can learn more about Crystal and her work at dirtygirlsministries.com.

Finding Help

The shame these addicted women feel often makes it more difficult for them to seek help. But, I'm asking you to trust God with this because there are many compassionate therapists and support groups that are ready to assist. Dirty Girls Ministries is just one. I list several other resources for women in the appendix. Taking that leap of faith to ask for help is the first step to recovery. Healing and recovery are possible. Don't be discouraged. Have hope! I want to leave you with a very special story from the Gospel of John 8:1–11:

> They went each to his own house, but Jesus went to the Mount of Olives. Early in the morning he came again to the temple; all the people came to him, and he sat down and taught them. The Scribes and the Pharisees brought a woman who had been caught in adultery, and placing her in their midst they said to him, "Teacher, this woman has been caught in the act of adultery. Now in the Law, Moses commanded us to stone such. What do you say about her?" This they said to test him, that they might have some charge to bring against him. Jesus bent down and wrote with his finger on the ground. And as they continued to ask him, he stood up and said to them, "Let him who is without sin among you be the first to throw a stone at her." And once more he bent down and wrote with his finger on the ground. But when they heard it, they went

away, one by one, beginning with the eldest, and Jesus was left alone with the woman standing before him. Jesus looked up and said to her, "Woman, where are they? Has no one condemned you?" She said, "No one, Lord." And Jesus said, "Neither do I condemn you; go, and do not sin again."

Jesus does not condemn the woman, but He does acknowledge her sin and admonishes her to "sin no more." He also treats her with love and compassion. No matter how much you've sinned, this is how our Lord will treat you. While He wants you to confess your sins and strive to stop sinning, He also wants you to know how much He loves you and wants to heal you. He has provided many wonderful people who are eager to help you. Allow God to love you by seeking help today!

If you are a spouse, family member, friend, or colleague of a woman who may be addicted to pornography and sex, please understand her shame and be compassionate toward her. Whether she comes to you for help or you discover her addiction by accident, she needs love and understanding. Remember, her sexual activity is really a symptom of deeper emotional wounds. You can help guide her to the help she needs. Be patient and listen to her story. Don't judge or condemn. You may be the only person she has ever told her story to, which is a wonderful privilege because you are someone that she trusts. It's also a great responsibility because your response can have a great impact on her recovery, and if she receives your love and compassion, it will be easier for her to seek help. If she receives shame and condemnation, she might dive deeper into her addiction. It's important for you to be Jesus to her.

5

How Pornography Affects Marriages and Families

I presented the story of Tom and Janet at the beginning of chapter one (p. 7). They are like many married couples I've counseled whose lives have been wounded by pornography addiction. In this chapter we will return to their story to show how pornography affects marriage and families.

Recall that Tom and Janet were married for fifteen years, had four children, and came to my office because of Tom's pornography use. Hurt and betrayed, Janet told Tom he either ends his pornography use or she would leave him. Tom knew that he was addicted. He was hurting Janet and their marriage, and he agreed to get help because he didn't want to lose her. This was their first step toward healing.

Different Views of Pornography

To better understand how pornography affects marriages and families, we need to examine the difference between how men and women view pornography.

Men have been viewing pornography for thousands of years. It has even been found on cave walls. While most women don't approve of this "guy thing" in western culture, they have tolerated it since the debut of pinup girls in the 1940s. I believe this acceptance has led men to believe that "it's okay to use pornography, as long as your wife doesn't find out about it." Men will often joke about this in the locker room. As we have already shown, even some men view pornography use as a rite of passage into manhood and as harmless adult entertainment. While most men are aware of women's disapproval of pornography, they often don't know why or how it hurts women.

Tom's view of pornography was similar to most men. He knew Janet wouldn't approve of it, and so he hid it from her. Notice he was more afraid of her disapproval and anger than of her pain. He was entirely unaware of how his pornography use would hurt her. He never saw it as committing adultery or contributing to the exploitation of women. Tom had much to learn.

Women, on the other hand, don't see pornography as harmless adult entertainment. They often see it as degrading toward women. Much of the pornography available today is very aggressive and abusive toward women, which is evident in many scenes depicting one or more men using a woman in sexually violent ways. Some forms of pornography go to extremes to hurt women by depicting scenes of verbal degradation, sadomasochism, rape, and even murder. Sex is never depicted as a warm and gentle expression of love between a husband and wife. While men may view the women in porn as simply images on a screen, women see them as real people. To women, using pornography is similar to being in a relationship with those women, and that is tantamount to adultery.

Janet's response to Tom's pornography use was similar to that of most wives. She was sickened by the very thought of her husband viewing pornography, because to her, he was not only using and condoning the sexual abuse of women, he also was committing adultery.

When a man and a woman fall in love and enter into a relationship, they give each other their hearts and expect the other to care for and protect it. When a wife discovers her husband's pornography use, she often feels heartbroken. He has neither cared for nor protected his wife's heart. He has betrayed her love and trust. She feels deeply hurt because she originally believed she had her husband's complete heart, and now she sees that only part of his heart belonged to her while the rest belonged to the women in porn.

When a woman considers a man as a possible mate, she doesn't simply judge him on his appearance, because women are relationally stimulated. They enjoy looking at handsome men, but they are not as visually stimulated as men are. Thus, when a woman evaluates a man, she discerns whether he is virtuous. Is he trustworthy? Will he protect her heart? Would he make a good husband and father? Will he take care of his responsibilities? What kind of family does he come from? Most women would not judge a man who uses pornography to be a suitable mate. They would avoid such a man.

Some women tolerate pornography use, justifying it by claiming "all men do it." They try to sound sexually liberated and open-minded. I believe these women are too afraid to put their foot down. They are afraid their husband or boyfriend will leave them. Their self-esteem is so low that they don't believe they could find better men. So they suffer in silence. In my clinical experience, no woman wants to share a man with the women in pornography. A study from the University of Florida found that young women who are dating or married to a man who looks at porn frequently are less happy in their relationships than women with men who don't. The study supports anecdotal evidence that men's porn use lowers the self-esteem of their girlfriends or wives (Huffington Post, 2012).

With that difference of how men and women view pornography fresh in our minds, let's now look at how pornography affects marriages.

Effects on Marriages

Broken Trust. The most prominent effect of pornography use on a marriage is the loss of trust. When a couple falls in love and marries, they do so believing they truly know each other. Without any hidden secrets, a deep level of safety develops within the relationship. This allows each person to fully give their heart to their spouse without fear of being hurt. It is the deepest form of intimacy in marriage (Laaser, 2008). Pornography use destroys this trust and is extremely painful for a wife. Without warning, her husband seems like a stranger and she feels like she never really knew him. Many questions arise in her mind:

How long has he been viewing pornography? Has he been to strip clubs or with prostitutes? Am I at risk for contracting a sexually transmitted disease? Has he had affairs? Am I no longer sexually attractive to him? Has he told me the truth about all his sexual activity? Her life becomes consumed with worrying about where her husband is and who he is with when he's not home. She wonders whether it is safe to leave their children alone with him. This sacred marital trust can take months or even years to rebuild. For some wives, this trust has been so deeply damaged that it can lead to divorce.

The pain of the loss of trust was very real for Janet. She always believed that she and Tom were best friends as well as spouses. She never thought he would ever keep secrets from her and she had always shared everything with him. Discovering his pornography use changed everything. She no longer felt emotionally safe with him and wondered if she would ever be able to trust him again. It was as if her husband moved out of her life and a stranger moved in.

Damaged Communication. Pornography use also affects communication in a marriage. Because most husbands keep their pornography use a secret, they cannot discuss everything in their lives with their wives. This prevents them from truly sharing their hearts, and it creates a vicious cycle in which many men get trapped: They turn to pornography because they feel alone, harming their communication with their wives and increasing their isolation, which further leads them deeper into pornography use and deeper into loneliness. Often a wife can sense that her husband is struggling with something, but she is left wondering because he doesn't talk about it. This lack of communication also leaves her feeling shut out of his life.

Tom's pornography use was fueled by a deep loneliness he had felt since childhood. He used pornography to ease the pain of that feeling, but it continued because he couldn't express this to Janet. He didn't realize she could have helped him resolve his loneliness without him turning to pornography. Janet's "woman's intuition" told her that Tom was struggling with something, but she couldn't get him to talk about it. When she eventually learned about Tom's pornography use, it was painful and damaged their marital trust, but it was also a relief because Janet no longer felt like she was in the dark about their relationship. They could finally communicate!

Increased Selfishness. This is especially evident in marriages. Men's attitude of entitlement today after a "hard day's work" leads them to close in on themselves, spending hours and money on viewing pornography while neglecting their wives and families. Their lack of communication is another form of selfishness, refusing to share all of themselves with their wives and families. Selfishness is rarely limited to one area of life. One can be stingy in sharing his time, attention, and resources, a fact that Tom and Janet experienced in their marriage.

Tom often told Janet he had to work late. Instead, he was really viewing pornography, which took him away from his family. He believed he deserved this time away, and his sense of entitlement expanded to playing golf with his buddies on weekends. This aspect of Tom's addiction angered Janet the most. While she could comprehend him turning to pornography like a drug to self-medicate his emotional pain, she could not excuse his selfishness. Fortunately, Tom was very remorseful and realized he had lost precious time with Janet and their children—time he could never get back.

Disordered Sexuality. Constant viewing of pornography can create a disordered view of sexuality in marriage. Along with making men believe their wives are there solely for their sexual pleasure, it can make them want to engage in forms of sex that are degrading to women, namely oral and anal sex. Many men have come to believe this is normal, healthy sex that women enjoy because it's what is shown so often in pornography. Clearly, this is not true. When I refer to "oral sex" throughout this book, I am referring to the illicit practice forbidden by the Church and widely accepted by our culture. While married couples can partake in oral or manual genital stimulation as a form of foreplay, engaging in "oral sex" as the culmination of sexual activity is a grave matter of mortal sin. To be clear, ejaculation should only occur in the vagina. Since the husband's biological make up can result in his reaching a climax before his wife does, he should then, in an act of charity of love for his wife, seek other forms of stimulation to bring his wife to climax. Pope John Paul II says that "if a woman does not obtain natural gratification from the sexual act there is a danger that her experience of it will be qualitatively inferior, will not involve her fully as a person" (*Love and Responsibility*, 273). This is all considered an integral part of their "complete" marital act. Anal sex is also a matter of grave mortal sin. For most people, anal sex is extremely painful and not sexually stimulating. Despite what the "sexperts" say, the anus was never meant to be a sex organ. Remember, women are relationally oriented, and there is really nothing relational about oral or anal sex. Many women claim that when they perform oral sex or receive anal sex, they really feel like sex toys for their husbands. The desire to engage in oral or anal sex may be a warning sign that a husband has been viewing pornography.

This was how Janet first suspected that Tom was viewing pornography. She believed they had a healthy and satisfying sex life, until one day Tom suggested she perform oral sex on him. She initially refused, but he persisted to badger her until she relented. She did not enjoy it and only did it to please him. Soon he wanted to try anal sex. Janet drew the line there. Her women's intuition told her there was something wrong with Tom, although she couldn't say what it was. On a hunch, she checked Tom's laptop computer and found his pornography stash. This led them into therapy.

The deviant sex promoted by pornography doesn't stop with oral and anal sex. It can include swinging, rape scene role playing, and sadomasochistic sex, which are degrading to both parties and physically and emotionally dangerous. A person who insists on engaging in these behaviors is probably deeply entrenched in sexual addiction and needs immediate professional help.

Decreased Sexual Satisfaction and Performance. The pornography industry wants men to believe that viewing pornography and masturbating helps their sex lives. It can actually have a detrimental effect. Pornography can change a person's view of beauty, and through repeated exposure to pornography a man can come to believe that the only beautiful women are the women in porn. These young women with massive amounts of plastic surgery damages a man's ability to see the true beauty of real women, such as his wife, and he comes to believe the fantasy is better than real love. It's as if they've conditioned themselves to believe that true fulfillment can only come from viewing the constant parade of beautiful women in porn, rather than from a healthy committed marital relationship with one woman. Some men even prefer masturbating with pornography over having sex with a real woman. As we showed in chapter three, it can even cause erectile dysfunction, leaving a man unable to perform when he tries to have sex with his wife, because the overstimulation from pornography creates changes in the brain that make him less responsive to the physical pleasures of a woman and hyper responsive to Internet porn (Wilson, 2012). When men become entrenched in pornography, it ends up deadening their libido. In the words of Dr. Mary Anne Layden (2004), "Having spent too much time in unnatural sexual experiences with paper, celluloid, and cyberspace, they find it difficult to have sex with a real human being. Pornography is toxic miseducation about sex and relationships."

These sexual problems caused by pornography are very damaging to marriages, and especially damaging to a woman's self-esteem. When a husband is unable to perform sexually with his wife, she may blame herself, believing he no longer finds her attractive. This is especially true for older wives. Discovering that her husband views porn only reinforces this belief. Most of the women in porn are between the ages of eighteen and twenty-five, and so when a middle-aged woman sees the porn stars her husband has been viewing, she may think she is too old and ugly for him. This is how Janet felt. It appeared to her as if Tom wanted to replace her with the women in porn. She felt rejected and cast aside.

Healthy sexuality is not only an expression of the love between a husband and wife, it also affirms each spouse in their beauty, desirability, and dignity. It says, "I love you, you are beautiful, you are the only one for me, and I reserve this special and intimate part of my life for you alone." Pornography use destroys this.

Increased Loneliness. We have seen how pornography use leads men and women into deeper loneliness. This has a dual effect on both spouses in marriage. The more a man's life is consumed with pornography, the less time he gives to his wife, who in turn becomes lonely. The man becomes more isolated as he chases the false illusion of intimacy in pornography, an illusion created by the women in porn who are always there, always beckoning, always promising love and intimacy. The excitement of pornography leads him to forget the true love and intimacy he once had with his wife. The draw of pornography is so strong that despite its constant failure to provide real intimacy, he still goes back to it believing "the next time will be better," resulting in a vicious downward spiral leading both spouses deeper into loneliness.

Emotional Effects on Wives

I have already listed many of the harmful effects that pornography has on marriages. There are deeper wounds that wives struggle with that can take a long time to heal. While there is overlap between what follows and the effects listed above, it's very important that both husbands and wives are aware of these deeper wounds and address them as part of the recovery process for the marriage.

Betrayal. This is the most obvious emotional wound that wives experience. To them and the Church, pornography use is adultery. When a man and woman marry, they make vows to love, honor, and cherish each other for the rest of their lives. To use pornography is to break those vows (CCC 2381). A woman cannot feel loved, honored, and cherished when her husband uses pornography, when he has taken something as sacred as their intimate sexual life and shared it with hundreds of women online. Her husband's betrayal raises many other questions for her: "How long has this been going on? How many women has he viewed in porn? Has he been with prostitutes? Have there been any extramarital affairs? Has he spent money on pornography and how much?"

Janet had all of these questions, and the betrayal was so deep for her that she felt she no longer knew Tom. Now, he was a stranger and she couldn't sleep in the same bed with him anymore. She no longer felt special in her marriage. To her, she was "just another bimbo that Tom has been with." It took a while for Tom to realize how deeply his actions betrayed her. This was clear to him only when he fully understood how women and men define pornography differently, and how injurious it was to Janet.

Anger. Along with betrayal is anger. Most women experience a strong rage when they discover their husbands' pornography use, a righteous anger. They have been betrayed, marital vows have been broken, and for some women this anger and betrayal are so strong that they want to end their marriages. Janet was tempted to do this. In therapy sessions she admitted that if it had been anything else, she probably could have handled it better. The effects of Tom's pornography use went to the core of her soul. She wanted to forgive him, but she knew it would take time despite his deep remorse. He repeatedly apologized, and she needed to hear it, but he also realized that while Janet was working through her anger, he would have to be her "punching bag" for a while, enduring her outbursts of rage. Most women are able to work through their anger and forgive their husbands, but it requires a lot of love and patience, and the understanding that holding onto anger, no matter how justified it is, will ultimately do more harm to a wife and to a marriage. More on the forgiveness process will be discussed later, but remember, there is a time to be angry and a time to forgive (cf. Ecclesiastes 3:1–8).

Loss of Trust. I discussed loss of trust earlier in this chapter, but let's look at how this specifically affects wives emotionally. When a wife loses trust in her husband, it affects her ability to feel emotionally safe and secure in her marriage. She no longer feels that she can count on her husband. This can lead to many irrational behaviors, including checking Internet history, phone records, credit card bills, and so on. She will regularly interrogate her husband to uncover all his sexual activity, while constantly questioning what he has told her and not knowing what to believe. She may fear leaving him at home alone, allowing him to go on business trips, or even go to work. All of this activity is done to try to regain some sense of safety and security for her, but it usually ends up wearing her out, and ultimately, she knows she cannot control every minute of his life. For some wives, this loss of trust leads them to live estranged from their husbands to protect themselves emotionally. Repeated violations in some cases can permanently damage trust and lead to divorce.

Janet's loss of trust in Tom was particularly painful because he was the one person she thought she could always trust. She never questioned him. He was her rock. When she discovered his pornography use, it felt like her world was destroyed and she didn't know who she could count on. Janet began to experience bouts of depression and anxiety. Husbands must understand that sacred marital trust can be easily damaged and can take months or years to restore. With Tom, this meant a life of total honesty and transparency. For months, he had to account for every minute of his day, his use of the Internet, and any other form of media.

Pain and Sadness. Wives who have been affected by their husbands' pornography use often say there is a deep aching in their hearts. They gave each other their hearts in marriage, and it is their responsibility to protect each other's heart. Discovering her husband's pornography use, a wife often is stunned at how he could have been so thoughtless, inconsiderate, and disrespectful. She can't believe how the man she loved and trusted the most could do something so hurtful. This pain is accompanied by a deep sadness. All at once the wonderful marriage she thought she had now seems like a farce. She now questions what is real in their marriage and what isn't, and whether the marriage can even be healed and if they will ever recover.

Janet felt this way. She thought Tom loved her. Now, she felt as if he threw her heart on the ground and stomped on it. She grieved over her marriage, or at least the marriage she thought she had. Many nights were spent lying awake and weeping. Seeing how hurt and sad Janet was deeply affected Tom. Had he known how much his pornography use would hurt her, he never would have entertained the thought of using it. This deep pain and sadness may seem unending, but healing is possible. Husbands can help heal their wives' pain and sadness by seeking forgiveness and making a firm commitment to never hurt their wives in such a deep way ever again.

Unable to Compete. Discovering her husband's use of pornography can severely wound a woman's self-image. A wife, who looks like a real woman and not a porn star, and sees these very young and beautiful women that don't exist in real life, often asks, "How can I compete?" She knows there is no way that she could ever look like the women in porn! This can leave her feeling sexually undesirable, and it is a no-win situation for most women. The women in porn are always young while real women age. In an interview with the Huffington Post, secular sex educator Carlin Ross even admitted, "We don't experience the same heights of pleasure as these porn stars, and we internalize this failure. We believe that there's something wrong with us. Then add the body-image issues created by watching idealized images of women with surgically enhanced bodies and genitals, and now we feel even worse. We believe that we're genitally deformed, we're broken, and we'll never have great sex" (Huffington Post, 2012). Because pornography damages a man's ability to appreciate true beauty in women, it leaves wives feeling unloved and rejected by their husbands.

Feeling like this, Janet began exercising more to lose weight. She also dressed sexier and had more sex with Tom. In the end, however, she knew she was only fooling herself and that she would never look like a twenty-year-old porn star. She also knew that all the sex she was having with Tom felt empty. She realized what she was doing and became angry with herself for allowing porn to dictate the type of wife she should be. For a while after that she refused to have sex with Tom or even sleep with him. Tom never imagined how deeply his actions would affect Janet emotionally. Recall, to him, the women in porn were just those images on a screen. But for Janet, they were real women with whom she needed to compete for Tom's love and attention.

Codependence. Many spouses of addicts become codependent, a disease that reacts to the addiction and results in a loss of self for the spouse. They may appear to be completely in control, but behind the scenes their worlds are falling apart. Patrick Carnes and colleagues

(2007) list nine signs of codependency in spouses. While I refer to the husband as the "addicted person" and the wife as "codependent," the roles can be seen in reverse.

1. *Collusion.* Codependent wives may enable their husbands' addiction by covering up for their behaviors. A wife may make excuses for him when he neglects important responsibilities. She might also join her husband in his sexual behaviors so as not to feel left out of his life. She may even try to convince herself that her husband's behaviors are not so bad. She may tell herself that viewing pornography is not as bad as going to strip clubs or prostitutes.

2. *Obsessive Preoccupation.* Codependent wives often obsess over their husbands' sexual activity, which can result in them playing detective by checking his mail, email, computer files, cell phone histories, bank statements, credit card and phone bills, etc. They will search Internet histories trying to identify every porn site their husband has ever visited. In addition to trying to control their husbands' lives, wives may do this to avoid facing their own painful feelings. This can consume a woman's life and prevent her from experiencing the healing she needs.

3. *Denial.* Codependent wives can also ignore what is really happening in their marriages. They may try to keep busy so as not to think about the problem. Some believe they will eventually change their husbands. They may attempt to dismiss the seriousness of viewing pornography by telling themselves that those women really are just images on a screen and not real.

4. *Emotional Turmoil.* Codependent wives often feel their lives are on an emotional rollercoaster. They can go through emotional binges where their emotions are out of control, quickly cycling through emotions of rage, sadness, fear, depression, anxiety, shame, humiliation, and so on. Often they feel they are in a

constant state of crisis, which is extremely frightening for wives who feel they are "losing control and going crazy."

5. *Manipulation.* Codependent wives can become very manipulative in their attempts to control their husbands' sexual acting out. A wife may use sex to control him, or threaten to leave altogether, often ending up in the martyr, hero, or victim role. She may try to regulate her husband's computer use by holding all the passwords, or installing a blocking or accountability software and being the only one to monitor Internet use. This ultimately leads to frustration since it is impossible to control every aspect of a person's life.

6. *Excessive Responsibility.* Codependent wives often blame themselves for their husbands' sexual behaviors, believing if they change, their husbands will stop. This can lead them to be hypersexual and trying to compete with the women in pornography. They may also take on excessive family and household responsibilities, making themselves indispensable to their addicted husbands.

7. *Compromise or Loss of Self.* Codependent wives often compromise their morals, values, and beliefs to keep their marriages afloat. They may change their dress or appearance to please their husbands, or join their husbands in viewing porn, or participate in the sexual acts depicted in porn despite feeling cheap and used. Codependent wives will give up interests, hobbies, and life goals to please their husbands, ultimately eroding their sense of self.

8. *Blame and Punishment.* Codependent wives can become blaming and punishing in their obsession with their husbands' sexual behaviors. They see themselves as victims and self-righteous in their anger. They may punish their husbands by withholding sex. Some may have affairs to prove to their husbands that they are sexually desirable. They view their behavior as acts of revenge and destructive toward their husbands. Some even experience homicidal thoughts and feelings, and although they

may see their actions as justified, they often don't see them as self-destructive.

9. *Sexual Reactivity.* Codependent wives often go to extremes in reacting sexually to their husbands' behaviors, sometimes becoming hypersexual, believing this will keep their husbands from acting out sexually with pornography or other people. Others simply shut down sexually. They will make excuses for not being sexual, change clothes out of sight of their husbands, and will rarely feel intimate during sex. For these women, if they do have sex with their husbands, it's just going through the motions. They are emotionally detached.

The purpose of all these behaviors is safety. Many codependent wives come from highly dysfunctional families that struggled with addiction. For example, it's not uncommon for a woman who grew up in an alcoholic home to marry an alcoholic. Although she may have made a vow to herself to never marry an alcoholic, she somehow ends up in such a relationship. People often tend to end up with what's familiar to them. It is believed that many of the codependent behaviors found in a marriage to an addicted person actually developed during childhood and are carried into the marriage. These wives have been deeply wounded by their husbands' pornography addiction, and to protect themselves from further hurt, wives will try to control their husbands by engaging in the codependent behaviors listed above. They may see their actions as irrational, but they don't know another way to deal with their situation, which is why they need to seek professional help and support.

Trauma. Not all wives of pornography addicts are codependent. Research has shown that most spouses of addicts actually struggle with trauma (Steffens, 2009). They generally do not come from dysfunctional families. This often is the reason why the trauma is so painful. They did not grow up with the pain and chaos of living in an addicted family, and this is a new experience for them. To label them as codependent leaves these wives feeling misunderstood. While they realize they need healing, such a label makes them feel like they are the "sick one."

Barbara Steffans and Marsha Means (2009) list three general reactions to trauma related to sexual addiction. Note that there is considerable overlap among the symptoms.

1. *Avoidance.* The traumatized wife will avoid activities or other reminders of the traumatic event, or avoid the conflict altogether by watching porn with her husband and hoping he will turn to her for sex. Others will avoid sex altogether. Still others will numb their feelings and deny the situation, detaching from their husbands emotionally. A wife may ignore her "intuition" or new evidence that her husband is acting out again.

2. *Re-experiencing.* These are recurrent and intrusive thoughts and memories of the traumatic event that cannot be controlled. A wife may be plagued with constant thoughts about what her husband has done, which can consume her energy and intensify her anxiety.

3. *Arousal.* This intense emotional pain can include feelings of depression, anxiety, fear, and shame. A woman may have panic attacks or uncontrollable crying. She may wonder what she did wrong to cause her husband to turn to pornography. The shame and embarrassment may keep her from telling others about her situation. She might try to control every aspect of her husband's life to prevent being hurt again, such as regulating when and how long he uses the computer and what websites can be accessed.

When a wife is traumatized by her husband's pornography addiction, her response is not limited to just one of the reactions listed above. Often she responds using a combination of the three.

As with codependency, these behaviors are meant to protect the wife from being hurt any further. The goal is to ensure safety. However, the difference between a person who is codependent and one who is traumatized depends on who or what they are trying to control. A codependent wife is trying to control her husband. Her focus is on him and what he is doing or not doing to hurt her. A traumatized wife is trying to control her environment, which is akin to a woman who has been sexually assaulted. Her main focus is ensuring that her environment is safe. Thus, even after her attacker is sent to prison, she may have the locks on her house changed, avoid certain parts of town, and constantly check the back seat of her car to make sure no one is back there. No one would call her sick or obsessed for doing these things, as they are seen as normal behaviors of a traumatized person.

Janet fits the description of someone who has been traumatized by her husband's behaviors. She came from a healthy loving home with no history of abuse or addiction. Her father was a strong, loving, protective man. When she discovered Tom's addiction, it was a new experience and particularly painful. Her attempts to feel safe focused on her environment. For a while she refused to have sex with Tom or even sleep with him. While much of this was due to the betrayal, anger, and sadness she experienced, it was also to help her feel safe. Not having Tom in their bedroom provided her with a safe refuge that she could escape to when she was feeling bad. She also cycled through many painful emotions including depression, anger, sadness, and anxiety, and at times she would cry uncontrollably. This frightened her as it left her feeling totally out of control. She just wanted to feel safe and secure.

Effects on the Family

Pornography use and addiction also has multiple effects on the family. A father's time away from his family has enormous effects on the family. Envision the father who sleeps through his son's Saturday morning baseball game because he was up for hours the night before viewing Internet pornography. Or the man who misses dinner with his family several nights a week claiming he has to work late when he is actually frequenting porn shops and strip clubs after work. This takes a toll on the family because children miss valuable time with their father. The father misses out on creating cherished memories watching his kids grow up, and the wives are burdened because their husband leaves them with additional parenting responsibilities. Consider the financial burden placed on the family because of money spent on pornography, strip clubs, prostitutes, and the rest. There is also the embarrassment and humiliation that all family members feel when the addiction is finally discovered.

The loss of Tom in their family life left Janet feeling both like a single parent and a fool for trying to explain his absence. All along she believed he was working overtime. She was angry because of all the wonderful times he missed out on because of his addiction—baseball and soccer games, school plays, family gatherings, and much more. Tom also felt bad because he realized these were times and experiences that he could never get back.

Pornography use also damages a man's ability to be a good leader, provider, and protector of his family. Instead of being a good role model for his kids, he is a hypocrite. Many fathers will preach to their kids on the dangers of pornography while they regularly use it behind closed doors. A wife may think, "If he believes it is okay to use pornography, will he allow our sons to view porn someday?" It contributes to her loss of trust in him as a father. To make matters worse, many fathers don't see viewing pornography as a problem. Others see it as a rite of passage and actually give their sons pornography on their sixteenth or eighteenth birthday. If a couple has daughters, it could be worse. A wife might think, "Is he looking at our daughters the way he looks at the women in porn?" While a son might not be too upset to learn that his father uses pornography, this can be devastating for a daughter. To think that the man she has always loved, trusted, and looked up to as her protector is using porn is repulsive to her. She loses all respect for her father.

Janet always felt that Tom was a good role model for their sons. He often spoke to them about respecting women and treating them properly. Tom's use of pornography destroyed this image. Janet had nightmares about their sons discovering Tom's stash of pornography and how he would explain it. While she knew he would never expose their kids to pornography, the trauma of Tom's addiction led her to fear leaving them alone with him. She had difficulty seeing him as a good leader, provider, and protector of their children.

Divorce

A man's use of pornography can lead to q3divorce in many cases. According to the American Association of Matrimonial Attorneys, pornography plays a significant role in 57% of all divorces (Eberstadt & Layden, 2010) and is correlated with a 318% increase in infidelity (Stack, 2004). This often happens when the husband doesn't see his pornography use as a problem and refuses to stop using it. They usually feel entitled to use porn and often blame their wives for being too prudish or not open-minded. Most wives won't put up with this and eventually they give their husbands an ultimatum. Their husbands must choose between their wives and the pornography. For many men, this ultimatum is a wakeup call. They are finally able to see how destructive pornography is to their marriage and are willing to find help for their addiction and their marriage. Other men deny that they have a problem with pornography and continue viewing it. In their selfishness, they continue to feed their addiction, choosing pornography over their marriages. They are totally unaware of the hold that pornography has on them. Wives of such men often file for divorce, which is extremely damaging to children as they witness their family break apart.

Pornography addiction doesn't have to end in divorce and the breakup of the family. In chapter eleven I will discuss healing for couples and show the process of healing and restoration in Tom and Janet's marriage. In the meantime, remember there is hope for healing and restoration in a marriage that has been wounded by pornography addiction.

God's Plan for Marriage

Even with all the pain pornography addiction causes in a marriage, we have to keep in mind God's plan for marriage. God wants healthy marriages and wants to bring healing and restoration to those marriages wounded by pornography. We must faithfully trust in God that His plan will come to fruition, regardless of the time it takes. This is a spiritual battle. Satan hates holy marriages and will do anything to destroy them. Pornography addiction is one of his most powerful weapons. We can't let Satan win! Wounded couples should turn their lives and their marriages over to the Lord, and He will take care of them and bring them comfort in the darkest hour. Asking the Blessed Mother and St. Joseph to intercede for wounded marriages and to protect these marriages during the healing process is also very powerful.

If you are experiencing the deep pain of pornography addiction in your marriage, know that you are not alone. God is with you. He knows your pain and wants to comfort you. He wants to take your wounded marriage and turn it into something wonderful. He will bring caring people into your life to help you. Not only can He heal your marriage, but He will also use you to help others. Somewhere down the road you might meet a hurting couple who is going through the same thing you are going through now, and you will be able to help them in their healing process. God will use you to "pay it forward."

6

How Pornography Affects Children and Teens

Pornographers are savvy business people who have learned early on that to earn the most money they need to get more and more people addicted to their drug, using all forms of media to peddle their goods. They have succeeded. They use magazines, books, films, videotapes, DVDs, telephone, cable and satellite television, strip clubs, porn shops, and now the Internet. Any device that has access to the Internet is now a portal for pornography. By getting younger and younger people addicted, they also realized they could make even more money.

Today, technology is an integral part of our kids' lives. We now have the first generation of kids coming of age that grew up with the Internet and cell phones. They cannot imagine a world without them and are often more technologically savvy than their parents. Kids use the Internet, video games, chat rooms, video chat, email, instant messaging, texting, Twitter, Facebook, Skype, Pinterest, and Face Time. They're doing this on their laptops, netbooks, iPads, tablets, iPods, MP3 players, cell phones, eReaders, and gaming systems. Whenever a new form of technology comes out, it's the kids who first make use of it. Even young children are taking advantage of new technology. Parents are often amazed at what their kids are doing today with technology!

ABC News reported that kids today begin watching porn from as early as the age of six, and begin flirting on the Internet from the age of eight, according to a survey of over nineteen thousand parents worldwide released by Bitdefender. Almost 25% of the kids in the study had at least one social network account at age twelve and 17% were social media users at ten. The survey also found that children lie about their age when creating social network profiles, specifically on Facebook where they're required to be at least thirteen (ABC News, 2013).

The intersection of kids, technology, and the pornography industry is very dangerous. Pornographers know this and are exploiting it, despite the obscenity laws deemed to protect minors. They are virtually unenforceable on the Internet. When a person logs onto a pornographic website, he is asked if he is over the age of eighteen. If he clicks "yes," he is let into the site. If he clicks "no," he is directed away from the site. This is really a no-brainer. When a fifteen-year-old boy is asked that question, how do you think he is going to answer? Naturally, he's going to lie and there is no way for the website to check his ID.

Another way kids are being introduced to Internet pornography is through pop-up advertisements that lead them to pornographic websites. Parents are often concerned about violence in video games, yet many video games are also very pornographic. Some kids are discovering pornography by accidently finding it on a family member's computer, while others are introduced to it by their friends. Pornography is an unavoidable reality in our culture. Here are some sobering statistics (Black, 2013; Family Safe Media, 2007):

- The average age a child is first exposed to Internet pornography is 11.
- By age 18, 60% of girls and 90% of boys have been exposed to Internet pornography.
- 57% of girls and 83% of boys have seen group sex on the Internet.
- 55% of girls and 69% of boys have seen homosexual pornography.
- 23% of girls and 39% of boys have seen online sex acts involving bondage.

- 29% of 7–17-year-olds would freely give out their home address online.
- 14% of 7–17-year-olds would freely give out their email address online.
- 9% of girls and 15% of boys have seen child pornography.
- 18% of girls and 32% of boys have viewed bestiality on the Internet.
- 89% of solicitations of youths in chat rooms are sexual.

These statistics are probably gross underestimates of what is really going on in our children's lives. There is no way to accurately measure kids' exposure to pornography and the effect it is having on them. We do know, however, that pornography can only have a negative effect on their lives.

Back in 1996, the United States Justice Department stated that, "Never before in the history of telecommunications media in the United States has so much indecent (and obscene) material been so easily accessible by so many American homes with so few restrictions" (U.S. Justice Dept., 1996). That was when the Internet was starting to take off. It was hard to imagine that the problem would get worse, but it has!

Many parents feel helpless in the battle for their kids' innocence; however, there is hope! We can protect our kids from pornography. First, we need to take an honest look at how pornography can affect minors. In this chapter I present the facts about pornography's impact on children and teens, and in chapter thirteen I present ways to protect children from pornography and how to train teens to say no to it.

Pornography and Narcissism

The problems of pornography use and narcissism are intertwined. It's the story of the chicken and the egg. While pornography use fosters narcissism, it's narcissism that can lead a person to feel entitled to view pornography. This is especially evident in young people.

Let's first take a look at the problem of narcissism, which is a strong form of selfishness. For almost forty years, America has seen a steady rise in narcissism among young people. Dr. Jean Twenge and colleagues (2008) studied the scores of 16,475 American college students who completed the Narcissistic Personality Inventory (NPI) between 1979 and 2006, and found that narcissism scores had risen steadily over that time period. Numerous books and journal articles have been written about narcissism in young adults since then. Because of their high rate of narcissism, Dr. Twenge calls young adults who were born between 1970 and 2000 "Generation Me." Others have referred to these people as "Millennials."

To understand how narcissism has grown over the recent decades, we have to look at how both the family and the educational system in the United States have changed. Starting in the 1970s, due to the increase in contraception and focus on careers, Americans began marrying later and having fewer children. Having children came to be viewed as a choice, not a duty. The positive result was that children were wanted and treasured, but unfortunately, they were also coddled (Twenge, 2006). Parents idealized their children rather than loving them. Parents fed their children's narcissism by being overly indulgent—their children became little princes and princesses (Young-Eisenrath, 2008).

Parental values have also changed. Children are taught to value their own opinions above all others. Personal happiness is most important. Social norms have been cast aside (Twenge, 2006). In 1924, when asked which traits they wanted to instill in their children, mothers said strict obedience, loyalty to church, and good manners. The same study was replicated in 1988. This time, mothers listed independence and tolerance as traits they wanted in their children (Remley, 1988). While these are not bad traits, one can see that the focus has shifted more toward self.

Parents of "Generation Me" place their children on pedestals. They shower them with praise, protect them from teachers' and coaches' criticisms, and spoil them with material possessions. Educational consultant Karen Hill Scott believes "this is really the era of the weak parent" (Picket, 2003). This view of modern parenting—overindulgence, excessive praising, and putting the child in charge—instills in children a sense of excessive self-importance and entitlement. This can lead to narcissism.

Society's emphasis on high self-esteem has also increased narcissism in young people, as is evident in the American education system. Since 1980, there has been a pervasive belief in America that all children should feel good about themselves at all times. Research articles on self-esteem in psychological and educational journals doubled between 1970 and 1990. They increased another 52% in the 1990s (Hewitt, 1998). School curriculums were designed around helping children feel special because it was believed that higher self-esteem would result in greater academic achievement. These self-esteem programs teach children that it is acceptable to be preoccupied with oneself, and many of the exercises in self-esteem actually make self-importance mandatory (Hewitt, 1998).

The push for greater self-esteem extends beyond school and to extracurricular activities. This can be seen in sports leagues where everyone wins a trophy. "There is something inherently good about trying to raise kids' feelings about themselves, but there has to be balance," says Leonard Zaichkowsky, a Boston University professor and director of its sport and exercise psychology training program. "We also have to teach kids to be mentally tough, to take criticism, to experience failure, to learn that somebody wins and somebody loses" (Reiss, 2006). While giving every child a trophy may help raise their self-esteem, it will not necessarily improve their athletic success. Growth in self-discipline and self-control are what truly lead to success, not self-esteem (Reiss, 2006).

When preparing to enter the work world, the narcissism young adults have embraced will lead to disappointment. Consider the following quote from the Wall Street Journal (2008):

> When Gretchen Neels, a Boston-based consultant, was coaching a group of college students for job interviews, she asked them how they believe employers view

them. She gave them a clue, telling them the word she was looking for begins with the letter "e." One man shouted out "excellent." Other students chimed in with "enthusiastic" and "energetic." Not even close. The correct answer, she said, is "entitled." "Huh?" the students responded, surprised and even hurt to think that managers are offended by their highfalutin opinions of themselves. (p. D1)

The narcissism that was instilled in young adults from doting parents, teachers, and coaches has even reached the workplace. Young adults want their careers to fit their lives rather than vice versa (Wall Street Journal, 2008). According to a survey conducted by Career-Builder.com, 87% of hiring managers and human resource executives believe that young adults have a stronger sense of entitlement than older workers. Young adults expect higher pay, flexible work schedules, a promotion within a year, and more vacation and personal time (Balderrama, 2007).

In American society it seems that narcissism is encouraged from all angles: family, school, extracurricular activities, etc. This has led many young people to have a great sense of entitlement. Personal needs and wants are considered paramount, and so if a man believes viewing pornography and masturbating will meet his needs or wants, he is entitled to it. When confronted by friends or family about how morally wrong this is, narcissistic people often accuse them of "being judgmental."

Pornography and Children

One autumn afternoon, Beth received a shocking and disturbing phone call from the principal of her son's elementary school. Her ten-year-old son Jason had been caught sexually molesting a seven-year-old girl. Beth was horrified. She knew, however, that Jason's actions were somehow tied to her husband's pornography use. Upon questioning her son, Beth learned that Jason had found the stash of "girlie" magazines her husband hid in the garage and his stash of online pornography on their home computer. Jason had been spending much of his unsupervised free time viewing pornography. He thought it was "cool" because it was what his dad did. Unaware of the dangers of the Internet, Jason's parents never monitored his computer use.

Stories like this are not uncommon. Although the average age a child first encounters Internet pornography is eleven, younger children are being exposed to it. Parents try to protect their kids, but often they are unaware of how their tech-savvy kids are using the Internet. So how are children being exposed to Internet porn? For many, they stumble upon it accidentally. They may find a family member's "stash" or discover it through a pop-up window or advertisement. In one study, the National Center for Missing and Exploited Children concluded that sexually explicit material on the Internet is "very intrusive" and can be stumbled upon while searching for other material or opening an email (Mitchell et al., 2003). Children also are introduced to it by their peers. Many times I've heard parents claim their children were viewing Internet pornography at a friend's house, and in most of these situations the children were using the computer unsupervised. I often tell parents that leaving a child alone with the Internet is like leaving him alone with a total stranger. There is no telling what can happen.

So what are the effects of pornography on children? While research is limited, what we do know tells us volumes.

1. *Loss of Innocence.* Viewing pornography at a young age robs a child of his innocence. It introduces him to a world that he is not ready for or able to understand. Unfortunately, our sexualized culture is forcing children to grow up too fast. Children don't have a chance to be children anymore. We see this in children's fashions. Designers are targeting tweens with more sexually provocative clothing. Some parents are offended by this, but many think it's cute. From clothing, to television, to video games, to pornography, our culture sexualizes children at increasingly younger ages and deprives them of healthy childhoods.

2. *Brain and Sexual Development.* During the childhood years, the brain is being "hardwired" for sexual arousal and attraction. Exposure to healthy sexual norms and attitudes by parents and educators during this period helps develop healthy sexuality (Kavanaugh, 1997). Information about sex in most homes and schools is often presented in age-appropriate increments, which the child understands. However, pornography bombards children with confusing, unhealthy, and even dangerous information about sex, and leaves them confused about their sexuality, sense of self, and body. It can leave a child "hardwired" for sexual deviancy (Hughes, 1997).

3. *Attitudes toward Relationships.* While children might not understand what is happening in a pornographic video, it can change the way they view the opposite sex and relationships. For example, we have previously discussed how women are often depicted as being sexually abused by one or more men in a very physically aggressive manner, and enjoying it. The message to boys is that women enjoy physical and sexual abuse, and a young boy will naturally conclude this is how women want to be treated. The message to girls is mixed and confusing. On one hand, they see men being abusive toward women. On the other, they see women loving this type of treatment. For some, the message is that men are dangerous and cannot be trusted. For others, the message is that this is how a woman must be to get a man. Because boys and girls are unable to fully understand what is going on in pornography, this exposure warps their view of sexuality and relationships.

4. *Attitudes toward Sex.* Prepubescent children are not sexual beings, but exposure to pornography can affect their attitudes toward sex once they do enter puberty. A warped view of sexuality may lead them to believe that violent sex, group sex, homosexuality, and even sadomasochistic sex are normal and healthy in a relationship.

5. *Trauma and Pornography.* Exposure to pornography for young children can be traumatic. Imagine a seven-year-old girl left alone with a computer and accidentally stumbling onto a pornographic website where she encounters a woman being brutally raped by half a dozen men. Because children have difficulty distinguishing fantasy from reality, to this little girl it's an actual rape she is witnessing. This can be extremely traumatizing for a child, and this child could easily exhibit symptoms of a sexually abused child.

6. *Sexual Violence.* While the trauma listed above can definitely be considered a form of sexual violence against children, exposure to pornography can leave children vulnerable to more physical forms of sexual violence as both victim and perpetrator. As we saw in the story of Jason who molested a younger peer, his exposure led him to become a perpetrator and the younger peer a victim. Studies show that exposure to pornography can prompt children to act out sexually against younger, smaller, and more vulnerable children (Carnes, 1991). Children often imitate what they see in the media: "You need just one film to tickle their curiosity and make them want to try what they have seen. Until seven years, they are walking sponges without any filters. Between seven and fourteen years, they model their behavior on what they have seen on the screen" (Wentzel, 2012). They may not realize that their actions can hurt another person because they may not be able to distinguish between reality and fantasy.

This was the case with Jason. He observed the people in pornography having a good time. It looked like fun and he wanted to try out what he saw with someone else. On one level he knew that touching private body parts was wrong, so he looked for a younger victim who wouldn't say no, without realizing how deeply this would hurt the little girl. He had no idea how violating his actions were, and unfortunately, cases such as this are growing. According to Luke Lambrecht, manager of the Teddy Bear Clinic, 90% of young sexual offenders (seven to fourteen years) have been exposed to pornography. According to the Durban Childline Sexual Abuse Treatment Centre, 42% of sexual assaults against children in 2002 were committed by adolescents and children younger than thirteen (Cape Times, 2002).

Parents have much to be worried about if their children are exposed to pornography. In addition to the grave moral consequences, pornography steals their children's innocence and childhood, can prevent them from developing healthy sexual attractions, warps their attitudes toward sex and relationships, and can lead to trauma and abuse. We must protect our children so they never come in contact with pornography. In chapter thirteen I present practical ways to protect children from this poison.

In the story above both Jason and the girl he molested were able to get the help they needed. The little girl and her family received counseling to help her recover from the traumatic event. Jason and his family also received counseling to help them understand the dangers of pornography, and Jason's father got rid of all his pornography. He also made the commitment to be more active in Jason's life and be a father who would raise Jason to be a virtuous man that respected women.

Pornography and Teens

Eric is a sixteen-year-old high school junior who was first introduced to pornography when he was in seventh grade. During a sleepover at a friend's house, they were left unsupervised with a computer, logged on to the Internet and simply typed "sex" into the search engine. This brought up a whole host of pornographic websites. Eric had never been so shocked, but as a young adolescent he also found it extremely exciting. This began several years of viewing pornography on their home computer, which unfortunately was kept in Eric's father's home office instead of a public area of the house. There was no Internet filtering or accountability software on it. Both his parents worked, so Eric often was alone at home in the afternoon, free to search for Internet pornography.

When Eric entered high school, he began dating and was engaging in oral sex and heavy petting. Among his peers, only intercourse was considered "sex." Everything else was just "fooling around." He was also using the internet more and more to seek sexual exploits. He and his friends were deeply immersed in all the latest technology. He had his own laptop computer, smartphone, and iPad. His cybersex activity really began to escalate during his sophomore year when he was viewing Internet porn, sexting with girls, and using several Facebook accounts for online sex where he posted nude photos of himself. He also began chats with girls he had friended who had also posted nude photos. Like many young teenagers, Eric and his buddies considered all of this "cool," like a rite of passage into manhood. His life was consumed with pornography and online sexual activity. None of his online activity was monitored by adults. He eventually stopped socializing with his closest friends, quit the school baseball team, spent more time isolating himself in his room with his computer, and his grades fell dramatically.

Eric's parents discovered some pornography he had saved on his computer, and a deeper search through his computer revealed his use of social media for his online sexual activity. When his parents brought him in for counseling, it was easy to see how embarrassed he was, and yet Eric knew he needed help.

Although Eric's parents were concerned about him, they had no idea he was addicted to pornography, and they were angry with him because they thought they had raised him with good Catholic values. They were angrier with themselves for being so naive about the dangers of the Internet and the amount of pornography online, and how deviant it was. They were clueless about how teens were using social media for sexual purposes and unaware of computer filters and accountability systems. Unlike Eric and his friends, they had not grown up with computers, the Internet, or cell phones, so technology was not a dominant part of their lives. They had a lot to learn.

So what kinds of porn are teens viewing and how are they accessing it? Pornography today comes in many forms. There's visual porn found in magazines, DVDs, Internet movies, video games, music videos, comic books, and anime. There is also written porn found in romance novels, magazines, blogs, and online erotic stories. Because our society is saturated with sexualized images, many people have progressed from viewing and reading pornography to making their own amateur porn. They are taking nude pictures and videos of themselves and their partners, often having sex, and posting them online. This is how many teens are using social media. Like Eric, they are using sites such as Facebook, Twitter, and Snapchat to exchange pornographic images, or using social media to chat and send pornographic messages to one another. This could be considered a written form of pornography. Thus, with social media, pornography has become interactive.

Both teens and pornographers have kept pace with the latest developments in technology. Whenever a new gadget comes out, teens often are the first to use them and pornographers find a way to peddle their wares through it. Teens are accessing pornography through desktop and laptop computers, netbooks, tablets, iPads, iPods, MP3 players, Xbox, Wii, PlayStation, Kindle, Nook, eReaders, portable video game systems, and cell phones. Any gadget that can access the Internet, download information, or be used to communicate with others can be used for pornographic purposes. The more portable the device, the more likely a teen will use it for pornography because it can be easily hidden from others. In 2012, Tru Research conducted over two thousand online interviews with teens ages 13–17, and their parents, and found 71% of teens have taken some form of action to hide their online activity from their parents, including clearing browser history, deleting items, lying, using a smartphone, blocking parents with social media privacy settings, using private browsing, disabling parental controls, and creating social media accounts without parental knowledge. Only 12% of parents were aware that their teens were viewing porn (Le, 2012).

Teens are naturally curious about sex. They will take any opportunity to learn more about it, and this curiosity, combined with their tech savviness, naturally leads them to the Internet for information that is often wrong and dangerous. Several studies have found that teenagers around the world report using porn to gain information about "real-life sex" (Giordano & Ross, 2012; Flood, 2009; Lauzus et al, 2007; Wade et al, 2005).

Even teens who don't seek sexual content online are often bombarded with it. In a 2002 Henry J. Kaiser Foundation report, 70% of teens between the ages of fifteen and seventeen claimed to accidently come across pornography online. And 23% of those teens claimed it happens "often" or "very often" (Kaiser, 2000).

While I place heavy emphasis on technology as the source and method of pornography use for teens, we cannot forget the many other ways teens have become sexualized by our culture. Other forms of pornographic images and messages can be found in the following mediums:

- Cable and satellite television
- Books, magazines, and catalogs
- Video games
- Popular music lyrics and videos
- Clothing
- Phone sex (while not as popular as it once was, some teens do engage in this)

As with children, exposure to pornography can be devastating for teens, but with teens it can be more serious because they are sexual beings. In order to discuss this impact we need to ask ourselves what messages teens are receiving from porn. These messages are also different for boys and girls. For boys, the messages are:

- Women are there for your sexual pleasure and it's okay to use them.
- Women don't have thoughts or feelings and they don't need to be respected.
- Women love sex and can't get enough of it. They beg for it.

- Women love all deviant forms of sex, especially anal sex.
- Women like violent sex, including rape.
- The sex in pornography is healthy and normal.
- One should be having lots of sex.
- Sex and pornography should be part of a relationship.
- True happiness and fulfillment comes from having sexual encounters with multiple partners, not through a committed marital relationship.

For girls, the messages are:

- In order to be loved and desired by men, you must look and act like a porn star.
- Sex equals love and intimacy.
- The sex in pornography is normal and healthy.
- One should be having lots of sex.
- You must learn to like deviant forms of sex, including anal sex.
- It's okay for men and women to use each other sexually.
- You must be just as sexually aggressive as men.
- Sex and pornography should be part of a relationship.
- Sexual fidelity in a relationship is almost impossible.

The degree to which teens accept these messages depends on the individual, but pornography is changing the way teens view sex and relationships. *Psychology Today* published an article in January of 2014 on how porn is influencing adolescent boys' views on relationships. It highlights the danger that they are no longer learning what it means to develop healthy romantic relationships because they're using online porn as their model for real-life sexual relationships. In porn, these boys don't see a storyline or an emotional connection. There is no concern for physical or emotional safety. There is no romance or tenderness.

Kissing and foreplay are entirely absent. "All that's there is an endless stream of idealized body parts and sexual acts." The article goes on to assert that this is rewiring these boys' brains not only to expect but to demand unrealistic levels of stimulation and excitement, resulting in boys "becoming totally out of sync with real-world romantic relationships." The article cites two large-scale surveys (2008 and 2010) that the issue is more prevalent than people think, and growing (R. Weiss, 2014).

There is also is a distinct double standard. While teenage girls are becoming more sexually aggressive, they are still being used sexually and are little more than sex toys for teenage boys. This is detrimental to both sexes because it prevents them from being able to establish and maintain healthy relationships as teens and adults.

For over forty years, studies have consistently shown how the sexualization of women is harmful, especially to teenage girls and young women. According to the American Psychological Association (APA), the sexualization of women leads to girls and young women feeling bad about themselves. There is evidence that sexualization contributes to impaired academic performance and can contribute to body dissatisfaction, eating disorders, low self-esteem, depression, and even physical health problems in high school aged girls and young women. Sexualizing treatment and self-objectification can generate feelings of self-loathing, anxiety, and even disgust toward one's physical self. Girls feel that they are ugly and gross. Furthermore, the APA makes the vital point that sexualization practices may function to keep girls in their place as objects of sexual attraction, limiting their free thinking and movement in the culture (APA, 2007).

The messages pornography presents are extremely harmful to both sexes. These effects include:

1. *Changing Attitudes toward Sex.* Pornography use misleads teens about the type of sex average people are having. They believe that deviant forms of sex are normal and healthy. This can lead them to engage in dangerous forms of sex including group

sex, oral and anal sex, violent sex, homosexual sex, and even sadomasochistic sex. It has even changed their definition of what sex is. For many, only sexual intercourse is considered "sex." Oral sex, anal sex, self and mutual masturbation, etc., are not considered sex, but simply "messing around." Boys now believe that women love sex and want it all the time, especially the deviant sex in porn. Because they see a woman in porn acting like she enjoys being brutally raped by half a dozen men, boys can come to believe that this is what women want, that this is normal. Girls are left believing that they have to engage in deviant sex in order to attract and keep a boyfriend, and that they should like this kind of sex. An analysis of forty-six independent studies concluded that pornography use directly contributes to sexually dysfunctional attitudes and behaviors. The adverse effects include developing sexually deviant attractions, committing sexual offenses, difficulties in relationships, and accepting rape myths (e.g. a rape victim deserved the rape or wanted it) (Paolucci-Oddone et al., 2000).

Eric's constant use of pornography over four years left him with deviant sexual attractions. He fantasized about tying women up, having anal sex with them, and even raping a woman. In the fantasy she would at first struggle to get away from him, but would eventually give in, love it, and beg for more. Fortunately, he never tried to act out this fantasy with a woman. He did, however, pressure his girlfriends into having oral and anal sex with him. This was normal sexuality to Eric, not dysfunctional sex where boys are using girls. Teenage boys and girls cannot learn healthy sex or relationships from this warped view.

2. *Changing Attitudes toward Women.* Several studies have found that when both boys and girls are exposed to sexualized media, they are more likely to view women as sex objects (Ward, 2006; Peter, 2007). It creates a cynical attitude toward relationships

with little hope for a stable monogamous relationship. This sexualization of girls is very harmful to them and reduces them to sex toys for boys. It's easy to see how boys can buy into this attitude because it naturally benefits them sexually. However, girls also buy into this. Why? Because it is where they find their self-worth. For many teenage girls and young women, the "hotter" they feel they look, the more self-worth they feel. This is a warped view of beauty and self-value because it is based on one's ability to be a sex object for others. It's scary to think that female porn stars have become the model for beauty to which girls believe they must aspire. A beautiful teenage girl may look at herself in the mirror and think, "I'm so hot! I'm just like a porn star! This is great!" Another beautiful girl who does not look like a porn star may think there is actually something wrong with her, that she is ugly. No consideration is given to either girl's true physical beauty, personality, values, gifts, talents, or to the simple fact that she is a child of God.

Eric felt this way toward girls and his use of pornography led him to view girls as personal sex toys. He would rate girls' appearances based on how closely they looked like porn stars. Deep down he wanted a true relationship, but his attitudes toward girls prevented it. While he was getting a lot of sex, he was still very lonely, and the girls he was with were also very lonely. For many girls, their purpose for having sex is to develop a relationship. When they realize that boys are just using them for sex, they feel hurt and betrayed.

3. *Increased Sexual Activity.* Exposure to pornography naturally makes a person want to engage in what they are viewing and is why sexual activity among teens has risen exponentially over the years. Sexualized media leads to an early onset of sexual activity in youth. Young people come to believe they should be having sex all the time, and if they are not "getting any" regularly, there is something wrong with them (Zillman, 2000).

This was the case with Eric. From what he saw in pornography and heard from his friends' bragging, he thought he should be having sex several times a week. This led him to pressure the girls he dated for sex. Although many girls don't want to be hypersexual, they give in, thinking this is what they have to do to keep a boy. In the end they only feel used, and as with adults, both teenage boys and girls feel lonelier.

4. *Increased Sexual Harassment.* Pornography use among teens has led to a rise in sexual aggressiveness and harassment in person and online. In a 2006 study of 1,500 teens, one in seven reported unwanted sexual solicitation online and one in eleven had been harassed online (Wolak et al., 2006). Another study of 804 Italian teenagers found that boys who viewed pornography were significantly more likely to have sexually harassed a peer or forced someone to have sex with them (Bonino et al., 2006). This shouldn't surprise us. Because pornography use leads teens to view women as sex objects, not as people, it makes it easier to harass them into having sex. And since the women in pornography are often used in sexually abusive ways, teens can come away thinking that it's okay to use women this way. Girls are pressured to tolerate physical, emotional, and sexual abuse in order to be accepted by boys (Manning, 2006). Harassment can also be the result of how kids are introduced to pornography. In one study, 101 sexually abusive Australian children claimed that an older sibling or friend showed them how to access pornography online, and another quarter said pornography use was their main reason for going online. Being introduced to pornography by an older person can make the sex portrayed in it appear to be normal and accepted (Goodenough, 2003).

5. *Teen Pregnancy and Sexually Transmitted Diseases.* As more teens are exposed to sexually explicit media, a dangerous message they are receiving is that sex can be enjoyed without responsibility or

consequence. The Catechism of the Catholic Church states that pornography "immerses all who are involved in the illusion of a fantasy world" (2354). Pornography is not the real world. It appears to be a consequence-free experience where no one gets hurt, pregnant, used, abused, or contracts a sexually transmitted disease. Because this make-believe world is projected to teens, pornography poses a threat to their health. Teenage pregnancies may be dropping, but those who use pornography are more likely to become teenage parents. This could also account for the many abortions performed on teens today. It's well known that sexually transmitted diseases (STDs) are on the rise among teens. In the United States, about 25% of sexually active teens contract a sexually transmitted disease each year, resulting in three million cases of teenage STDs annually. According to the Centers for Disease Control (2011), nearly half of all STDs are contracted by young people between the ages of fifteen and twenty-four. The deviant forms of sex promoted in pornography make teens vulnerable to most sexually transmitted diseases including HIV/AIDS. While parents and schools warn teens about STDs, few see the relationship between STDs and pornography use.

Eric was lucky. He did not contract any sexually transmitted diseases, but the thought of contracting one never crossed his mind when he was sexually active, which is quite scary. In his mind, "nice people" like him don't get STDs, an attitude that unfortunately many teens share.

6. *Inability to Have Healthy Relationships.* All of the risks listed above can hinder a person's ability to maintain a healthy relationship. If pornography only teaches young people to use others sexually, they will not be able to trust one another. They will only be in a relationship for what each can get out of it, not for what they can contribute. Pornography teaches selfishness. Like adults, teens crave intimate relationships too, but they

never learn how to have one. They're only out for what they can get. Pornography is also damaging girls' ability to trust and relate to boys. In order to feel like equals, girls must be sexually aggressive, and the quality of a relationship is then judged on how good the sex is. This leads to very cynical attitudes toward relationships, and as they get older they lose hope for having a healthy long-term relationship let alone a happy marriage.

Sexting

Sexting is a particularly dangerous activity among teens today. Chris and Julie were two fifteen-year-old teenagers who were dating. One day Chris said to Julie, "Babe, you're so hot! You're like a porn star. Why don't you take some naked photos of yourself and send them to me." Julie thought, "This is great! He thinks I'm as hot as a porn star!" So late that night, Julie went into the bathroom, undressed, took nude photos of herself with her smartphone, and emailed them to Chris. That is sexting.

Unfortunately, the story didn't end there. After Chris received Julie's photos, he emailed them to all his buddies and soon the photos were all over school. Mortified, Julie tried to commit suicide. Luckily she didn't succeed.

Sexting is a direct result of teen exposure to pornography. Teens get the idea that it's normal and okay to create their own porn because there's so much amateur porn on the Internet. Sexting is a form of amateur pornography. Cell phones aren't the only methods teens use for this purpose. They also use social media, such as Facebook. Some teens are so caught up in the false glamour of porn stars that they see nothing wrong with posting graphic pornographic photos of themselves online. They have no sense of morality. They may even believe it's a good thing when other people are using their images for selfish sexual pleasure. These people are often very narcissistic.

Aside from the moral problems, teens often are unaware of the legal ramifications of sexting. For example, when Julie took those nude photos of herself, she was actually creating child pornography, a felony. When she sent them to Chris, she distributed child pornography, another felony. When Chris received and opened the photos, he was in possession of child porn, a felony, and then he distributed this pornography by sending the photos to his buddies, committing another felony. Neither Julie nor Chris would have ever considered themselves child pornographers.

Eric was also guilty of sexting. He used his cell phone for sexual chats, texts, and emails. Fortunately, he never used his real name or posted photos of his face on his three Facebook accounts. If he had and was caught by authorities, he could have been charged with the production, possession, and distribution of child pornography.

Sexting can have lifelong consequences for teens. Many states have very strict laws regarding sex offenders, and sexting could lead to conviction for child pornography and being listed on a state's sex offender registry for life. This can impact where a person may live, where they can travel, and the type of career they can have.

Root Causes

We've seen how children and teens can accidently find pornography, yet once introduced to it they will often continue to seek it out. Why is this? Recall the Five "A's" (pornography is affordable, accessible, anonymous, accepted, and aggressive). In addition, teens are naturally curious, and that is particularly true about sex. As they grow into their sexuality they want to know and experience as much about it as possible. While this curiosity is normal, it does make teens highly susceptible to becoming regular users of Internet pornography and becoming addicts.

Furthermore, like adults, many teens become addicted to Internet pornography because they use it to self-medicate deep emotional wounds. While all of the wounds I listed in chapter two on the addictiveness of pornography apply to teens, there are a few that I have found particularly common in teenagers.

1. *Narcissism.* Parents are to blame for this. This deep wound is inflicted by parents who place their kids on pedestals and spoil

them. These kids can do no wrong and are rarely disciplined. If anything bad happens in their lives, it is always viewed as someone else's fault. These kids are taught that their wants and needs come first. Naturally, then, what follows shouldn't surprise anyone. If they believe that using someone for their own sexual pleasure will meet their needs, then it's okay. Society is also to blame for this, daily bombarding teens through mass media with messages that convince them to place their personal needs and wants first. Narcissism leads teens to believe that pornography use is good and healthy.

2. *Family-of-Origin Wounds.* We've mentioned these wounds as including abuse, addiction, neglect, abandonment, death and/ or divorce in a family. All of these wounds can leave a teen feeling alone, insecure, and unwanted. Abuse can be physical, emotional, or sexual, for which sexual is the most harmful. Most of the time, the child knows the abuser. Imagine how traumatic it is to know that the people who are supposed to love and protect you most are the ones who violate you. Addiction brings chaos into a home. A child or teen growing up with an alcoholic parent often doesn't know what will happen from day to day. Will their parent come home drunk? Will he be violent? Did he spend the rent money on liquor? Neglect and abandonment leave a child feeling insecure, unloved, and unwanted. It's extremely frightening for a child to feel that no one will care for him. Death and divorce damage a child's sense of safety and security because they break up the family. While some try to downplay the effects of divorce, we have decades of research on its harmful effects. Kids often blame themselves for the divorce, believing that if they had behaved better, earned better grades, or been more helpful at home, their parents wouldn't have divorced. Divorce leaves kids feeling frightened and insecure. They worry about if the family will survive financially, or if the parent moving out will still love them, or if they will ever see that parent again. This brings about fears of neglect and

abandonment. For these teens, pornography is the drug that quickly eases their pain.

3. *Loneliness.* During the teenage years, peer relationships become more important than family, which is quite natural. Thus, peer acceptance is vitally important. However, many teens do not feel accepted by their peers. They feel like outcasts. Many are victims of bullying. While their peers are going to parties and football games, these teens spend much of their time alone at home, and to ease their loneliness and boredom, they turn to pornography. Remember, these women are beautiful, always available, and controlled by the viewer, which is a huge plus for teenage boys who may have been rejected by girls or may be too insecure to ask a girl out on a date.

4. *Weak Spiritual Life.* Unfortunately, many kids today are raised without any religious faith. They may claim to be Christian or Catholic, but they rarely attend Mass or church functions and lack any relationship with God, which leads to a very lonely existence and little self-worth. They don't know there is a heavenly Father who loves them unconditionally. They don't know how *fearfully and wonderfully made* (cf. Psalms 139) they are. They cannot see other people as beloved children of God. Without any sense of greater purpose in life, they focus on satisfying their own immediate wants and needs without any consideration of others. This makes it easy to use people for sexual gratification. Since they don't know there is a loving God that they can turn to in their pain and loneliness, they self-medicate emotional wounds with pornography.

Along with the Five A's, Eric struggled with all of the above wounds. Both of his parents are successful professionals who always gave him whatever he wanted, and justified it by claiming they wanted him to have everything they never had growing up. However, they did have everything. Their overindulgence of Eric led him to believe he was entitled to do whatever he wanted to meet his needs and wants, including using girls for his own gratification. Eric also felt neglected by his parents, and spent much of his time at home alone because of their busy work schedules. Rarely did they do things together as a family. They didn't even have regular meals together, which contributed to his deep loneliness. While Eric and his family did attend Mass together, he had no real sense of God in his life. He attended religious instruction classes long enough to be confirmed, and then stopped going. There was no real practice of their Catholic faith at home, which also led to his loneliness and a lack of self-worth. Because Eric had spent his whole life in this environment, he had become so accustomed to living with these wounds that he didn't know they were there. However, they were there and he used pornography to self-medicate.

These wounds can lead to five core beliefs in children and teens that fuel pornography use. We listed these core beliefs earlier as:

1. I am unworthy of being loved.
2. If people really knew me, they would reject me.
3. I cannot trust anyone, including God, to meet my needs.
4. I must find something that I can control that will meet my needs.
5. Pornography/Sex is my greatest need and source of comfort.

Many can see how the Five A's lead a person into pornography use, but often it's difficult to recognize the emotional wounds and core beliefs that lead to pornography because these wounds and beliefs are on the subconscious level. A person has lived with them for so long that they don't even know they're there.

This was true for Eric. He believed he came to use pornography simply because all of his friends were doing it (the Five A's). The clue that there was a deeper issue present with Eric was that it was virtually impossible for him to stop. Whenever he would try to stop in the past, his sobriety lasted only three weeks and he would fall back into pornography use. Furthermore, the sobriety he did experience was a "white knuckle" sobriety because he was not addressing the root causes of his pornography use: his emotional wounds and core beliefs.

Hope for our Kids

The pornography epidemic in America is severe and our kids are most at risk for becoming its victims. We need comprehensive recovery programs for teens. While there are many good recovery programs, few are open to minors because some of their members are sex offenders. However, if more programs were designed only for teens, they could receive the help they need without risk. But there is hope! We can protect our children from this cancer. This will be addressed in depth in chapters thirteen and fourteen.

Eric's Story

Eric's story does have a happy ending. Eric was able to enter a comprehensive recovery program that helped him overcome his addiction. Eric's parents became educated on the dangers of pornography and how today's youth use technology. This helped them monitor their kids' use of technology and ensure that their kids weren't viewing pornography or sexting. Eric's parents also made a commitment to be more active in their kids' lives, to stop overindulging them, and to begin practicing their Catholic faith as a family. All of this helped heal Eric's emotional wounds and maintain his sobriety. He also learned about healthy sexuality, healthy relationships, and respect for women, which enabled him to have happy and fulfilling relationships with them. Most of all, Eric came to know the Lord on a much deeper level, and this gave him a great sense of hope and purpose in life. He neither felt lonely nor felt the need to use pornography.

If there is one message I can leave with parents, it's the truth that no child or teen is immune to the dangers of pornography. Our high tech world puts everyone at risk. We need to understand how dangerous pornography is to youth and we must do everything we can to protect them. Chapters thirteen and fourteen offer detailed plans for protecting kids.

7

The Church and Pornography

M att, a twenty-four-year-old graduate student, sought counseling for his uncontrollable pornography use and masturbation. His addiction began as a college freshman, and despite
attending a college that identified itself as being Catholic, most of the
guys he knew in his dorm regularly used pornography. None of his
religion classes ever mentioned sexual sin, and many of his religion pro-
fessors promoted relativism and political correctness. Thus, if a person
chose to use pornography, masturbate, or have sex outside of marriage,
no one was to correct that person or judge his actions. In his psychology
classes Matt was taught that very little sexuality could be considered
deviant, and with the exception of pedophilia and incest, all sexuality
was "normal and healthy." Pornography use was promoted as a way of
exploring sexuality and enhancing one's sex life, which was confusing to
Matt, since he learned exactly the opposite at home growing up.

Matt grew up in a devout Catholic family and attended Catholic
schools all his life. His family attended Mass on Sundays and all holy
days of obligation. They prayed at home daily and went to Confession
monthly. His parents helped him develop a strong faith in God, but
they didn't instill in him a healthy view of sexuality. In his family, sex
was viewed as something dirty. It was rarely talked about, and when
the subject did come up, the response was that it was something sinful
and he shouldn't do it until marriage. That was difficult for Matt to
understand. As an adolescent, he had a natural curiosity about girls

and sex, yet he received no sex education at home and the education he received at school was weak. At home, the computer and all media were heavily monitored. Matt had seen some sexually suggestive material, but he was very ignorant about pornography. His view of sexuality was limited and skewed, and his knowledge of the Church's teaching was just as limited.

When Matt went to college, he was unprepared for the tidal wave of sexual material he would encounter because his parents never prepared him for it. They simply sent him off to school believing he would be safe at a Catholic college. Upon arriving, he immediately discovered pornography and began to masturbate to it. He was still able to keep his grades up, but he spent much of his free time online searching for more and more porn. Understandably, this affected his relationships. Although he wanted to date, Matt didn't know how to communicate with and relate to women in a healthy way. His only friends were a small group of guys who also viewed pornography regularly. What he was taught about pornography and sex in his religion and psychology classes also made it seem perfectly acceptable. Still, Matt continued to struggle with an internal conflict. The world said that using pornography and masturbating was perfectly okay, but Matt knew this was not God's plan for men, women, relationships, or sexuality.

After college, Matt's pornography use and masturbation continued. He knew it was a sin and went to Confession, but the addiction was so strong that he continued to fall soon after receiving the sacrament. Confessing seemed pointless. He began to think, "It's useless. I can't stop sinning. God must hate me. How could He ever forgive me? I'm doomed!" This led Matt into a deep depression. Finally, when Matt could no longer stand the emotional pain and turmoil, he sought help.

For Matt, recovery began with the standard practices of attending support group meetings and counseling sessions, ridding himself of all access to pornography, and identifying the root causes of his pornography use and masturbation. It also included straightening out his confusion about the Church's teaching on pornography, and how God views the human person, including Matt himself. The information

Matt received at home and college came from two unhealthy extremes. His understanding that using pornography and masturbating are mortal sins was correct; however, he needed to know that God still loved him and wanted him to recover. Knowing this gave Matt hope and the strength needed for recovery. Although it would take a while for him to achieve sobriety, he kept going to Confession and Mass, and he prayed daily for God's strength and guidance in recovery. Matt also needed to learn about God's plan for sexuality, and how it is a wonderful gift that should be used in the correct context. Working with his spiritual director, a priest, was a great help to Matt throughout recovery.

Matt's story is not uncommon. It has been my clinical experience that people who struggle with pornography are unaware of the Church's teaching on it. There are those who follow societal beliefs about sexuality and believe there is nothing wrong with pornography or masturbation, a view which is promoted in many supposedly Catholic colleges and universities. This view can lead many Catholics into pornography use and eventually addiction. Then there are those who follow a very legalistic view of Church teaching. They believe sexual sin is the "unforgivable sin," especially if they are addicted and cannot overcome their compulsions to act out. They believe there is no hope for them, which can prevent them from seeking the help they need. Most people, like Matt, struggle with a combination of both views. The secular influence leads them into pornography and their legalistic view of God prevents them from seeking help. In the end they are left in hopelessness and despair.

How the Church Protects Us from Pornography

The truth is that God and the Church have clear rules against the use of pornography and masturbation (CCC 2352) because of their great love for all people. They are there to protect us. We can see this by looking to the Church's definition of pornography that we presented in chapter one.

- Pornography consists of removing real or simulated sexual acts from the intimacy of the partners, in order to display them deliberately to third parties. It offends against chastity because it perverts the conjugal act, the intimate giving of spouses to each other. It does grave injury to the dignity of its participants (actors, vendors, the public), since each one becomes an object of base pleasure and illicit profit for others. It immerses all who are involved in the illusion of a fantasy world. It is a grave offense. Civil authorities should prevent the production and distribution of pornographic materials (CCC 2354).

Looking deeper into each sentence will help us discover why the Church wants to protect us from pornography.

Pornography consists of removing real or simulated sexual acts from the intimacy of the partners, in order to display them deliberately to third parties.

God designed sex to be an intimate expression of the love between husband and wife. It is both unitive and procreative. It is unitive because it brings the couple together in a deeper, more intimate loving bond, mirroring the unitive love between the Father and the Son in the Trinity. Because the love expressed in the sexual act is so deep, God has made it life-giving through the conception of children. This is the procreative aspect of sex. This also mirrors the procreative love of the Trinity as the Holy Spirit proceeds from the Father and the Son.

Pornography is, essentially, two or more people using each other for selfish reasons that defiles God's beautiful plan for sex. The consumer simply uses the people in pornography for his own sexual pleasure, and the people in pornography use each other and the consumer for financial gain. The sexual acts in pornography defile God's plan for sex because there is nothing unitive about oral sex, anal sex, group sex, rape scenes, bondage, fetishes, and bestiality, even if they are practiced by "consenting adults." The sexual acts in pornography also defile God's plan for sex because the actors use contraception to preclude procreation.

In order for love and intimacy to exist, there must be a relationship between two people who are fully acknowledged and respected by each other. Love and intimacy cannot exist in pornography because the actors are reduced to mere body parts. Paraphrasing Pope St. John Paul II, Bishop Robert Finn (2007) wrote, "The problem with pornography is not that it reveals too much of the person (exposed in the image), but that it reveals too little of the person. The person in the image is reduced to their sexual organs and sexual faculties and is thereby de-personalized."

God's beautiful plan for sex is truly fulfilling and satisfying. God and the Church want people to have healthy marital relationships where the sexual act is an expression of a couple's deep love for each other and is open to human life. Satan is the father of lies, and he leads people to believe that happiness can come from using others in sexual ways. Although the sex in pornography may appear exciting, it always leaves people lonely and unfulfilled. The Church wants to protect us from that.

It offends against chastity because it perverts the conjugal act, the intimate giving of spouses to each other.

Chastity is a beautiful gift from God and part of the cardinal virtue of temperance. It calls us to use our sexuality within the limits of our state in life. Many people incorrectly believe that the purpose of chastity is to prevent any expression of sexuality. Chastity actually enables us to use this life-giving power for a worthy goal, calling us to respect ourselves and others. The Catechism defines chastity as "the successful integration of sexuality within the person and thus the inner unity of man in his bodily and spiritual being. Sexuality, in which man's belonging to the bodily and biological world is expressed, becomes personal and truly human when it is integrated into the relationship of one person to another, in the complete and lifelong mutual gift of a man and woman. The virtue of chastity therefore involves the integrity of the person and the integrality of the gift" (2337). Thus, chastity calls us to use our sexuality in a way that enables us to connect deeply and lovingly with others. It protects love and enables us to be fully human.

In *Love and Responsibility*, Karol Wojtyla (before he was Pope St. John Paul II) wrote that "the opposite of love isn't hate, it's use." If you do not love someone, you will end up using them. The Pope refers us to what he calls the "personalistic norm": One may never use another person for his own pleasure, and the only proper way to treat a person is to love the person. John Paul II asserted that chastity is always about people. He argued that if love is not about affirmation of the person, it is not love at all. Chastity ensures that we always love others and not use them (Wojtyla, 1993).

Chastity is needed by all regardless of their state in life. It brings fidelity to the marriage and a deep love and respect for one's spouse, and never treats the other as an object. This is similar to the love between Jesus and His Church. For those called to live a celibate life, such as priests, religious, and consecrated virgins, chastity frees them to love on a much broader level. Their love for God and neighbor is a sign of the love we will experience in heaven. For those who are single, chastity means reserving sex for marriage and not acting out in sexual ways. This is very difficult in today's world because single people are constantly bombarded with messages saying they should be having sex frequently. Admitting that one is single and chaste is often met with ridicule from peers. I know this personally. I decided to wait until I was married to have sex and I didn't get married until I was forty!

For married people, pornography violates chastity because it takes their sexuality outside their marriage. It is adultery (CCC 2380). It desecrates the most sacred and personal gift one can give to their spouse. This is why so many wives feel hurt and betrayed when they discover their husbands using pornography. Pornography use can lead to infidelity in the form of husbands patronizing strip clubs, using prostitutes, and entering into extramarital affairs.

For priests, religious, and consecrated virgins, pornography violates their vows to forgo sex for the sake of the kingdom. It is also a form of infidelity because their love is supposed to mirror Christ's love for the Church, and by using pornography they cannot love as Christ loves—He never uses people. This compromises their effectiveness in their vocations.

For single people, pornography use is a form of fornication. They are taking something that is reserved for the marriage covenant and using it for their own egocentric pleasure (CCC 2352). Single people must understand that while this kind of chastity may seem like a cross to bear, it is actually life-giving. Pornography use fosters self-centeredness and prevents people from loving as God wants them to love. Thus, the man who uses pornography for sexual relief until he finds a wife might actually be sabotaging his ability to have a healthy relationship. In addition, few women would want to date or marry a man who uses pornography.

By taking the conjugal act outside of the bonds of marriage, pornography use and masturbation are a form of adultery or fornication (CCC 2352–53, 2380). To reduce sex to a recreational activity that uses people for self-centered pleasure is clearly an offence against chastity, which is designed to protect people and promote authentic love and intimacy.

It does grave injury to the dignity of its participants, since each one becomes an object of base pleasure and illicit profit for others.

Dignity is the state of being esteemed or honored (Webster, 1984). The human person has inherent dignity as a singular creation of God's hand, even beyond the higher animals, as our greater dignity lies in our free will and ability to self-legislate. God has given us free will, something that we share only with the angels, and with free will we can choose to love, honor, and respect others. The flip side of free will is that we can choose not to love. We can choose to sin. We are violating the dignity of all involved when we use people through viewing pornography. Pornography takes a sacred part of a person—their sexuality—and reduces it to a thing to be used and discarded.

Pope Benedict XVI wrote in *Deus Caritas Est* (2006): "Eros, reduced to pure 'sex,' has become a commodity, a mere 'thing' to be bought and sold, or rather man himself becomes a commodity. This is hardly man's great 'yes' to the body. On the contrary, he now considers his body and his sexuality as the purely material part of himself, to be used and exploited at will. Nor does he see it as an arena for the exercise of his freedom, but as a mere object that he attempts, as he pleases, to make both enjoyable and harmless. Here we are actually dealing with a debasement of the human body: no longer is it integrated into our overall existential freedom; no longer is it a vital expression of our whole being, but it is more or less relegated to the purely biological sphere."

The participants in pornography are both those who produce pornography and those who consume it. Pornography producers include actors, directors, producers, film crews, investors, and marketers. Of these people, those who are hurt most are the actors, especially women. While the pornography industry portrays these women as modern liberated women who are choosing this profession, the fact remains that the industry is preying on the weak and vulnerable. Most of the women in pornography come from very abusive, dysfunctional families. They are deeply wounded. Many are addicted to drugs, alcohol, and sex. Former porn star Shelley Lubben describes this in her book, *Truth Behind the Fantasy of Porn* (2010). The pornography industry does not see its actors as people but as commodities to be used and thrown away. The lack of care for these people is evident in their short lifespan of only thirty-seven years. The producers of pornography don't care about the trauma, abuse, addiction, STDs, or suicide that is rampant among porn stars. When they are done with one porn star, they simply toss her aside and find another to exploit. This is truly an act of violence.

The producers of pornography also violate their own dignity by being involved in this industry. God created us to love, serve, and protect one another. By exploiting others, pornography producers are sabotaging their own dignity by refusing to live as God created them. Obviously, if they cannot respect their own dignity, how can they respect the dignity of others?

The consumers of pornography are those who view it. Consumers don't have to pay for pornography to consume it and be complicit with an industry that exploits people. Like the pornography producers, consumers violate their own dignity because they refuse to see the actors in pornography as human beings who deserve to be loved and respected. When a woman's human dignity is denied, she is no longer seen as a person. She becomes an object to be used. When love and intimacy are removed from sexuality, it becomes nothing more than base pleasure.

There is reciprocity among producers and consumers of pornography, which perpetuates their lack of respect for human dignity. On one hand, producers disregard the dignity of consumers, providing millions of men the opportunity to use weak and vulnerable women for their own sexual pleasure. The wide distribution and acceptance of pornography in the media has convinced men that they aren't committing a crime. This has also led to the acceptance of strip clubs, prostitution, and extramarital affairs. On the other hand, consumers disregard the dignity of producers by providing a market for pornography. Many pornographers claim they are in this business because there is strong demand for it, but their financial greed leads them to disregard the dignity of the consumer. In the United States alone, pornography is a multibillion-dollar industry exploiting weak and vulnerable people—actresses, actors, young consumers, and addicted men—and turning them into commodities to be used for profit. Whenever a man engages in pornography, he is supporting an industry that dehumanizes all involved simply for financial gain.

It immerses all who are involved in the illusion of a fantasy world.

Pornography presents the consumer with many false promises, but as we've seen in earlier chapters, the biggest one is intimacy. Like the Sirens who beckoned sailors with the promise of love only to meet their demise, pornography promises to fully meet one's need for intimacy—a clever illusion. Viewing pornography is very exciting for a man, but after he has viewed it for a while, masturbated and climaxed with an orgasm, he is left feeling lonelier and unfulfilled. No matter how enticing pornography is, it never satisfies. Men who use pornography and sex as a way to receive intimacy are putting the cart before the horse. God designed sex to be an outpouring of the love and intimacy between a man and women in marriage. Thus, intimacy precedes sex, not vice-versa. To believe that one can receive intimacy by viewing pornography is a grand illusion.

Pornography immerses men in a fantasy world of unhealthy sex that is not found in the bedroom of a loving husband and wife. Pornography often portrays people using each other in sexually deviant ways, and repeatedly watching it leads men to think it's the most intense and satisfying kind of sex a person can experience. While this might seem like the ultimate sexual experience, it usually leaves men feeling empty because it is not real sex. Real sex is designed by God and it emerges from a deep, loving, and intimate relationship between a husband and wife.

The fantasy sex in pornland is like a matchstick. When struck, it flares up bright but burns out fast. The sex in marriage is like a slow burning flame that is never extinguished. It may not appear as exciting, but it is infinitely more satisfying.

It is a grave offense.

The Church teaches that using pornography is a mortal sin (CCC 2354). The Catechism defines sin as "an offense against reason, truth, and right conscience; it is a failure in genuine love for God and neighbor caused by a perverse attachment to certain goods. It wounds the nature of man and injures human solidarity. It has been defined as 'an utterance, a deed, or a desire contrary to eternal law' [St. Augustine, *Contra Faustum* 22:PL 42,418; St. Thomas Aquinas, *STh* I-II,71,6]" (1849). The Catechism goes on to state that mortal sin "destroys charity in the heart of man by a grave violation of God's law; it turns man away from God, who is his ultimate end and his beatitude, by preferring an inferior good to Him" (1855).

Sin separates us from one another and from God. It is an abuse of freedom and a failure to love. God gave us the incredible gift of free will so that we all could be in loving relationships with one another and with Him. This was God's plan from the very beginning. In Genesis 1:26 God says, "Let us make man in our image, after our likeness." The "our" in this verse refers to the Trinity. God loves us so much that He created us in His image. This means more than simply physically "looking" like Him. He wants us to experience the true life-giving love of the Trinity.

When a man uses pornography, he is misusing his freedom and ability to love God and others. He is using this freedom for selfish reasons. This refusal to love separates him from God and others. What's sad is that the very thing a man believes will bring him happiness (pornography) actually brings him more loneliness, isolation, and despair. He neither knows nor can experience authentic love and intimacy. This problem is not new. Proverbs 13:19 tells us, "Lust indulged starves the soul." The man choosing to use pornography is "preferring an inferior good" to God. Consequently, he cannot give or receive love as God intended.

Pornography use is a grave sin against the dignity of the human person and human sexuality. Pornography use by married people is adultery because it takes sex outside the marriage covenant. Pornography use by single people is fornication because neither partner is married. Pornography use by celibate people is fornication and infidelity. Although most people understand the seriousness of committing adultery and infidelity, many have never heard the word "fornication" and are unaware that unmarried people (both single and celibate) having sex is a sin. Fornication is defined by the Catechism as the "carnal union between an unmarried man and an unmarried woman. It is gravely contrary to the dignity of persons and human sexuality which is naturally ordered to the good of spouses and the generation and education of children" (2353). By using pornography, a single person is using his sexuality outside the bonds of marriage. He is fornicating. He is committing a mortal sin.

The Church also teaches that lust is a mortal sin in many ways. Pornography always involves lusting after others for narcissistic pleasure, a sin against chastity. Lust is one of the seven deadly sins, also known as a capital sin. Capital sins are serious because they engender other sins (CCC 1866). Lust is a "disordered desire for or inordinate enjoyment of sexual pleasure. Sexual pleasure is morally disordered when sought for itself, isolated from procreative and unitive purposes" (CCC 2351). Pornography is a sin against chastity because it excludes love, intimacy, and bonds of marriage for which sex is reserved, and reduces sex to a mere recreational activity.

The Church also teaches that masturbation is a mortal sin. Masturbation almost always accompanies pornography use. While most people know what masturbation is, the Catechism defines it as "the deliberate stimulation of the genital organs in order to derive sexual pleasure. . . . The deliberate use of the sexual faculty, for whatever reason, outside of marriage is essentially contrary to its purpose . . . mutual self-giving and human procreation in the context of true love" [CDF, *Persona humana* 9] (2352). There is no love, intimacy, or relationship with masturbation, and it is not open to the creation of new life. Masturbating with pornography is simply a way of using other people for one's own pleasure. Avoiding masturbation is difficult for many, especially young single people, because our culture has led many to believe that sexual release is a necessity of life. The media presents masturbation as "healthy self-pleasuring." However, if we look at it through the lens of God's plan for sexuality, we see it is an inherently selfish act. How? The person is communicating that he doesn't want to reserve his sexuality for the one he loves most.

Avoiding the grave sins of pornography use, lust, and masturbation, and choosing to love as God calls us, opens people up to experiencing life-giving love and intimacy with God and others. They are choosing God over self. The benefits are striking! Married couples are led to a deeper level of intimacy through their sexual fidelity to one another. Celibate people are able to love God and others more deeply through their service to the kingdom. Single people are able to truly love and respect others and foster healthy relationships that can lead to healthy marriages.

Avoiding sexual sin need not be difficult. If a person's goal is to constantly live a virtuous life, then avoiding sin becomes easier because we grow in maturity and self-mastery. Our culture presents pornography use as something that all "real men" do. But "real men" have the strength and control to reject pornography and masturbation because they know those are grave sins and selfish pursuits. Weak men view pornography because they have no control over themselves and give into their base urges. Virtuous men strive to be the men God created them to be, men who can fully love God and others and receive their love. Virtue will be discussed in greater detail later.

Civil authorities should prevent the production and distribution of pornographic materials.

While the United States Constitution guarantees us the right of free speech, this is not without limits. What many people don't realize is that obscenity is illegal in the United States. According to Morality In Media (M.I.M.), Federal Obscenity Laws prohibit the distribution of hardcore obscene pornography on the Internet, cable, and satellite television, including hotels, sexually oriented businesses, and other retail shops. These laws, however, are not currently being enforced (M.I.M., 2013), partially because there is no clear and accepted definition of hardcore pornography. Consequently, the federal government has left the job of defining hardcore pornography to individual communities.

Most communities do have obscenity laws to protect their citizens. These laws prohibit the sale of pornographic materials to minors, regulate who can sell pornography, and where such businesses can be located. Thus, in many communities, businesses that sold pornography were usually banned from residential neighborhoods, video rental stores prohibited minors from entering the "adult room," and porn shops and strip clubs were relegated to undesirable areas of town. The Internet has changed all of this. Because few websites actually check the ages of their viewers, it is virtually impossible to prevent minors from being exposed to pornography. In addition, the growing acceptance of pornography in our culture has led to the establishment of porn shops and strip clubs in residential communities and near schools and churches. This has left millions vulnerable to the dangers of pornography.

Lawmakers need to be made aware of the dangers of pornography and be pressed to enforce obscenity laws at every level of government. Laws that would prohibit the operation of pornographic businesses in any community should be passed and rigorously enforced. Because the Internet provides access to the entire world, it might be impossible for the government to eliminate access to online pornography. Notwithstanding, the government can pass laws that would require the ages of viewers be verified before they can access a pornographic website. Warning labels on the dangers of pornography could be made mandatory on pornographic websites just as they are for tobacco products.

The most powerful thing that governments can do to protect the public from the dangers of pornography is to educate it. Programs could be designed to educate the public on the dangers of pornography similar to programs on drugs, alcohol, and tobacco.

Scripture and Pornography

Scripture doesn't directly address pornography, but it does speak about the importance of a clean heart and mind. God warns us most clearly in Galatians 5:19–21 about the dangers of an immoral life: "Now the works of the flesh are plain: immorality, impurity, licentiousness, idolatry, sorcery, enmity, strife, jealousy, anger, selfishness, dissension, party spirit, envy, drunkenness, carousing, and the like. I warn you, as I warned you before, that those who do such things will not inherit the kingdom of God." In this passage, immorality, impurity, licentiousness, idolatry, selfishness, and "orgies" (included in the NAB translation) all pertain to pornography use.

Scripture also talks about the value of striving to maintain a pure heart. Bishop Robert Finn talks about this in his Pastoral Letter, *Blessed are the Pure in Heart* (2007). Throughout Scripture, the Lord admonishes us to remain pure of heart, which is most clearly found in the beatitude, "Blessed are the pure in heart, for they shall see God" (Matthew 5:8). The beatitudes challenge us to follow a higher moral calling. They are the way of discipleship. Purity of heart doesn't just mean avoiding sexual sin. It means pursuing a virtuous life. This allows us to more fully maintain loving relationships with God and with others. God's ultimate plan for us is to enjoy pure happiness forever with Him in heaven. To achieve this, we cannot have any stain of sin on our souls. Even the Old Testament teaches this: "Who shall ascend the hill of the Lord? And who shall stand in his holy place? He who has clean hands and a pure heart, who does not lift up his soul to what is false" (Psalms 24:3–4).

To be pure of heart, we must love God with our whole heart, soul, mind and strength (Deuteronomy 6:4–5). We must also love our neighbor as our self (Mark 12:29–31). This means focusing our love on the good of others. This is a tough calling, but it's not impossible. With God all things are possible (Matthew 19:26). If we focus on living a virtuous life all for the love of God and others, we will experience that love in return one hundred fold. This is the value of having a clean and undivided heart.

Living a life of virtue is a daily challenge and requires daily practice. It calls us to get outside of ourselves and focus on others. "Every athlete exercises self-control in all things. They do it to receive a perishable wreath, but we an imperishable" (1 Corinthians 9:25). This requires daily prayer and sacrifice. By denying base urges (sexual sin) for a greater good, we can grow stronger in our faith and ability to maintain a pure heart. "Create in me a clean heart, O God" (Psalms 51:10). Even if we fall along the way, we shouldn't get discouraged. God is patient and merciful, and has given us the Sacrament of Reconciliation to reunite us to Him when we sin. "I said, 'I will confess my transgressions to the Lord'; then you forgave the guilt of my sin" (Psalms 32:5). Thus, God has given us all the resources we need to live a pure life.

Scripture admonishes us to pursue a pure life, reminding us of the price our Lord paid for our redemption from sin. "Shun immorality. Every other sin which a man commits is outside the body; but the immoral man sins against his own body. Do you not know that your body is a temple of the Holy Spirit within you, which you have from God? You are not your own; you were bought with a price. So glorify

God in your body" (1 Corinthians 6:18–20). In that passage our Lord affirms the sacredness of our bodies. To use sex for any purpose other than its intended purpose defiles the sacredness of sex and our bodies. Sex within marriage is both sacred and sacramental. Every time we commit a sin of immorality, it is as if we are nailing Jesus to the Cross again, but our love for the Lord should compel us not to want to hurt Him again. By striving to live a pure life, a man glorifies God in his body, and this includes his heart, mind, soul, and strength.

Through Scripture, God calls every person to be a light to the world and not to place our light under a bushel basket (Matthew 5:15). We are to show others the joy of living a pure life. "[B]e blameless and innocent, children of God without blemish in the midst of a crooked and perverse generation, among whom you shine as lights in the world" (Philippians 2:15). Many people caught up in the immorality of our culture believe that leading a sexually immoral life will lead to happiness. However, as we have shown repeatedly, it always leads to loneliness and despair. When we live pure lives, we are able to truly love God and others; we shine like lights to the world, which is ultimately God's light. This will glorify God, preserve us from sin, and lead others to Him.

Spiritual Battle

The Church recognizes there is a true spiritual battle occurring in our world, and sexual impurity is one of Satan's strongest weapons. He knows how weak and vulnerable we are to sexual sin. When an enemy attacks a fortress, he focuses on the weakest point. For men, our eyes are our weakest point for impurity, and this is why it is crucial to guard our eyes. Like a thief in the night, Satan is always waiting to catch us off guard and lead us into sexual sin. He is the father of lies that leads men to believe that pornography and masturbation will bring them happiness and fulfillment. We need to remember that when we sin, we are telling God, "I will not serve you. I will serve Satan and my own selfish desires." Our Lord understands this battle and speaks clearly about it in Ephesians 6:10–12: "Finally, be strong in the Lord and in the strength of his might. Put on the whole armor of God, that you may be able to stand against the wiles of the devil. For we are not contending against flesh and blood, but against the principalities, against the powers, against the world rulers of this present darkness, against the spiritual hosts of wickedness in the heavenly places."

God knows temptation is a serious problem among all people. We are weak. In 1 Peter 5:8–9 we read, "Be sober, be watchful. Your adversary the devil prowls around like a roaring lion, seeking someone to devour. Resist him, firm in your faith, knowing that the same experience of suffering is required of your brotherhood throughout the world." Fortunately, God has given us everything we need to fight the battle and succeed. We need to put on the whole armor of God. Ephesians 6:13–20 says, "Therefore take on the whole armor of God, that you may be able to withstand in the evil day, and having done all, to stand. Stand therefore, having fastened the belt of truth around your waist, and having put on the breastplate of righteousness, and having shod your feet with equipment of the gospel of peace; besides all of these, taking the shield of faith, with which you can quench all the flaming darts of the Evil One. And take the helmet of salvation, and the sword of the Spirit, with all prayer and supplication. To that end keep alert with all perseverance, making supplication for all the saints."

Let's look closer at that passage from Ephesians. It's logical that God would first have us put on "the belt of truth." If we are to resist Satan's lies, we must know the truth about sin, especially sins of impurity. This means understanding all the ways that pornography and masturbation hurt us, others, and God. We need to embrace the truth about God's perfect plan for sexuality, which is unitive, procreative, and reflects the love of the Trinity. Referring to truth as a belt reminds us of the value of chastity, which enables us to have healthy relationships with others and prevents us from using people sexually.

Next we "put on the breastplate of righteousness." This means we both understand the truth and live it. We stand up for what is right and just and condemn evil. This can be difficult in today's society, because a person who stands up against sexual immorality can be labeled a "prude" or "religious fundamentalist." In these situations we need to remember the beatitude, "Blessed are the pure in heart for they shall see God." Our primary goal is union with God where we will see Him face to face.

For shoes for your feet, God calls us to use whatever makes us ready to proclaim the gospel of peace. We must evangelize using whatever means possible, and in the fight against pornography, this means using all our available resources. Not everyone makes fighting pornography his full-time ministry, but there are other things the average person can do. One can educate young people on the dangers of pornography, organize a protest outside a porn shop, or start a men's ministry in his parish.

Our faith is truly a shield against the flaming arrows (temptations) of Satan. Our faith enables us to proclaim, "Jesus is Lord!" With a strong faith we can turn to the Lord when tempted, rebuke Satan and his empty promises, and through God's grace overcome temptation and sin. 1 John 4:4–5 states: "Little children, you are of God, and have overcome them; for he [God] who is in you is greater than he [Satan] who is in the world." We can overcome Satan's flaming arrows if we turn to God daily in faith.

"Take the helmet of salvation, and the sword of the Spirit, which is the word of God." Salvation is referred to as a helmet to be worn on our heads, reminding us that in Christ we are new creations. We are not slaves to Satan or the world. We can walk with our heads held high as adopted sons and daughters of the Father, something we should never take for granted, for Christ's suffering and death on the Cross bought us our salvation. Jesus paid the price for our sins and gave us the incredible gift of the Holy Spirit to dwell within us. Through this wonderful gift we are never alone. We must always be grateful for everything God has done for us. Any sin of impurity is a sign of ingratitude, for it leads us to focus solely on ourselves and forget all that God has done for us. Again, we read in 1 Corinthians 6:19–20, "Do you not know that your body is a temple of the Holy Spirit within you, which you have from God? You are not your own; you were bought with a price. So glorify God in your body."

The Word of God is referred to as the sword of the Spirit because it conveys God's truth and combats Satan's lies. Many people consider Scripture alone as the only Word of God, yet God also speaks to us through the magisterium, the teaching authority of the Church. We have already seen what the Church teaches about pornography, lust, masturbation, and chastity in the Catechism of the Catholic Church. We also learn about God's perfect plan for love and sexuality in papal writings, such as Pope St. John Paul II's *The Theology of the Body* and *Love and Responsibility*. More recently, pastoral letters such as *Blessed are the Pure in Heart* by Bishop Robert Finn (2007) and *Love Undefiled* by Bishop Paul Loverde (2006) speak specifically about pornography.

Finally, God admonishes us to: "Pray at all times in the Spirit, with all prayer and supplication. To that end keep alert with all perseverance, making supplication for all the saints" (Ephesians 6:18). We constantly should turn to God for help and protection in the fight for purity. We also need to pray for each other because we cannot win this battle alone. If we are constantly keeping God in our hearts and minds, we will more easily avoid temptation, and by praying for each other we can gain more strength. In the above passage, "the saints" refer to the other early Christians, but I believe it also means the communion of saints in heaven. We can turn to them for intercession and protection. Here I reiterate Ephesians 6:12, "We are not contending against flesh and blood, but against the principalities, against the powers, against the world rulers of this present darkness, against the spiritual hosts of wickedness in the heavenly places."

Back to Matt

Matt was very confused with the Church's teaching on pornography when he first entered recovery. He thought the Church always condemned sex. This gradually changed as he learned why the Church was against pornography and discovered that the Church wants to protect people. The Church wants people to experience true love and intimacy, because it understands sex as a holy gift from God that celebrates the love between a husband and wife, which is open to the gift of new life. Matt began to realize that living a chaste life would enable him to have healthy relationships that were much more fulfilling than he ever imagined. He knew from experience that pornography use sabotages this and only leads to more selfishness. Matt began to hope he would one day meet a woman with whom he would fall in love and marry. His sexuality would be a precious gift he would give to her alone. He learned how the Church's view toward human sexuality is not only logical, but worth following with all his strength.

8

Priests, Religious, and Seminarians Addicted to Pornography

In 2010, a priest in Massachusetts was accused of stealing over $80,000 from his parish. Most of this was taken from parish collections. He admitted that he was addicted to pornography, and much of the money he stole went to support his addiction. The priest's credit card had a balance of $25,000 that he used to purchase online pornography. A review of his cable bills revealed that he spent over $4,000 on "adult" movies. As a result of his conviction, this priest was placed on probation for three years and was required to perform community service during that time. He was also sent to a psychiatric treatment facility for priests for six months to begin his recovery (Tennant, 2010). Getting caught was actually a blessing in disguise for this priest because it helped him to realize just how sick and in need of help he was. Thankfully, he was able to get help.

While this true story is an extreme case, it does illustrate that clergy are not immune to pornography addiction. I did not treat this priest; however, in my practice, I have worked with countless priests and seminarians who struggle with pornography use. I even run a phone support group for priests. Today, priests face numerous challenges in their vocation. Many are isolated in remote areas of the country and are working long hours with little time off. Because of their position as moral leaders, they have difficulty asking for help when they struggle.

Currently, there is little research published on Catholic priests, religious, and seminarians who struggle with pornography addiction. However, there are several good studies on this disease in Protestant clergy. According to Dr. Lynn Anne Joiner (2008), "Surveys of Protestant evangelical clergy in the United Stated reported that 33% to 43% admitted to viewing Internet pornography. Of these numbers, approximately 6% to 18% viewed pornography multiple times per month and one survey cited 37% of clergy who described Internet pornography as a current temptation."

The National Coalition for the Protection of Children and Families (2000) reports, "In an informal survey of pastors in Seattle, WA, 11% of the 58 pastors surveyed intentionally had accessed a sexual explicit website; 9% viewed by choice and felt that it may be a problem for them." Five thousand pastors were questioned through the website with 55% indicating they had visited a pornographic site within the last year; 33% had visited a sexually explicit site within the previous three weeks (Weiss, 2000).

According to national surveys by Christianity Today and Leadership Journal (2001), "four in ten pastors with Internet access reported they have visited a pornographic website . . . and more than one third have done so in the past year. Slightly over half of the pastors (51%) say Internet pornography is a temptation for them; 37% admit it is a current struggle. Among the laity, 11% report at least occasionally viewing pornography."

This epidemic among Protestant clergy is probably much worse than the statistics show. Moreover, if this is a problem among Protestant clergy, it could be just as severe among Catholic clergy. My personal experience counseling Catholic priests, religious, and seminarians leads me to believe this is so.

These studies among Protestant clergy also shed valuable light on priestly celibacy. Many people believe that Catholic clergy turn to pornography because they cannot marry and therefore substitute pornography for a wife. However, most Protestant clergy are married and they still struggle with pornography, leading us to deduce that celibacy is not a major issue in sexual addiction. There are much deeper root causes.

Root Causes

As with any addiction, remember that we need to view pornography use as a form of self-medicating. Many of these clergy struggle with deep emotional wounds too, and this can lead to addiction. Often they don't even realize these wounds are there, and then one day they discover pornography and realize how good it makes them feel. It eases their pain, but because the effects are only temporary, they continue to go back time and again. They become addicted.

Addiction in Priests and Religious

While all the root causes for pornography use listed in earlier chapters apply to priests and religious, there are some that affect them in unique ways.

1. *Family-of-Origin Wounds.* Many people believe that a man who becomes a priest must come from a loving Catholic family. Unfortunately, this is a stereotype. There are priests who came from very tragic family backgrounds and have had to contend with divorce, death, rejection, abandonment, addiction, and abuse in their families. Many priests have recovered from these wounds and use their experiences to effectively minister to those suffering from similar wounds; however, there are those who have not healed and have turned to pornography to ease their pain.

   a. *Divorce.* Ever since the sexual revolution of the late 1960s, the divorce rate in America has steadily risen. Catholic families have not been immune to the effects of this, and many priests today come from families that were torn apart by divorce. Divorce is painful for all parties, especially children. One of the deepest wounds is the inability to trust

163

others, which makes it difficult to develop healthy relationships. The result is deep loneliness. Children of divorce often struggle with a deep guilt. They blame themselves for the breakup of their parents' marriage. In many divorces the father moves out and sees his children rarely after that. This leaves children feeling rejected and abandoned. Children of divorce carry these wounds into adulthood and can affect them for years.

Fr. Bill is a forty-five-year-old diocesan priest whose parents divorced when he was ten years old. His father had been serially unfaithful to his mother, and she was deeply wounded by this and bitter. Subsequently, Fr. Bill learned not to trust people. After the divorce, he rarely saw his father and felt rejected by him. During high school, Fr. Bill joined his parish youth group and had a religious conversion. While his experience of God's love was very comforting, Fr. Bill was still sorely wounded. He became a loner because of his inability to trust others. This continued into seminary. He never thought the divorce wounded him so deeply. In fact, he saw himself as pretty successful despite his upbringing. However, after a few years of priesthood, the stresses of ministry brought to the surface his old wounds of guilt, mistrust, and loneliness, and he turned to pornography for comfort. Soon he was viewing porn almost every day and was addicted.

b. *Abuse.* There are also priests who grew up in abusive homes and have turned to pornography for relief. Recall the comprehensive research on sex addicts we presented in chapter two finding that 97% were emotionally abused, 74% were physically abused, and 81% were sexually abused. Based on people's stereotype of a priest's family, it's hard for many to believe that a priest could have been abused as a child. Unfortunately, many are.

When Fr. Ed was seven years old, he was repeatedly sexually abused by his grandfather. Fear and gifts were used to ensure Fr. Ed's silence. The abuse went on for three years and ended when his grandfather died. While Fr. Ed never told his family about the abuse, he carried guilt, fear, and shame into adulthood, and his silence left him feeling alone and isolated. After several years of priesthood, Fr. Ed became an alcoholic to ease his pain, blaming his drinking on the stresses of ministry. With the help of Alcoholics Anonymous he was able to stop drinking. However, he was still hurting inside from the abuse and turned to pornography, which led to this new addiction.

c. *Addiction.* I have treated many priests who came from families with addictions. A common theme I have found in their families is the need to appear to the public as "perfect, faithful Catholics." To the outside world, they are model families, but behind closed doors, it's total chaos. This leaves the families of addicts suffering in silence.

Fr. Lou grew up in such a family. His father was an angry alcoholic who would get drunk and violently terrorize the family at night. Because they had to maintain the façade of being the perfect family, Fr. Lou couldn't talk to anyone about it. He felt alone and helpless. He vowed to never drink, but as an adult he found himself turning to pornography to ease his pain. Thirty years later, his family still didn't acknowledge his father's alcoholism and its effect on them, and yet its effects left Fr. Lou addicted to pornography.

2. *Loneliness.* This can be a trigger for anyone to use pornography. Many believe that a person addicted to pornography is searching for a romantic or sexual relationship, but as we've seen in earlier chapters, this is not necessarily true. Recall that pornography addiction is also a serious problem among Protestant

clergy, and most of them are married and not seeking a romantic or sexual relationship. The real need is for intimacy. They are seeking a deep emotional connection. Sex and romance are just one way to experience intimacy. It can also be experienced in close friendships, among family members, and with God. You would be surprised how many priests don't experience intimacy with God. They have a deep faith in God, but it is an intellectual faith (of the head), not an emotional one (of the heart). This results in profound spiritual loneliness that many priests struggle with due to a lack of good friendships. People tend to connect most with others who share the same vocation. Married couples tend to have more friends who are married. Single people tend to have more single friends. Thus, a priest's closest friends should be other priests. Priests can also have good friends who are laypeople, as long as these relationships don't compromise his role as a spiritual father. Unfortunately, because of the shortage of priests and the busy lives they lead, many priests don't have time to work on developing healthy friendships. Others may have difficulty making friends in general because they lack self-confidence.

Fr. Nick became addicted to pornography shortly after he was ordained. He was assigned as parochial vicar of a large suburban parish with a wonderful pastor, but they were both so busy they rarely saw each other. Parish work kept Fr. Nick from getting together with priests from other parishes, and he had little time to socialize with any laypeople. After a long day, he would retire to his room and surf the net to relax. Before he knew it, he was spending several hours a night viewing pornography. He didn't want a wife. He wanted to connect with some genuine friends. Pornography was used to ease the pain of his loneliness.

3. *Isolation.* This is a unique form of loneliness. Many priests find themselves ministering to Catholics in remote areas or rural areas, such as the desert or deep in the mountains. They don't

have priest brothers nearby and only have limited contact with laypeople.

Fr. Ron is pastor of three parishes in the rural Midwest where the parishes are roughly seventy miles apart. Fr. Ron spends much of his time in his car traveling from parish to parish. Each parish has one employee, a part-time secretary, and several lay volunteers. Aside from the secretaries, the only times he sees the volunteers and his parishioners are on Sundays, and with the exception of the occasional funeral, he spends most of the week alone working around the parishes. Because he was not raised in a rural community, Fr. Ron had great difficulty adjusting to the remoteness and isolation of his pastorate. This led him to turn to pornography for comfort. He also got into online chatting just so he could experience some form of human interaction. Before long, he was addicted.

4. *Ministry Stress.* Many priests are being asked to do a lot more because of the shortage of priests. Like Fr. Ron, they are pastors of multiple parishes. Others are also ministering in hospitals, nursing homes, prisons, schools, colleges, homeless shelters, soup kitchens, and food pantries. Due to their heavy work load, many are unable to take a regular day off, which leaves them struggling under mountains of stress. Some of this stress is self-imposed. These priests feel overly responsible to minister to people and have difficulty saying no. They tend to take on excessive amounts of responsibility, even jobs that a layperson could easily handle. If they do say no, they feel guilty, as if they were neglecting their vocation.

Fr. Ben was a pastor of two small inner city parishes with innumerable needs. Along with his regular pastoral duties, he started a food pantry, literacy program, and a youth group. He liked the excitement of his ministry, but soon the responsibility was wearing on him. He would work up to eighteen hours a day, and despite having every Tuesday off, he always found some work that needed to be done that day. The responsibilities of ministry also took time away from prayer. While he didn't feel burnt out, the stress became overwhelming. He was physically and emotionally drained by the time he got back to his room late at night. He would surf the net to relax, and this soon led to viewing pornography and addiction.

5. *Ministry Burnout.* Many priests and religious neglect healthy self-care because of the demands of ministry. They forgo having days off to relax and rarely take a vacation. Some priests feel pressured to meet all their parishioner's needs and feel guilty if they say no. Then there are those who are left with more responsibilities than one man can handle. These priests are put in charge of large parishes that should be staffed by two or more priests, and they are often given additional assignments, such as hospital ministry. Then, there are priests who truly love an exciting fast-paced ministry, but take on more responsibility than is necessary or healthy. The result for all three is burnout.

   Fr. Stan was a pastor of two parishes because of the shortage of priests in his diocese. Although both parishes had good lay staffs, the workload for Fr. Stan was exhausting. Canon law and bishops mandate that priests take vacations and retreats each year; however, because of the tremendous sense of responsibility Fr. Stan had toward his parish, it had been years since he took a restful period of relaxation. This left him angry and burnt out. He began neglecting his pastoral duties, doing only the bare minimum, and to escape from the burnout he turned to viewing pornography late at night. Of course it led to addiction.

6. *Anger.* Anger is a key trigger for many addictions. Often when a person is mistreated and feels he can do nothing about it, he becomes bitter and resentful. For a priest, this anger can be toward his parishioners, staff, bishop, or even God, and he can turn to pornography to ease the emotional pain caused by the anger. Pornography use can also be a form of rebellion for a priest, a way of getting back at those who hurt him. Some priests may not even be aware they are carrying anger.

Fr. Peter sought treatment for pornography addiction when his secretary discovered pornography on the parish computer. After the staff would go home at night, Fr. Peter would spend hours surfing for porn on the office computer. He had originally been in the navy, and after an honorable discharge he entered seminary with the hope of becoming a navy chaplain. However, after he was ordained, his bishop instead assigned him to a parish. Fr. Peter loved being a priest and serving his parishioners, but he was angry with God and very angry with his bishop, which he openly admitted to. He used pornography both to ease his pain and as a form of rebellion. Even if his bishop never found out about it, Fr. Peter still felt, subconsciously, that in some way he was getting back at his bishop. He definitely knew he was defying God, but he was so angry he didn't care. Fr. Peter's use of pornography soon escalated into a full-blown addiction.

7. *Lack of Confidence.* Some priests use pornography to ease the pain of having little self-confidence. They may have done well in seminary, but the real world of ministry frightens them and they feel inadequate. When comparing themselves to other priests, they don't believe they measure up, and they deeply fear that people will eventually discover how incompetent they believe they are.

Fr. Jude has been a religious priest for fifteen years, and in all that time he has been an assistant pastor of several parishes. He never felt confident enough to be a pastor, so whenever the opportunity to become a pastor arose, he managed to convince his superior that another priest would be a better choice. Deep down, Fr. Jude felt like a failure. He didn't think he would ever amount to anything as a priest. He turned to pornography to ease his guilt and pain. He knew viewing pornography was wrong, yet he would imagine himself as the men in pornography. To Fr. Jude, male porn stars were strong, take-charge men who weren't afraid of anything. He saw them as "real men." This gave Fr. Jude a false (and very temporary) sense of confidence that led him to become addicted to pornography. He soon began engaging in online chatting and even made plans to meet a woman from a chat room. Fortunately, he didn't have the courage to go through with the rendezvous. That was his wakeup call and he immediately sought help.

8. *The Five A's.* As stated earlier, the Five A's have made pornography the new drug of choice in our culture, and this is true for priests as well. Thirty years ago, it wasn't uncommon to find a priest self-medicating his emotional pain with alcohol, and the media would often poke fun at the drunken priest. Pornography has changed all this. Alcohol must be purchased. Pornography is free. While a priest must be careful not to be seen intoxicated in public, pornography use is easily hidden and has become the new drug of choice for many priests.

Seminarians and Pornography

Many seminarians who struggle with pornography addiction were addicted before they entered seminary. For others, the stress of seminary triggers deep emotional wounds that can lead to pornography addiction. While all the root causes I've cited above and in earlier chapters apply to seminarians, there are a few that affect seminarians in a unique way due to their age and the culture in which they were raised.

1. *Narcissism.* This is not a new phenomenon in the ministry. History is riddled with extremely selfish clergy. Catholic seminarians, most of whom are young adults, are not immune to this, and many of them are raised in small families and over-indulged by their parents. Despite their deep faith and desire to serve the Lord, this treatment can lead to a strong sense of entitlement and is further fueled while they are in seminary. Imagine a young man who announces to his family and parish that he will be entering seminary. From that moment on, his family and parish treat him like a celebrity. This can also lead him to believe he is a special person who was chosen by God to

do great things, which only enhances his sense of entitlement. In 2010, I conducted a study of narcissism in seminarians and found that about 16% are highly narcissistic. During times of high stress, this sense of entitlement can lead a seminarian to seek relief by using pornography.

Kyle is a second year theology student at a prominent Catholic seminary and is well known in his parish. He enjoys helping in his parish during breaks from school because everyone treats him like a rock star. Parishioners invite him to their homes and offer him gifts, and while he knows he needs to work on remaining humble, Kyle admits he likes this treatment. This led him to expect special treatment all the time. As his narcissism grew, Kyle began to feel entitled to "some relief" after a long day at school, and he subconsciously used this to justify viewing pornography. As his studies became more challenging, Kyle began to view pornography more often and it became a full-blown addiction.

2. *Perfectionism.* The stress of their state in life can be very intense for many seminarians. As future priests, they are held to a higher standard of moral behavior. Here is where being treated like a celebrity has its down side. Many seminarians feel as if their lives are being examined by the public under a microscope. This can lead to a struggle with perfectionism. This always results in failure and disappointment because they constantly set the bar too high. To deal with this constant sense of failure, many turn to pornography for comfort.

As a young college seminarian, one of Justin's apostolates was to work with a local parish youth group. He realized how tough it was to be a teenager today and wanted to show the teens that they could live a chaste life and be very happy. In wanting to appear perfect before the teens, he set standards for himself that no one could meet. For example, he decided that he should never get angry or show any kind of temper.

So as not to appear a hypocrite, he decided to practice this in all of his relationships and not just with the youth group. Soon the stress of being perfect was too much for him to bear. When Justin would return to his room late at night, he would be extremely exhausted and the desire to rebel was intense. He was primed for getting caught in the web of pornography and its addiction.

3. *The Five A's.* The Five A's have a special impact on seminarians. Technology is an integral part of young people's lives. Most seminarians grew up with computers, cell phones, and the Internet, which has made the affordability, accessibility, and anonymity of pornography more prevalent for them. Many were exposed to Internet pornography at a young age. To their generation, pornography use is acceptable. All of this has made justifying pornography use too easy for young adults and seminarians. This allows pornography to aggressively move into their lives and lead them into addiction.

Mark is a true tech guru. Growing up, he always seemed to have the latest gadgets, and whether it was a computer, cell phone, or video game system, he was always on top of technology. His parents encouraged him in this, believing that this knowledge would be needed to succeed in the 21st century. However, his parents didn't realize the negative consequences. In buying him all the gadgets he wanted, they were spoiling him and leading him into a sense of entitlement. They were also unaware of the danger in giving him unrestricted access to the Internet. Mark began viewing Internet pornography when he was thirteen. The easy access and peer acceptance made pornography use perfectly okay. Mark knew his parents would not approve, and with his knowledge he could easily hide his pornography use from them. His pornography use went unchecked for several years. In college Mark had a conversion experience and felt God calling him to become a priest. Although he wanted to stop using pornography, he couldn't. He was already addicted.

Obstacles to Getting Help

As with all addictions, getting help for pornography addiction can be very difficult. There is much fear, guilt, and shame associated with admitting that one has an addiction. Then there is the challenge of finding adequate help, be it support groups, counselors, accountability partners, and others. However, for priests, religious, and seminarians there are unique challenges.

1. *Shame.* While all addicts struggle with shame, I believe clergy struggle with it to a much greater degree because they are public figures whom society holds to much stricter standards of moral living. Shame is the emotion that leads us to believe we are terrible people because of the bad things we've done. Discovering that a priest is struggling with pornography addiction creates a large scandal in the Church, especially if he is well known or a bishop. There is great fear about what others will think of them, so to preserve their reputation and protect the Church from scandal, many priests do not seek help.

   Fr. Bill is the pastor of a large suburban parish that prides itself in its many ministries. He is loved by his parishioners who see him as a holy priest. The love and esteem of his parishioners made seeking help for his pornography addiction almost impossible. Fr. Bill feared what they would think if they found out about this dark side of his life. He couldn't bear how disappointed everyone would be in him. It wasn't until his assistant pastor discovered him viewing pornography one night that he was compelled to seek treatment. Fr. Bill is now grateful for this because had he not been discovered, his shame may have prevented him from ever seeking help.

2. *Fear of Scandal.* The sexual abuse crisis in the Catholic Church has kept many priests from seeking help for pornography addiction. If anyone discovers their addiction, they fear they will be labeled a pervert or a sexual predator. They also fear the public knowledge of their addiction will cause additional scandal in the Church.

That's why it took Fr. Howard many months to muster up the courage to seek help. He feared the public knowledge of his illness would cause a scandal and his reputation would be ruined. Several priests in his diocese had been placed on administrative leave because of sexual issues, and a few were deemed unfit for ministry. Fr. Howard feared that his bishop would also find him unfit for ministry. He feared losing his vocation and being laicized if he sought help. Finally, he realized how much his guilt and shame were preventing him from being an effective priest, and he didn't want to shortchange his parishioners, so he sought help.

3. *Fear of Treatment.* Some priests refuse to seek help because of the treatment they may undergo. Priests who admit to having a pornography or sexual addiction are often sent to special treatment centers for priests. Unfortunately, these treatment centers often overdiagnose or misdiagnose priests. Their usual treatment recommendation is four to eight months of inpatient treatment with extensive outpatient follow up, which unfortunately violates all current standards in the mental health profession. The majority of pornography and sex addicts can be successfully treated in an outpatient program. For those who need inpatient treatment, the best programs in America usually only keep a person for thirty days and then continue with outpatient treatment.

Fr. Brian struggled with pornography addiction for several years before seeking help. He confessed this to his superior who responded with much care and compassion. He assured Fr. Brian that he would help him find a good recovery program, and referred him to a treatment center for priests. Fr. Brian went there for an evaluation that lasted three weeks. Along with pornography addiction, Fr. Brian was given the ambiguous diagnosis of "unintegrated sexuality." This diagnosis was never clearly explained to Fr. Brian or his superior. The treatment recommendation was six months of inpatient treatment. Two months into the program, Fr. Brian began to feel more like a prisoner. He was unable to leave the treatment center without being accompanied by a staff member, and his communication with people outside of the center was limited. He also didn't believe he was being helped by the program and began to view it as a great waste of money for his religious community. After three months, he left the treatment center and entered an outpatient recovery program where he was able to achieve and maintain sexual sobriety. The outpatient program was far more effective and a mere fraction of what the inpatient program cost. When I asked Fr. Brian why his superior sent him to the inpatient program, his response was, "That's where we've always sent priests who struggle with emotional problems." Dioceses and religious communities need to rethink treatment options for priests.

4. *Denial.* Although a priest may admit he has an addiction to pornography, he may be in denial regarding his need for outside help, believing that through more intense prayer, the sacraments, spiritual direction, and sheer will power, he can overcome his addiction. While this can be fueled by unhealthy shame, fear, and perfectionism, it can also be fueled by pride. A man may think that because he is a priest, he should be able to deal with sexual temptation. This type of pride only leads a man deeper into addiction. With continued failures he becomes more depressed and discouraged. This leads him back into pornography use to ease his pain.

Frank is a second year seminarian who struggles with pornography addiction. The rector of his seminary referred him to me for help, yet he was resistant to treatment. Although he has been presented with all the facts about pornography addiction and proper treatment, he was determined to overcome it on his own. It is as if he is saying, "Don't confuse me with the facts when my mind is already made up." Needless to say, we only had a few sessions. Fortunately, God usually intervenes in the lives of such men and places them in situations that will humble them. Then they are ready to seek help. For men like Frank, we can only pray that God will intervene soon.

5. *Family Loyalty.* This is a unique obstacle to recovery that I have found in many priests, religious, and seminarians. Family-of-origin wounds are a key factor in the development of any addiction, and a successful recovery requires a man to face these wounds and work on healing them. However, because priests are supposed to come from "good Catholic families," some priests, religious, and seminarians have difficulty admitting that their families are human and flawed. To them, making such an admission is an act of disloyalty to the family. This was the case for Fr. Lou.

Throughout his childhood, his family covered up his father's alcoholism and presented to the public an image of the perfect Catholic family. Maintaining that image was the number one rule in the family. Fr. Lou would be breaking that rule if he admitted to others that he grew up in an alcoholic home. It would be a sign of disloyalty and bring shame to his family, crushing the image they spent years maintaining. Through counseling, Fr. Lou came to understand how damaging this unspoken rule was. This gave him the courage to honestly look at how his father's alcoholism deeply wounded him, and it was the key to Fr. Lou's healing and recovery.

Healthy Self-Care

A key factor in preventing pornography use in priests, religious, and seminarians is healthy self-care, for which there are four facets. First, it's a fact that everyone on this planet is deeply wounded. It's part of being human. Healthy self-care acknowledges one's wounds and works towards healing those wounds. This helps prevent deep wounds from interfering with one's vocation. The second facet of self-care is maintaining healthy relationships. Priests need to have close-knit circles of friends, especially with other priests. This can help eliminate loneliness and isolation, while giving priests a safe place to vent frustrations, receive advice, and be supported. The third facet is not taking on excessive responsibilities in ministry. One must have balance in life, which means doing one's best in ministry, making time for prayer every day, and taking time for rest and relaxation. We would do well to follow the example of Pope Saint John XXIII who, after a particularly long day, is noted for having looked up to heaven and said, "It's your Church, Lord, you run it, I'm going to bed." This helps reduce ministry stress and can prevent burnout.

Getting Help

For clergy struggling with pornography addiction, getting help means letting go of unhealthy shame, fear, denial, and family loyalty. It means facing the truth that they are struggling with a disease that requires treatment. This entails much humility and honesty, because pride and unhealthy shame are the most difficult barriers to overcome. Priests represent Christ and are supposed to be models of virtuous living, yet they are also human. If you are a priest, religious, or seminarian struggling with pornography addiction, I urge you to seek help. Don't let the obstacles listed above prevent you from recovering. God loves you. He doesn't condemn you. He wants to help you get better so you can continue to serve the Church. It has been my experience that those who seek help become even better priests. They have a unique understanding of suffering and of God's mercy and forgiveness. They are extremely compassionate. Many start men's ministries in their parishes where they can help other men struggling with pornography. God has a special plan for your life. It doesn't matter how much of a mess you may think your life is, God can turn it around and create something beautiful. Reaching out for help is the first step.

Bishops, vicars for clergy, religious superiors, seminary rectors, and vocation directors need to treat those struggling with pornography addiction lovingly and compassionately. They must empathize with these men, recognizing how tremendously difficult it is for them to ask for help. These addicted men should never fear seeking help. If a man avoids seeking help because of the possible repercussions, his addiction will only get worse, and this might result in a huge scandal and cost thousands in legal fees and settlements. If a man knows he will be treated with love and compassion, he will seek help early in his addiction before it can turn into a huge scandal. Perhaps dioceses can be proactive in reaching out and fostering a genuine sense of compassion and concern. One practical way to do that could be an open letter from the Bishop to each of his priests, something along these lines: "Brothers, it is no secret that a large percentage of the male population of our country struggles with pornography addiction. If you share in this struggle, please know that help is available." Remember, God often uses the most wounded among us to do great things, and I believe that God has special plans for addicted persons. Once in recovery, God can use them to reach out to people experiencing any kind of suffering. They can see the suffering Christ in others and they can be Christ to others.

Another reason why priests fear seeking help is the type of treatment they receive, which currently is a paradigm from the 1950s. A typical stay in a psychiatric treatment center can cost as much as $1,000 a day and insurance rarely covers the entire cost, which leaves a diocese or religious community with a huge bill. Simply because a treatment center specializes in treating a specific population doesn't mean it is the best at treating every disorder that population may have. For example, if a priest had a serious heart condition, should he be sent to a general hospital that treats Catholics or to a secular hospital that specializes in treating that heart condition?

Newer treatment programs are just as effective, shorter in duration, and much less expensive. Most pornography and sex addicts can be effectively treated in less expensive outpatient programs, which include counseling, support groups, accountability partners, education, and a strong spiritual component. Effective Catholic outpatient programs include the Integrity Restored Recovery Program and the My House Recovery Groups. For priests who require inpatient treatment, the best programs in America are usually only about thirty days with outpatient treatment afterward. One excellent program is the Keystone Center Extended Care Unit in Chester, PA. It was founded by Dr. Patrick Carnes, the foremost expert in sexual addiction, and has an excellent reputation for effectiveness. It is also much less expensive than the eight-month programs that many priests are currently in.

No one is immune to the pornography epidemic in America, including priests and seminarians. They need to be educated on the dangers of pornography and taught ways to protect themselves and their parishioners. Effective recovery programs must be made available and priests should not fear seeking help. Bishops, vicars for clergy, and religious superiors need to have frank discussions with their priests about this issue, encouraging them to get help if needed. Seminary rectors and vocation directors should do the same with seminarians. All of this will help ensure a healthy priesthood now and in the future.

INTEGRITY RESTORED

HELPING CATHOLIC FAMILIES WIN
THE BATTLE AGAINST PORNOGRAPHY

PART II
ADDRESSING THE PROBLEM OF PORNOGRAPHY

9

The Church, God, Recovery, and Hope

Rob was confused, frightened, and filled with shame when he sought help for his pornography addiction. His father was a violent alcoholic, and when Rob was two years old his parents divorced and he rarely saw his father afterwards. He craved fatherly love, affirmation, and acceptance. To make matters worse, Rob was repeatedly sexually abused by an older boy in his neighborhood. It began when Rob was nine. His babysitter, a fourteen-year-old boy, began to show an interest in him, and they would play video games, watch TV, wrestle, and play catch in the yard. Rob loved the attention. One day, the older boy began touching Rob in sexual ways, and despite knowing this was somehow wrong, Rob enjoyed the physical touch and attention. He did not know it was sexual abuse. This went on for three years and left him feeling guilty, ashamed, and confused. The older boy introduced Rob to pornography when he was twelve. This was exciting for Rob as a young adolescent beginning puberty. He saw it as a rite of passage into manhood. The sexual abuse ended when Rob was twelve, but the pornography use continued. He often would view Internet pornography and masturbate. He didn't realize that he was using pornography to ease the pain of losing his father, as well as the guilt and shame from the sexual abuse. Rob was addicted by the time he entered high school.

Rob's mother tried to raise him in a good Catholic home. They attended Mass every Sunday and Rob attended a Catholic grade school.

He believed in God, but felt guilty and ashamed because of the sexual abuse and his pornography addiction. He blamed himself for the sexual abuse because he enjoyed it. He also blamed himself for becoming addicted to pornography. Knowing his sexual activity was sinful, he believed God would never forgive him. Tears welled up in Rob's eyes as he shared this with me, as he felt he didn't deserve God's love, mercy, and compassion. Because of his past, Rob didn't think anyone could ever love him. He had no hope of ever having close friends or a girlfriend, and the thought of marriage and a family in the future weren't even on his radar screen. The loss of his father, sexual abuse, pornography addiction, and self-hatred had truly fueled the five core beliefs of an addict in Rob. Recall:

1. I am unworthy of being loved.
2. If people really knew me, they would reject me.
3. I cannot trust anyone, including God, to meet my needs.
4. I must find something that I can control that will meet my needs.
5. Pornography/Sex is my greatest need and source of comfort.

Rob stopped going to church because of his guilt and shame, thinking he would only experience more rejection and condemnation there. The only way he believed he could return to church and be reconciled with God was to completely stop all pornography use and masturbation, and complete some severe form of penance. However, because his addiction made it almost impossible for him to stop acting out, Rob thought he was doomed to hell. His depression led him further into his addiction and ultimately to despair.

Rob is not unlike many other Catholic men I've treated. They feel guilty and ashamed of their addictive behaviors. They believe that God could never love or forgive them for what they've done. They feel trapped and hopeless. These feelings are often compounded by the root causes of their addiction for which they also blame themselves, such as parents' divorce or sexual abuse. Unfortunately, these people often do not know about the Church's teaching on addiction or about God's tremendous love, mercy, and compassion for those who are addicted.

A large part of the recovery process is educating men on the Church's teaching on addiction. From this they learn that the Church is very compassionate toward addicted persons. They learn that instead of being a place of rejection and condemnation, the Church is a place of love and healing for anyone who is wounded. This gives them great hope for recovery and helps them return to the Church and the sacraments, especially the Sacraments of Reconciliation and the Eucharist. Understanding the great love that God has for them can help change the first faulty core belief—that they are unlovable—to believing they are truly lovable. This begins the process of changing the other four core beliefs to healthier ones, which helps ensure a healthy and successful long-term recovery.

The Catechism and Addiction

Most of the men I've worked with clearly understand the sinfulness of their sexual behavior. They have repeatedly gone to Confession and have tried to stop acting out. While they may succeed for a little while, they eventually fall again, and they feel hopeless because they cannot stop their sexual acting out. This is how Rob felt. Fortunately, there is hope!

Addictive behaviors are not necessarily sinful because an addiction can rob a person of his freedom and relieve him of his responsibility for sinning. This, however, doesn't relieve the addicted person from his freedom and responsibility to get help. To be clear, when we talk about addicts having "free will to get help," it's not meant in the sense that just one day out of the blue an addict of his own volition says, "You know, instead of accessing my porn sites I habitually visit, today I think I'll go get help." Rather, for most true addicts, the "decision" to get help comes after a "rock-bottom" experience, such as a humiliating experience of being discovered or losing one's job or one's family. When presented with some external forces like those, in most cases the addicted person has the free will to choose to get help, and thus has the responsibility for doing so.

To understand this, we need to look at what the Catechism says about mortal sin, freedom, and responsibility.

We know that pornography, lust, masturbation, fornication, adultery, and the like are mortal sins. The Catechism states that three conditions must be satisfied in order for a sin to be mortal: "Mortal sin is a sin whose object is a grave matter and which is also committed with full knowledge and deliberate consent" [*RP* 17 § 12] (1857). The Catechism also states, "Mortal sin is a radical possibility of human freedom, as is love itself" (1861). The key word here is "freedom." We have the freedom to choose whether or not we will love others. When a man lusts after a woman in porn, he is freely choosing not to love her. Instead, he is choosing to use her for his own selfish pleasure. With masturbation, he is freely choosing not to use his sexuality according to God's beautiful plan. Instead, he is using it for his own self-centered pleasure. He is responsible for it because he is freely choosing to sin.

The Catechism also states:

> Freedom is the power, rooted in reason and will, to act or not to act, to do this or that, and so to perform deliberate actions on one's own responsibility. By free will one shapes one's own life. Human freedom is a force for growth and maturity in truth and goodness; it attains its perfection when directed toward God, our beatitude. (1731)
>
> As long as freedom has not bound itself definitively to its ultimate good which is God, there is the possibility of *choosing between good and evil,* and thus of growing in perfection or of failing and sinning. This freedom characterizes properly human acts. It is the basis of praise or blame, merit or reproach. (1732)
>
> The more one does what is good, the freer one becomes. There is no true freedom except in the service

of what is good and just. The choice to disobey and do evil is an abuse of freedom and leads to "the slavery of sin" [cf. *Rom* 6:17]. (1733)

Freedom makes man *responsible* for his acts to the extent that they are voluntary. Progress in virtue, knowledge of the good, and ascesis enhance the mastery of the will over its acts. (1734)

Imputability and responsibility for an action can be diminished or even nullified by ignorance, inadvertence, duress, fear, habit, inordinate attachments, and other psychological or social factors. (1735)

Now let's bring together the Church's teachings on sin, freedom, and responsibility as they relate to addiction. When a person freely chooses to use his sexuality outside of God's plan, he is responsible for committing a mortal sin. However, with an addiction, a man's freedom is compromised, thus lessening his responsibility. The Catechism tells us that "freedom makes man responsible for his acts to the extent that they are *voluntary*" (1734, emphasis added). When pornography addiction takes over a man's life, the need for a "fix" can be so great that he cannot stop himself. He has no voluntary control over his actions and has lost his freedom.

The Catechism also says, "*Imputability* and responsibility for an action can be diminished or even nullified by ignorance, inadvertence, duress, fear, habit, inordinate attachments, and other psychological or social factors" (1735). Here, "habit, inordinate attachments and other psychological or social factors" can apply to pornography addiction. Thus, when a man is addicted to pornography, his responsibility for committing mortal sin can be diminished or even nullified because he has lost his freedom.

It was important for Rob to understand that having an addiction was not sinful. He never wanted to become addicted to pornography and despised his acting out. He wanted to stop but could not. The addiction had taken control of his life, and in doing so it had stolen his freedom. This helped Rob understand the great love and compassion that God and the Church have for addicted persons. In the eyes of God and the Church, people addicted to something are afflicted with a terrible disease and are in need of help. Rob began to feel more at ease with going to Mass and receiving the sacraments, knowing he needed God and the Church for his recovery.

God's Love and Mercy

People suffering with pornography addiction need to know that having an addiction is not a sin, and that God is loving and merciful. Because of the five core beliefs that addicted persons often live by, they need to know that regardless of what they have done, God still loves them. Scripture is full of references to God's love and mercy. Over and over again man has sinned and broken covenants with God, yet God is always faithful. He never breaks a promise or a covenant. Although sin separates us from God, He is always ready to forgive and welcome us back. The parable of the prodigal son in Luke 15:11–32 illustrates this love wonderfully, and is worth quoting in full:

> And he said, "There was a man who had two sons; and the younger of them said to his father, 'Father, give me the share of the property that falls to me.' And he divided his living between them. Not many days later, the younger son gathered all he had and took his journey into a far country, and there he squandered his property in loose living. And when he had spent everything, a great famine arose in that country, and he began to be in want. So he went and joined himself to one of the citizens of that country, who sent him into his fields to feed the swine. And he would gladly have fed on the pods that the swine ate; and no one gave him anything. But when he came to himself he said, 'How many of my father's hired servants have bread enough and to spare, but I perish here with hunger!

I will arise and go to my father, and I will say to him, "Father, I have sinned against heaven and before you; I am no longer worthy to be called your son; treat me as one of your hired servants.'" And he arose and came to his father. But while he was yet at a distance, his father saw him and had compassion, and ran and embraced him and kissed him. And the son said to him, 'Father, I have sinned against heaven and before you; I am no longer worthy to be called your son.' But the father said to his servants, 'Bring quickly the best robe, and put it on him; and put a ring on his hand, and shoes on his feet; and bring the fatted calf and kill it, and let us eat and make merry; for this my son was dead, and is alive again; he was lost, and is found.' And they began to make merry.

"Now his elder son was in the field; and as he came and drew near to the house, he heard music and dancing. And he called one of the servants and asked what this meant. And he said to him, 'Your brother has come, and your father has killed the fatted calf, because he has received him safe and sound.' But he was angry and refused to go in. His father came out and entreated him, but he answered his father, 'Behold, these many years I have served you, and I never disobeyed your command; yet you never gave me a kid, that I might make merry with my friends. But when this son of yours came, who has devoured your living with harlots, you killed for him the fatted calf!' And he said to him, 'Son, you are always with me, and all that is mine is yours. It was fitting to make merry and be glad, for this your brother was dead, and is alive; he was lost, and is found.'"

It's easy to take the older son's side in this parable. Asking for an inheritance early was akin to wishing his father dead, and then the younger son went out and wasted all his money on wanton living. Why should the father take him back, even as a servant? The answer is simple. The father's love was so great that it didn't matter what his son did. He would always love him, no matter what! The father knew the dangers of the world but loved his son enough to allow him to make his own choices. He loved him enough to take him back again. I can just imagine the father standing by the side of the road each day watching and waiting for his son to return. As soon as he saw his son, he ran to greet him. He wouldn't even let the son finish his sentence. By all rights, the younger son should have been treated as a servant because he had squandered all his inheritance, yet this didn't matter to the father. All that mattered was his lost son had returned home.

Valuable Lessons

No matter what we've done, God will always forgive us and take us back. He is also ready to teach us valuable lessons to draw us back to Him. If this parable recounted a true to life story, the father might have known how his son would fare in the world and that he would eventually return home. He had to let his son go and experience hardships to let him learn valuable lessons. The son eventually learned that the life he had with his father was far better than anything he could ever experience out in the world, and upon learning this lesson, he returned home and probably never took his father for granted again.

In life we often make decisions that can hurt us in many ways. God cares for every aspect of our lives. He wants us to be healthy. However, He often allows our lives to spin out of control to gain our attention. Don and Sylvia experienced this in their marriage.

When Don's pornography addiction was discovered, Sylvia was devastated. In an instant her whole world seemed to crumble. At first she wanted things to go back to the way they were before Don became addicted to pornography, but after examining their relationship, she and Don discovered that it was never healthy to begin with. They both came into the marriage with deep emotional wounds. Don had been physically abused as a child and turned to pornography for comfort. His pornography addiction was a symptom of his woundedness. Sylvia grew up with a father who was an alcoholic, which made it difficult for her to trust men. She often was cold and distant toward Don. It took many months working together in therapy before they eventually healed their individual wounds and their marriage. Today, Don and Sylvia have the healthy marriage they always wanted. Although it initially seemed as if there was no hope, God had a bigger plan for them. His plan for them was for healing, restoration, and a healthy marriage.

Responsibility

Let's be clear with the distinction between "pornography use" (acting out = sin) and "having an addiction" (= not a sin). While acting out is a sin, the addicted person's culpability or responsibility for that sin, as the Catechism teaches, can be diminished or even nullified due to the erosion of his freedom. Knowing that having an addiction is not a sin and that addicted persons often cannot be held responsible for acting out, it is vitally important for them to know that they are responsible for getting help. I often have encountered men who use addictions as an excuse for not getting help. They claim, "I can't help myself. I have an addiction." God will not have mercy on lame excuses. Remember, as we showed earlier in this chapter, addiction can take away a man's freedom when it comes to viewing pornography, but it doesn't take away his freedom to seek help when he is presented with external forces to get help. Scripture tells us to: "Shun immorality. Every other sin which a man commits is outside the body; but the immoral man sins against his own body. Do you not know that your body is a temple of the Holy Spirit within you, which you have from God? You are not your own; you were bought with a price. So glorify God in your body" (1 Corinthians 6:18–20).

God has charged us with being good stewards of every aspect of our lives. This includes our physical, emotional, sexual, and spiritual health, as well as our relationships. Even if we fall, God will bless our best efforts to overcome addiction and get healthy. The key is to keep trying and never give up. Commitment is key to success.

Help from the Church

God uses people and the Church as instruments of His healing power. The Church offers many valuable resources that can help a man end his pornography use. The Church helps men understand how much God loves them by providing a place where a man can find love, mercy, compassion, and forgiveness, a place where he won't find ridicule, humiliation, or condemnation. It's a safe place where a man can begin the healing process.

Many men who I have worked with had an unhealthy view of God. They saw Him as an angry taskmaster who was there to punish all sinners. Through prayer, Scripture study, spiritual direction, the sacraments, and compassionate people, the Church helped these men develop healthy relationships with God and to see Him as a loving Father. These men learned that God loves them unconditionally, but like all fathers, He often needs to discipline His children. While this can be painful, the men understood that it was ultimately for their own good.

When Rob began his recovery program, he felt that God had given up on him and that if he were to die tomorrow, he would go to hell. He stopped going to church and receiving the sacraments. Realizing that having an addiction was not a sin helped Rob to be a little more open to seeking help from the Church, and I recommended he first talk with a priest to allay his fears about God. Rob began meeting with a priest monthly for spiritual direction. The priest helped Rob develop a healthy image of God as a loving Father who is both just and merciful, and by studying Scripture Rob came to realize just how much God loved him—enough to die for him. It excited Rob to think that he could be a new creation in Christ, an adopted son of God! Scripture tells us in Ephesians 1:3–8, "Blessed be the God and Father of our Lord Jesus Christ, who has blessed us in Christ with every spiritual blessing in the heavenly places, even as he chose us in him before the foundation of the world, that we should be holy and blameless before him. He destined us in love to be his sons through Jesus Christ, according to the purpose of his will, to the praise of his glorious grace which he freely bestowed on us in the Beloved. In him we have redemption through his blood, the forgiveness of our trespasses, according to the riches of his grace which he lavished upon us."

Having this new understanding of God gave Rob hope for his recovery and his future. He began attending Mass again and received the Sacrament of Reconciliation weekly. Going to Confession was easier because the priest was both his spiritual director and his confessor. Along with offering absolution, the priest was a source of support and accountability. Rob also developed a deep love for Eucharistic adoration, often saying little and just simply sitting with the Lord feeling His love.

Because of Rob's history of abuse, I collaborated with his spiritual director. It was important for Rob's healing and recovery to forgive the neighborhood boy who abused him, despite still being extremely angry with the boy for violating him. Rob's spiritual director reminded him that we all fall short of the grace of God. We don't deserve God's forgiveness, yet He offers it anyway because of His great love for us. It was difficult for Rob to believe that God loved the boy who abused him just as much as He loved Rob. In therapy Rob came to understand that his abuser was also deeply wounded, and through counseling and prayer Rob was able to see his abuser through the eyes of love, mercy, and compassion. This allowed him to understand God's love for that boy and helped him forgive the boy, let go of the past, and move on with his life.

For married people, the sacraments are very important in the healing process. They are a source of God's grace, healing, and forgiveness. I recommend attending Mass as often as possible. Through counseling, many deep personal and marital wounds are identified that led to the addiction. At Mass, men and women can bring these wounds to the Lord for healing. Married couples attending Mass together is also a reminder of the marriage covenant, which is not only a covenant between a husband and wife but a covenant with God as well. An addicted husband violated this covenant, but Mass reminds us that God never breaks His covenant. No matter how wounded a person or marriage is, God can heal it.

Receiving the Eucharist is exceptionally healing because it is God within us. John 6:53–58 tells us, "Truly, truly, I say to you, unless you eat the flesh of the Son of man and drink his blood, you have no life in you; he who eats my flesh and drinks my blood has eternal life, and I will raise him up at the last day. For my flesh is food indeed, and my blood is drink indeed. He who eats my flesh and drinks my blood abides in me, and I in him. As the living Father sent me, and I live because of the Father, so he who eats me will live because of me. This is the bread which came down from heaven, not such as the fathers ate and died; he who eats this bread will live forever."

It's easy to see the Eucharist as a necessary part of the healing process when we understand how powerful it is. Many men and women who I've worked with have shared its efficacious effects upon their lives. It gives men the strength to persevere in recovery. It helps wives forgive their husbands and persevere in their marriages. Whether married or single, receiving the Eucharist is an essential element for Catholics in the recovery process.

Rob was fortunate enough to attend Mass daily. As he grew in his relationship with God, he came to look forward to attending Mass. Recall that Rob didn't have a close relationship with his earthly father, so Rob needed to know that he had a heavenly Father who loved him. Every Mass was an encounter with his loving heavenly Father. Receiving the Eucharist became very special to him as it reminded him that Jesus loved him enough to die for him. Many times Rob would get choked up because of the incredible love he felt.

Attending Mass together and receiving the Eucharist was also important for Sylvia and Don. Sylvia's whole world crumbled when she learned of Don's addiction. She had no sense of safety and security and no idea what would happen to her, Don, their children, or their marriage. Attending Mass with Don helped her realize that God is always in control, and despite the pitfalls of life, God could fix every problem and heal every hurt. This, along with the knowledge that God had an imperishable covenant with her and Don, gave Sylvia much peace. Receiving the Eucharist was healing medicine from God that gave her hope and strength to carry on in recovery. Like Rob, Don needed to learn how much God loved him and wanted his healing and restoration. Attending Mass with Sylvia at his side helped Don recognize that God had a special plan for them and their marriage, as well as the incredible gift Sylvia was to him from God. Don was deeply saddened that he simply discarded this wonderful gift, and it left him with a greater resolve to never hurt Sylvia or offend God in that way ever again. Don resolved to always be grateful to God for Sylvia and protect her from any future harm.

The Church also offers the invaluable Sacrament of Reconciliation where we experience God's mercy and forgiveness. It's also a form of support and accountability. Knowing he would have to confess his sin helped Rob stay clean. It was a good deterrent. However, whenever he did fall, he knew he would not be shamed or ridiculed in Confession, but instead he would experience love and compassion. As Rob progressed in recovery, he didn't want anything to keep him from growing in his relationship with God, especially sin. Rob learned through spiritual direction that when God forgives, He forgets our sins. This gave Rob great hope. He knew that once confessed and forgiven, God would never hold his sins against him. They were completely gone! Weekly Confession became a joyous occasion because he knew he would walk out with his relationship with God completely restored.

Don had a similar experience with Confession. Restoring his relationship with God gave him the drive to persevere in recovery. Sylvia found a different kind of healing. Her anger toward Don was justified, but she realized it was preventing her from experiencing both personal healing and the healing of her marriage. Every week she would bring her anger to Confession, and her penance often was to meditate on God's love for her and Don and His desire to bring healing into their lives. This helped Sylvia to let go of her anger and focus on healing.

In addition to spiritual help, there are many other practical ways that those with addictions are helped by the Church. Support groups can include men's and women's ministries, Bible studies, accountability groups, and 12-step groups. Rob joined a men's group sponsored by his parish, and although it was not specifically a group for men with pornography addiction, many there admitted to struggling with viewing pornography. They decided as a group to keep each other accountable for remaining pure. Each week they would report on their progress. If a man fell, the group would discuss how it happened and how he could prevent a future fall. They all exchanged phone numbers so if a man was struggling with temptation, he could immediately call one of the other members for help. All of the men in the group found this extremely helpful in maintaining chastity. During their group meetings they also discussed Pope St. John Paul II's *The Theology of the Body* and *Love and Responsibility*, which gave them a clearer understanding of God's beautiful plan for sexuality.

While such groups are excellent for men who struggle with occasional pornography use, they are usually not enough for someone with pornography addiction. Men like Rob also need the help of a 12-step recovery group. Going to meetings can be quite scary for most men; however, because Rob had received much support from his therapist and priest, he was able to muster up the courage to go. In addition to his parish men's group, Rob began attending a *My House Recovery Group* meeting. He felt safe discussing his addiction there because he knew he was surrounded by men who understood his struggle. They were there to support him and were committed to keeping him accountable for his sobriety. Rob found more accountability partners there with whom he made regular phone calls.

Don and Sylvia also began attending group meetings. Don attended a Sexaholics Anonymous (SA) meeting and Sylvia attended a Co-Dependents of Sex Addicts (COSA) meeting. The meetings were safe places where they could work on their healing in an environment that respected their faith. In fact, both groups encouraged them to use their faith in the recovery process. Detailed information on these and other support groups will be provided in the next chapter and in the appendix.

Advice for Clergy

If you are a priest, you will probably agree that pornography use is one of the most common sins heard in Confession. You have also probably seen how pornography has damaged marriages, families, and careers. Many ask me what they can do to help people who struggle with pornography use and those affected by it. Here are some practical things you can do to help:

1. *Be committed to preaching and teaching the truth about sexuality as presented by the Catholic Church.* To do this, I recommend studying Church documents, such as *Humanae Vitae* and *The Theology of the Body.* For more specific information on the Church's position on pornography, I recommend reading pastoral letters, such as *Blessed are the Pure in Heart* by Bishop Finn (2007) and *Bought with a Price* by Bishop Loverde (2006). Another invaluable book on the subject is *Love and Responsibility* written by Karol Wojtyla, long before he became Pope John Paul II. Unfortunately, there are many priests who refuse to follow the Church's teaching on human sexuality, which I believe is a result of poor formation. Many say they are "following their conscience;" however, their consciences are often improperly formed. Presenting the Church's teaching on human sexuality will give addicted persons hope and a reason to enter recovery. They will understand God's plan for human sexuality that is life-giving as opposed to the world's view on sexuality that leads to hopelessness and despair. Preaching about the dangers of pornography from the pulpit can be a bit tricky because priests need to warn parents of the dangers without piquing kids' curiosity. Priests can teach about the dangers of pornography more directly in men's ministry meetings, Bible study groups, and youth group meetings. It takes much courage to address this issue, but I guarantee that people will be grateful for it.

2. *Become aware of the resources available to protect families and help those struggling with pornography addiction.* Along with looking

to priests as being spiritual leaders, many people also look to them for help with personal issues, such as marital problems, employment, food, clothing, housing, adoptions, social services, and addictions. Many dioceses offer directories listing local resources to help people with various needs, including therapists, supports groups, food pantries, homeless shelters, social service agencies, and others. Many now include resources for those struggling with pornography addiction. Priests should familiarize themselves with these resources so they can direct parishioners to the appropriate help. The Archdiocese of New York created an excellent website specifically for those struggling with pornography use: www.FLRL.org/TrueFreedom. htm. If there is no such directory available, I recommend that a diocese's family life office create one. Having this directory greatly reduces a priest's stress because it helps relieve him of the responsibility for addressing the problems directly and personally. Priests should also familiarize themselves with helpful websites, books, DVDs, CDs, and software. In the appendix I provide an extensive list of resources that help protect families from pornography and aid those who struggle with addiction. Additional advice is offered in chapters thirteen and fourteen where I discuss how to protect children and teens from pornography.

3. *Provide an environment where struggling men are welcome.* Many men are afraid to come back to the Church because they feel they will be condemned. Let them know that the Church is a place of healing and God's love, where they can have their value and dignity as children of God validated. I have worked with many men who claim that the love and compassion they experienced from their pastor made it easier to seek help for their addictions.

4. *Address the issue directly in Confession.* Many priests in Confession are unsure of what to tell a man who struggles with pornography use. They want to show penitents compassion while admonishing them to get help. Here is a script that priests can use in the confessional that can help men.

Thank God for your strength in coming forward and admitting you have a problem. This is the first step in your journey to recovery. You're not alone. Thousands of men struggle with compulsive pornography use. Do you want to be free from this sin? Are you willing to pay the price? (Don't be afraid to challenge men.) Healing and freedom from sin are possible, but you can't do it alone. It takes God's grace, professional help, and support from other men who understand your struggle. Here is a card * that will direct you to helpful resources. If you're serious about overcoming pornography use, I urge you to check them out. Know that God, the Father of mercy and love, will provide the grace to overcome this sin.

*Several dioceses have created small cards that list local resources for men who want help overcoming pornography use. An excellent example is the card I helped develop for the Archdiocese of New York. On the card is printed, "I can do all things in him who strengthens me" (Philippians: 4:13), a "battle plan" for purity, and their website for pornography addiction. If the Confession is face to face, the priest can hand a card to the penitent. If the Confession is behind a screen, the priest can leave a stack of cards on the penitent's side and recommend he take one. I have known priests who have assigned looking up the resources on the card as penance. While it may take a while for a man to actually seek help, the priest can plant some valuable "seeds" in Confession for getting help.

5. *Begin a parish men's support and accountability group.* This is extremely helpful for men who struggle with occasional pornography use. In the group meetings, men can discuss the dangers of pornography and what they should do to protect themselves and their families from it. I recommend that the group not focus solely on pornography. If it does, few men will attend. Instead, the focus should be on becoming virtuous men of God, which opens the group up to discussing a variety of issues that help the members become the men God intended

them to be. This will help them become better husbands, fathers, employees, and friends. Priests today are extremely busy in their ministries, so the thought of starting a men's ministry can be daunting. Fortunately, there are many established men's groups that can be started in any parish. Here is a list of excellent groups:

- Crossing the Goal's Spiritual Workout Groups
- The Knights of Columbus
- Paradisus Dei's That Man is You! Men's Leadership Program
- St. Joseph's Covenant Keepers
- The King's Men Groups

More information on these groups is in the appendix.

6. *Help men develop a healthier relationship with God.* I cannot emphasize enough how important it is for those with addictions to have a healthy, intimate relationship with God. Through spiritual direction, priests can help them let go of old unhealthy notions of God and understand Him as He really is. This will make it easier to turn to God for strength when they are tempted and unafraid to seek forgiveness when they fall. Understanding that God has a wonderful plan for each person's life can give addicted persons the incentive to work on their recovery and achieve that wonderful life. Priests have a vast collection of tools they can recommend to help people with addictions, including prayer, sacraments, retreats, Scripture study groups, the daily practice of *Lectio Divina*, which is the slow, prayerful reading of Scripture and meditating upon what one has read, and ways to serve in their parish. For addicted individuals who need inpatient treatment, priests can visit them and offer the Anointing of the Sick.

7. *Host a 12-step recovery group.* Many churches host a variety of recovery group meetings, such as Alcoholics Anonymous, Gamblers Anonymous, and Overeaters Anonymous. I want to encourage pastors to also host group meetings for those recovering from pornography and sex addiction, and for their family members, such as Sexaholics Anonymous, My House Recovery Groups, and Celebrate Recovery. Groups for spouses and family members of addicted persons include S-Anon and COSA. See the appendix for more information. Many priests are reluctant to host such meetings for fear of how parishioners would react if they found out about them. Some would not like having a "club of perverts" meeting at their church. However, the groups are closed and not advertised to the public. And if parishioners did find out about the meetings and objected, the pastor should be strong and remind them that the Church is open to everyone, especially those who are sick and in need of love and compassion. Many people with addictions have returned to the Church because of the love and compassion from the pastor who allowed meetings to be held in his parish.

God's Plan for Healing and Restoration

I love the Book of Nehemiah in the Old Testament. It tells the story of the Prophet Nehemiah who was a servant to King Artaxerxes. Nehemiah was deeply saddened when he heard about the destruction of Jerusalem, but he knew God would not forsake the Israelites or His covenant with them. King Artaxerxes allowed Nehemiah to return to Jerusalem, giving him an army of men to accompany him on his journey home. When Nehemiah returned, he found the city in ruins. Things looked pretty bleak. However, God was faithful to His covenant and He helped Nehemiah organize the Israelites to rebuild Jerusalem, starting with the walls. While there were hostile plots against the Israelites, God did not allow those plots to prevail. Work continued until the walls and the city were finally restored.

The lesson we can learn from the Book of Nehemiah is that no matter how bad things might be, God is always faithful to His promises. His love is never-ending, and no matter how messed up our lives may be, He can bring healing and restoration. All we need to do is trust God and work with Him in the recovery process. While there may be some permanent consequences to choices we've made, God can still bring good out of any situation. I have seen God transform the lives of many people. So many men have told me if it were not for God's love and promise, they would probably be dead by now. Instead, God has transformed their lives.

If you or someone you love is struggling with pornography addiction, don't lose hope. Healing and restoration are possible. People can and do recover from addiction and God will be with you all the way, providing strength, grace, forgiveness, and healing. However, you will have to do your work. In the next chapter I present the Integrity Restored Recovery Program that has helped countless individuals, couples, and families. You will find that God and the Church are an integral part of the program. Healing can begin today!

10

The Integrity Restored Recovery Program

Almost ten years ago I first identified the need for an effective Catholic recovery program for pornography addiction. At that time there was a noticeable change in my clientele. More men were coming to me seeking help for pornography addiction. With the married men, it was often their wives who came to me for help. I searched for recovery programs that utilized Catholic spirituality, but could find none. There were several excellent evangelical Protestant programs available, so I adapted them to my Catholic clients. In fact, all my formal education in the diagnosis and treatment of sexual addiction is from evangelical Protestant training programs. I didn't set out to develop a Catholic program, but I discovered, over time, that I had developed one that was very effective in helping men recover from pornography addiction. That program is the Integrity Restored Recovery Program.

In developing this program I looked at several Christian and secular recovery programs, identifying what worked and ignoring what didn't. I also incorporated Catholic spirituality into the program, and the result was a comprehensive 7-point recovery program that has helped hundreds of men overcome pornography addiction. In this chapter I present an overview of the program, discuss each point, and use case studies to show how each point is applied in the program. The program is not complicated. I call them seven "points" and not seven "steps" because each point is of equal importance, and all are worked simultaneously. Men can find freedom from pornography by working each point daily. Initially, men need to be vigilant about working the points; however, after a while it becomes second nature, and when this happens, men find they can avoid pornography without any problems.

Most men who find themselves addicted to pornography live two lives. There is the life the world sees where they appear to be competent, healthy, virtuous men with wonderful families, friends, careers, and a strong faith in God. There is also the dark, secret life they lead where they view pornography regularly and are unable to stop. They may hate themselves for it and feel unworthy of being loved. They fear anyone finding out about this secret life because of the inevitable hate and condemnation they believe will follow. So they suffer in silence, using all their energy to maintain the façade the world sees while trying to keep their pornography use a secret. However, the façade eventually cracks, the man ends up with a life that is totally out of control, and in the end he may lose his wife, family, friends, and career.

When a man enters recovery for his addiction, he has the opportunity to leave his dark, secret life behind. He no longer has to keep any secrets. There is great freedom in this. He often finds he truly is loveable and that people will accept him as he is. I named my recovery program Integrity Restored because a man who doesn't live two lives is a fully integrated man. What you see is what you get. He is able to be fully authentic with everyone. He is a virtuous man who is able to love and be loved deeply. He is the man God created him to be. This is a wonderful place to be in. This is the goal of recovery.

Josh's Story

Josh was a thirty-five-year-old single man who had been viewing Internet pornography every day for at least an hour and masturbating. He also had gotten into online chatting and phone sex with women. Josh's wake-up call came when he received his credit card bill totaling over two thousand dollars for one month of pornography and phone sex. Josh had a girlfriend, Karen, whom he loved deeply and hoped to marry someday. He didn't want to bring this addiction into his marriage. Karen had been hurt in a previous relationship with a man who was an alcoholic, but it wasn't the alcoholism, *per se*, that was the problem for her. It was the lies and deceit that came with the addiction that hurt her. Josh didn't want to hurt her the way she had been hurt in the past. He wanted to overcome his addiction and be honest with her. He wanted to recover from his addiction, save his relationship, and be the man God intended him to be.

Defining Sobriety

Before discussing recovery, we need to define sobriety, which really boils down to what behaviors you will or will not tolerate. Some people define sobriety as simply not looking at Internet pornography, but they will still watch R-rated movies or masturbate. The definition for sobriety I recommend is comprehensive, respects Church teaching, and protects the dignity of all involved. My definition is:

> *Not engaging in any activity that would lead to lust and using others for selfish sexual pleasure.*

This definition covers use of pornography or any sexually suggestive behaviors, fantasizing, masturbation, or even just ogling women. This allows an addicted person to know his primary goal.

The 7-Point Plan

Below is a diagram of the 7-point plan I developed for recovery. As I stated earlier, each point is of equal importance and all of the points are worked simultaneously.

Now let's review each point and how Josh applied them in his recovery.

Point 1: Self-knowledge and Commitment

Self-knowledge begins with admitting one has a problem. In recovery there can be no denial. This means admitting to himself and at least one other person that he has a problem with pornography. It requires honesty, courage, and humility. If a man is not sure if he is actually addicted, he should be evaluated by a therapist who is trained in the diagnosis and treatment of sexual addictions. Seeking help is extremely difficult for many men, and to admit that they have a problem leaves them responsible for getting help and facing the shame associated with the addiction. However, this is also the first step to breaking the chains of addiction.

In addition to admitting one has a problem, the person struggling with pornography addiction must acknowledge the harmful effects pornography use has had on his life: emotionally, in relationships, financially, in school or at work, and sexually. This can be difficult for addicted persons, but it is necessary to be totally honest with themselves and others about the effects of their addiction. This helps them realize how serious it is and how much they need help.

Self-knowledge also means knowing one's weaknesses. Everyone has triggers that can lead to acting out with lust, pornography, and masturbation. Knowing what these triggers are and being proactive to avoid or successfully deal with them helps prevent acting out. While there are countless triggers for acting out, I have broken them down into two groups: sexual triggers and nonsexual triggers.

> ➤ *Sexual Triggers.* These are the easiest to identify. A sexual trigger could be a day at the beach where there are young women in bikinis, walking past the Victoria's Secret store in the mall, or the beer commercials during a football game. While these triggers are different for every man, they are all visibly sexual in nature.

➤ *Nonsexual Triggers.* These are more difficult to identify and can even be more powerful than sexual triggers. I identified these triggers earlier with the acronym, BLAST:

Bored or Burnt Out

Lonely

Angry, Apathetic, Afraid, or Alone

Sad, Stressed, or Selfish

Tired

Often it is not one but a combination of these triggers that can lead a person to act out. By monitoring when one is tempted to use pornography, common triggers can be identified and addressed.

In addition to triggers, "danger zones" must be identified. A danger zone is a specific time, place, or situation where one is more likely to be triggered. Common danger zones can include:

➤ Late at night

➤ Alone on a Sunday afternoon

➤ After a rough day at work

➤ Alone in a hotel room

➤ After a fight with one's spouse

➤ Stressed out by school or work

➤ Grieving over a loss

➤ Taking on excessive responsibility

Everyone has their own unique danger zones; the common denominator is that these danger zones all activate the triggers for acting out.

By identifying the triggers and danger zones, a person can proactively address them and avoid acting out. For example, if a college student often acts out on Friday nights because he is stressed, burnt out by school, and very lonely, he can take active steps to alleviate his stress, burnout, and loneliness. This could include taking regular study breaks, developing new hobbies, and making plans to go out with friends on Friday nights.

As with any addiction, recovery begins with detoxing the brain. We discussed thoroughly in Part I the effects pornography has on the brain (see pp. 38–40). Because the brain has become dependent on operating at an abnormally high level of chemical stimulation and needs regular doses of pornography to maintain that level of dopamine, withdrawal symptoms occur when the dopamine level drops: depression, anxiety, anger, irritability, insomnia, headaches, and/or the uncontrollable urge to use pornography and masturbate. This is when a man can be triggered to use pornography.

Detoxing helps the brain return to a normal level of chemical stimulation. By identifying and effectively addressing triggers and danger zones, an addicted person can successfully get through the detox process and deal with withdrawal symptoms without turning to pornography. Adhering to the 7-point program for recovery can greatly aid this process.

This leads us into the second part of the first point in the recovery program: commitment. A man must be committed to doing whatever it takes to recover, and to have this commitment he must first want to recover. John 5:2–6 says, "Now there is in Jerusalem by the Sheep Gate a pool, in Hebrew called Bethzatha, which has five porticoes. In these lay a multitude of invalids, blind, lame, paralyzed. One man was there, who had been ill for thirty-eight years. When Jesus saw him and knew that he had been lying there a long time, he said to him, 'Do you want to be healed?'" Obviously Jesus can heal the man, and He does. However, there must first be the desire to get well. God respects our free will and never forces His healing on us. We have to want recovery and we do have to do whatever it takes to cooperate with God in the healing process.

A man must admit he has the problem, seek help, identify his weaknesses, including triggers and danger zones, and be committed to take whatever steps are necessary to avoid acting out. He must be committed to the entire recovery program, which includes eliminating all pornography in his life, attending counseling sessions and support group meetings, and growing in his relationship with God. A man must persevere and not give up in times of discouragement during the recovery process. I have found that most men who are completely committed to recovery conclude that anything is better than the life they are currently living. They have hit rock bottom. They also realize they deserve to recover and understand that no matter how much of a mess they made of their lives, a better life is within reach. This brings them great hope for freedom from pornography.

Seeking help was difficult at first for Josh, but he knew if he didn't get help he would continue on the path of destruction. He would lose Karen, accrue more and more debt, and jeopardize his eternal salvation. At first he was reluctant to admit how much his pornography use had affected his life, but as he opened up about it he began to see how it had disturbed many areas of his life. He already knew he spent thousands of dollars on pornography. Then there was the guilt and shame he carried that kept him from getting close to people out of fear that they would find out about his secret and reject him. It also affected his confidence, which he believed kept him from excelling at work. Most of all, he knew it hurt his relationship with Karen and God. Knowing how pornography had hurt so many areas of his life strengthened Josh's resolve to break free of it.

Josh was able to identify his triggers through counseling. Sexual triggers included some of the women he worked with who tended to dress very provocatively. He also subscribed to *Sports Illustrated* and always saved the Swimsuit Issues. Lingerie ads in the newspaper were also sexual triggers. Nonsexual triggers included being tired, lonely, burnt out, stressed, and selfish. A danger zone here, for example, included Josh being alone late on Friday nights. Karen was a nurse and often had to work on weekends, and naturally, during those times Josh would feel lonely and tired. A third danger zone was discovered in counseling: It was just after he got home after a rough day at work, when again he would feel tired, angry, stressed, and burnt out.

To combat his sexual triggers and danger zones, he worked on averting his eyes at work from women dressed provocatively, reminding himself daily that they were God's daughters who should not to be used sexually, and if he did lust after them, he would have to answer to God! Josh cancelled his subscription to *Sports Illustrated* and got rid of all his back copies of the Swimsuit Issue. He also cancelled his subscription to the Sunday newspaper to avoid tempting lingerie ads. Throughout this process Josh became aware that sexual triggers could be anywhere and that he always needed to be on guard. What made it a little easier for him was knowing that each woman out there was a person, and as a man it was his duty to respect her and not to use her for his own selfish pleasure.

To deal with his nonsexual triggers and danger zones, Josh would always make plans for Friday nights. If he couldn't spend them with Karen, he would go out with friends or visit family. Fortunately, Josh had two good accountability partners who understood his struggle. They were always ready to meet him at a local coffee shop if he was alone in the evening. Josh also joined a local YMCA and started going there after work. Working out daily helped Josh reduce his stress and anger while giving him something to look forward to every day. Finally, he started looking for new positions within his company that would be more interesting and challenging for him than his current job.

Josh's commitment didn't end with dealing with triggers and danger zones. He was committed to the entire recovery program. As we discuss the following six points in the program, we will see his commitment and how it helped him to succeed in recovery and to finally free himself from the chains of pornography.

- Point Review: Six choices were the key to Josh's success with this point:
    1. Admitting he had a problem with pornography
    2. Being willing to seek help
    3. Understanding his weaknesses

     a. Sexual and Nonsexual Triggers

     b. Danger Zones

4. Understanding that detox and withdrawal is part of recovery

5. Being committed to doing whatever it takes to avoid acting out

     a. Proactively addressing triggers and danger zones

6. Being committed to his entire recovery program

Point 2: Purifying Your Life

In my last book, *The Pornography Epidemic: A Catholic Approach*, I listed this point as "Purifying the Environment." However, I changed it to "Purifying Your Life" because this point encompasses more than just one's environment. Purifying your life starts with the mind. It requires one to recognize how pornography leads us to use others for selfish pleasure. God did not intend for us to use each other. He intended for us to love each other. Thus, we purify our lives by making the commitment not to use others by lusting after them. A man can protect women from being visually used even if the only person he is protecting them from is himself. Purifying your life also means living a chaste life. By reserving sex for its proper context—a loving marital relationship—a man purifies himself for his spouse (or future spouse) and makes his sexuality a far more valuable gift to her. For those living vowed celibate lives such as priests, religious, and consecrated virgins, purifying their life allows them to love God and the people they serve more deeply. Whatever vocation a person may be called to, purifying his life allows him to love more fully because there is no competition with a dark secret life.

More practically, purifying your life requires eliminating all pornography and all access to pornography, including any pornographic books, magazines, videos, DVDs, and all such material. Keep in mind our definition of pornography: "Any image that leads a person to use another person for his own sexual pleasure." Based on this definition, the image doesn't have to be of an unclothed person. Any image that is used for sexual pleasure is pornography and must be eliminated from a person's life. The individual must also delete or block any phone sex numbers or prostitute numbers from their phone. If a man drives past a porn shop or strip club on the way to work each day, he needs to find another route. He might even need to end certain relationships that can lead to acting out with pornography. If an addicted person has friends who view pornography, frequently talk about it, or go to strip clubs, he needs to end those friendships. They are toxic and could lead him back into pornography use.

The biggest area of purification needed today is with the Internet. This is the primary source of pornography for most Americans today. For most people, living without the Internet is impossible. It has become a necessity, and while it's a morally-neutral tool for accessing information, it's how we use this tool that gets us into trouble. There must be accountability, and fortunately there are many software programs that can help with this. I recommend an Internet accountability service. (We'll discuss an Internet filtering service for children in chapter thirteen.) Unlike a filtering service, an accountability service does not block anything on the Internet. Instead, one subscribes to the email addresses of trusted friends and family members, and if anyone logs onto even the slightest questionable website, those people get email reports. This is an excellent deterrent. For men struggling with pornography addiction, an accountability service can greatly aid them in recovery. They can have their accountability partners receive email reports and they can do the same in return. This way they all work together to remain sober. I'll discuss who can be accountability partners and how wives can participate in the next section.

I have evaluated many filtering and accountability services and the one I recommend most, which I briefly mentioned in chapter one, is CovenantEyes.com. Covenant Eyes can be used on any PC, Mac, smartphone, iPhone, tablet, iPad, MP3 Player, iPod, and more. Along with software, Covenant Eyes provides excellent information on protecting families from pornography. In addition, I collaborated with

Covenant Eyes on the development of an excellent Parish Education Kit, which I believe should be in every parish library. It's excellent for use with parents groups, youth groups, and men's groups. Information on this and other resources are listed in the appendix.

Over the past five years, social media has exploded in America with email, texting, instant messaging, Facebook, Myspace, Twitter, Face Time, Instagram, Craigslist, Pinterest, countless chat rooms, and blogs. While social media is a great way to communicate with friends, family, and colleagues, it also can be very dangerous. Many people are now using it for sexual purposes, including pedophiles and sexual predators. Social media needs to be monitored. I recommend that parents, spouses, and accountability partners have access to any form of social media a person may use.

Television and video games are also dangerous sources of pornography. Offensive television programs and networks should be blocked. For some people, getting rid of cable and satellite television altogether is necessary.

Josh went home and immediately began purifying his life after our first counseling session. He made the commitment not to use women sexually by ogling them and made a point each day to respect the women he worked with and not to lust. It took a while but Josh eventually broke the habit, which improved his relationships with women at work. He noticed them starting to respect him more. His commitment to respect women extended beyond work. Wherever Josh went he reminded himself that every woman is a daughter of God and deserved to be respected. This was his duty as a man of God.

Josh subscribed to Covenant Eyes on his computer, cell phone, and tablet, and asked two friends from his men's group to be his accountability partners. In the beginning of his recovery Josh fell several times into viewing pornography. When his accountability partners received the email report, they would each immediately call Josh and ask if he was having a bad day and if there was anything they could do to help. They also challenged him to remain faithful to his recovery program and to call them before he acted out. As an extra measure of protection,

Josh decided to use the Internet for specific business and not to surf the web for pleasure, which he often did hours at a time. At first he surfed for sports scores and political news, but it invariably led to viewing pornography. He even threw out his Xbox gaming system so he wouldn't be tempted to play pornographic video games. Now, when Josh is not spending time with Karen, he spends time with family or friends, goes to the gym to work out, rides his bike, or reads books on his tablet. Not only has this helped him to avoid pornography, but he feels healthier because he is more physically active. Viewing porn led him into a very sedentary lifestyle.

- Point Review: Six choices were the key to Josh's success with this point:
    1. Cancelling his subscriptions to *Sports Illustrated* and the Sunday newspaper
    2. Throwing out his back copies of the *Sports Illustrated* Swimsuit Issue
    3. Making the commitment not to use women sexually by lusting after them
        a. Guarding his eyes wherever he went
        b. Recognizing that every woman is a child of God who deserves respect
    4. Installing Covenant Eyes Accountability Software on his computer, cell phone, and tablet
    5. Only using the Internet for specific business and not for idle surfing
    6. Throwing out his Xbox system
    7. Finding healthier pursuits to replace using the Internet

Point 3: Support and Accountability

Support and accountability are crucial for recovery. Ask anyone who has successfully recovered and they will admit that one can't do it alone. People who struggle with pornography addiction need to surround themselves with others who understand their struggle, support them in their efforts to remain clean, and make them accountable for their actions. This is especially important when working through detox and withdrawal symptoms. Here is where support groups and accountability partners play important roles.

Spouses and family members can be extremely effective as accountability partners. God gives us spouses as helpmates for all areas of life. Having a wife present to help in dealing with the triggers that can lead to acting out is very helpful, even though it may be difficult for a man to admit to his wife that he is struggling with temptation. Most women want to be there for their husbands for support and accountability. Being part of the recovery process gives them hope for healing their marriage because total honesty and transparency are needed for recovery as well as restoring trust and intimacy. When a husband and wife work together in recovery, they can build a new marital relationship that is happy and healthy. One thing I don't recommend is that a wife be the person to receive accountability software email reports. This puts her in the position of being the "policeman" in the marriage. Instead, another accountability partner should receive the report. A wife should then be able to contact that person at any time to find out how her husband is doing with his sobriety.

Accountability partners can include friends, siblings, neighbors, colleagues, or support group members. Men who suffer from addiction should have at least one male accountability partner since they will naturally understand a man's struggle with pornography better than a woman. They can also challenge a man to remain pure without sounding like they are nagging. Scripture tells us, "Iron sharpens iron, and one man sharpens another" (Proverbs 27:17). Check in with accountability partners daily in the beginning of recovery. This can be a short phone call where the person addicted reports on his day, talk about triggers, danger zones, avoiding falls, and so on. If a man does fall, they can talk about the triggers and how to avoid them in the future. The accountability partner should also receive accountability software email reports, and if there is a reported fall he should call the addicted person immediately to discuss the fall and how to prevent future falls. An accountability partner cannot be afraid to ask tough questions, such as "How are you guarding your eyes and avoiding lust?" "Have you been masturbating?" "How are you working your recovery program today?" "Why haven't you been working your recovery program?" I have found the best accountability partners are men who are also struggling with pornography addiction because they truly understand the struggle and what it takes to remain clean.

Support groups are excellent places to find accountability partners, but the type of support a man needs depends on whether he has a pornography problem or an addiction. A man with a pornography problem may occasionally fall into viewing pornography; however, he is not addicted to it. He doesn't actively search for it, there is no escalation in pornography use, and there is no craving for it. Such a man might be online looking up sports scores and confront a pop-up window for pornography. Out of curiosity he clicks on it and ends up spending several minutes viewing porn. While he might not be addicted, if such activity continues, it could turn into an addiction. Thus, he needs support and accountability to stay clean.

A man with a pornography problem can find support and accountability in Catholic men's groups. Many parishes have active men's ministries where men meet weekly to study Scripture and the Catechism, and learn how to be better men, husbands, and fathers. The problem of pornography use is often discussed in these group meetings, and men can commit to hold each other accountable and help each other remain clean. Excellent men's ministries that address this problem were listed in the last chapter and can also be found in the appendix.

Men with a pornography addiction need stronger forms of support and accountability. These men seek out pornography daily, a few times a week, or go on long binges every few weeks. The amount of time a man spends viewing pornography has steadily increased and the type of pornography has become more extreme. He has become dependent on viewing pornography just to function in daily life. His life is out of control. This man needs a support group specifically for people with sexual addictions. Bill Wilson, the co-founder of Alcoholics Anonymous, discovered the best way for one alcoholic to stay sober was to help another alcoholic stay sober. In a pornography support group every member helps each other remain sexually sober. With support a man can find specific accountability partners and call each other daily, if necessary, to remain clean.

Many support groups follow the twelve steps of Alcoholics Anonymous, which have been modified for sexual addiction in the following twelve steps of Sexaholics Anonymous (SA, 2013):

1. Admitted that we were powerless over lust—that our lives had become unmanageable

2. Came to believe that a Power greater than ourselves could restore us to sanity

3. Made a decision to turn our will and our lives over to the care of God as we understood Him

4. Made a searching and fearless moral inventory of ourselves

5. Admitted to God, to ourselves, and to another human being the exact nature of our wrongs

6. Were entirely ready to have God remove all these defects of character

7. Humbly asked God to remove our shortcomings

8. Made a list of all persons we had harmed and became willing to make amends to them all

9. Made direct amends to such people wherever possible, except when to do so would injure them or others

10. Continued to take personal inventory, and when we were wrong, promptly admitted it

11. Sought through prayer and meditation to improve our conscious contact with God as we understood Him, praying only for knowledge of His will for us and the power to carry that out

12. Having had a spiritual awakening as the result of these Steps, we tried to carry this message to sexaholics, and to practice these principles in all our affairs

Going to the first meeting can be pretty scary. For many it feels as if they are making their addiction public. However, confidentiality in a 12-step group is automatic, almost like the seal of Confession. People will not talk outside of the meetings because everyone there wants confidentiality. After a man has gone to meetings regularly for two to three months, he can request a sponsor who will help him work through the twelve steps. In this process the addicted person often journals about each step as it applies to his life, and may share this with the group. This experience can lead to significant healing, growth, and change in a man's life, which can be especially seen after he works through all twelve steps and then goes back and reads his journal. Living out the twelve steps helps a man successfully take responsibility for his recovery, deal with many of the root causes of his addiction, remain sober, and aid others in recovery. Popular support groups for men addicted to pornography include:

- Sexaholics Anonymous
- My House Recovery Groups
- Sex Addicts Anonymous
- Sex and Love Addicts Anonymous
- Celebrate Recovery

Each group has a different definition of sobriety, yet I prefer the definition used by Sexaholics Anonymous: No sex with yourself or anyone else except your spouse. Information on these and other recovery groups is in the appendix.

If those support groups cannot be found in one's community, there are many meetings held by phone and online. If those are not an option, I recommend going to an Alcoholics Anonymous (AA) meeting. The steps are the same and the people will be just as compassionate and ready to help a person with a sexual addiction. Because many people struggle with dual addictions, one might find other people addicted to pornography at an AA meeting, and they can support each other.

Support and accountability began for Josh when he attended a Sexaholics Anonymous (SA) group. Aside from admitting he had a problem with pornography, this was the hardest thing he had to do for his recovery. Josh feared that he would meet someone he knew in the group meeting and that his friends, family, or colleagues would find out about his addiction. This fear was allayed shortly after he arrived at the meeting. He learned that everyone else had the same concern, so they were all committed to maintaining confidentiality. Josh also feared he would be surrounded by "perverts" and "dirty old men" in the meeting. Instead, he found good people from all different walks of life struggling just like he. Several men gave him their phone numbers and encouraged him to call them if he was struggling with temptation. Josh was amazed at how the group members cared about each other. He felt unconditional love from them and looked forward to returning for more meetings. Josh attended three meetings a week and became an accountability partner with three other men. After three months, he asked another member who had four years of sobriety to be his sponsor and they worked on the twelve steps.

The SA group was very important to Josh in the beginning of his recovery when he was going through detox and experiencing symptoms of withdrawal. Whenever he felt the strong urge to use pornography, he would remind himself that this was just his brain getting back to a normal level of chemical stimulation. Despite the difficulty, he knew he couldn't give in to the urge. Here is where he would turn to his support system for help and regularly call on his accountability partners to help him through these difficult times.

In addition to his SA meetings, Josh joined his parish men's ministry group. While the group wasn't specifically for men who struggled with pornography addiction, they did address it in the group, and the members decided to keep each other accountable for remaining clean. Josh was amazed at how many men struggled with pornography. He found he was not alone. He was even able to assist another addicted man in the group to get help.

Finally, Josh told Karen about his addiction. She was understandably upset, but it helped her to know that Josh was taking full responsibility for his recovery and was in a comprehensive recovery program. She vowed to support him in his recovery as long as he promised to be honest with her and let her know when he was struggling. He agreed. Working through Josh's recovery was difficult for both of them at times, but it actually brought them closer together. They were able to share their deepest fears with each other and experience love, forgiveness, and acceptance.

Having support and accountability from many sources helped Josh achieve sobriety. He knew many people loved him and wanted him to succeed. Although Josh fell several times in the beginning of his recovery process, his support and accountability system immediately helped him get back on the road to recovery. They loved him unconditionally while challenging him to diligently work through his recovery program.

It is the combination of the first three points of the Integrity Restored Recovery Program that helps people overcome the physical side of the addiction and helps the brain return to a normal level of chemical stimulation. The next point, counseling, can help a person recover from the emotional side of the addiction.

- Point Review: Four choices were the key to Josh's success with this point:
  1. Joining Sexaholics Anonymous
     a. Attending group meetings
     b. Finding accountability partners
     c. Finding a sponsor and working through the twelve steps

2. Turning to his accountability partners whenever he felt tempted to use pornography

3. Joining his men's group

4. Telling Karen about his addiction
   a. Taking responsibility for his addiction and recovery
   b. Being honest with her and letting her know when he was struggling

Point 4: Counseling

Therapy is imperative to the recovery process and is where the addiction is formally diagnosed and a comprehensive recovery program developed. The therapist begins by listening to the story of how the person became addicted and how the addiction has affected his life. A complete sexual history is taken, and tests such as the Internet Sex Screening Test (Delmonico, 2001) can be administered to help in the diagnosis.

Along with diagnosing the addiction, the therapist educates the addicted person on pornography addiction, the physical side of the addiction (including brain chemistry), and the emotional side (self-medicating emotional wounds). The full recovery program is then presented and discussed.

The therapist discusses sexual and non-sexual triggers and danger zones to help the addicted person avoid acting out with pornography. Effective strategies are developed for the person to avoid and/or deal with those triggers and danger zones. Because deep emotional wounds led to developing bad habits and self-medicating pain with pornography, now, new habits are developed to help the person use healthier and more effective ways to deal with his pain. We often refer to this as creating new neural pathways. This can include calling on accountability partners, exercising, new hobbies, prayer, etc. Of course the therapist will also recommend that the addicted person find accountability partners and participate in a support group.

From here the therapist moves on to help uncover the root causes of his addiction. Many men in America have viewed pornography, gotten bored with it, and ultimately rejected it. But as we discussed in earlier chapters, those who keep going back to it are self-medicating deep emotional wounds to ease their pain. They become emotionally addicted to it and this allows the physical side of the addiction to set in. To refresh your memory, these deep wounds include:

1. Selfishness/narcissism
2. Family-of-Origin Wounds
    a. Abuse
        1. Physical
        2. Sexual
        3. Emotional
    b. Addictions
    c. Abandonment
    d. Rejection
    e. Divorce
3. Loneliness
4. Insecurity
5. Body Image
6. Marital Conflicts
7. Excessive pressure in life
8. Perfectionism
9. Peer Rejection
10. Grief
11. Anger
12. Sadness
13. Shame
14. Mistrust of women/men
15. Lack of fulfillment in life
16. Lack of confidence

While it's important for the therapist to address triggers and danger zones to help prevent acting out, more is needed. To identify and resolve the emotional wounds to ensure long-term sobriety, the therapist helps the person struggling with pornography addiction to recognize the cycle that is perpetuating the addiction. Recall the cycle: (1) Sexual and non-sexual triggers activate the pain of the deep emotional wounds, which (2) feed the five faulty core beliefs (see p. 51), which then (3) lead a man to self-medicate with pornography and act out sexually with lust and masturbation, and afterward (4) he experiences deep shame, guilt, and despair, and this in turn (5) reinforces the emotional wounds.

Abuse wounds often result in deep trauma and lead to using pornography to self-medicate. Some struggle with Post Traumatic Stress Disorder (PTSD) because of their wounds. Recall the eight general ways people use pornography to cope with trauma: (1) Trauma Pleasure, (2) Trauma Blocking, (3) Trauma Shame, (4) Trauma Repetition, (5) Trauma Splitting, (6) Trauma Reaction, (7) Trauma Abstinence, (8) Trauma Bonding (see pp. 88–89).

When pornography addiction is the result of trauma, the therapist can work with the client to tap into the pain of their trauma, release it, and heal it. This requires a therapist who is trained in the treatment of trauma and PTSD.

Because the addicted person is self-medicating the pain of his emotional wounds and his lack of intimacy, many experts have referred to sex addiction as an "intimacy disorder." The person feels unlovable and lacks healthy intimacy in his life, and when he gets his fix from porn to ease the pain of loneliness, the temporary nature of the substance leaves him feeling lonelier, isolated, and more unlovable. The therapist can help the person see that healthy intimacy in marriage fosters satisfying sex, but sex alone does not foster true intimacy.

In counseling, a therapist can help addicted individuals uncover emotional wounds that led to pornography use and keep them going back to it. A treatment plan can then be designed to help them heal from those wounds, which can include forgiving those who hurt or betrayed them, growth in confidence and self-esteem, ending unhealthy relationships, developing healthy intimate relationships with God, spouse, family, and friends, working on achieving new life goals, and creating a positive vision for the future. As their wounds are healed, there is no longer a need to self-medicate with anything. This fosters healthy sobriety. Without uncovering and resolving the root causes of pornography use, any sobriety will be a "white-knuckle" sobriety, which is usually short-lived.

Letting Go of Shame
In addition to helping an addicted person heal from the emotional wounds that led to pornography use, a therapist can help the individual

let go of the shame associated with the addiction. Pornography/Sexual addiction carries with it more shame than any other addiction. Recall that society now views drug and alcohol addiction as a disease that requires treatment, and people with those addictions can seek help without experiencing much condemnation and ridicule. However, persons struggling with pornography addiction are often treated as "sick perverts," and regrettably this is also how pornography addicts see themselves. They tend to believe that no one, including God, could ever love them. In therapy they eventually come to see that their actions don't make them bad people, that they are actually good people who are struggling with a terrible disease, and that God still loves them very much. This can help them let go of their shame.

A Vision for Life

When I work with an addicted person in recovery, I help him develop a positive and attainable vision for life that gives hope for the future. I help him develop a vision statement, which is uniquely tied to the seventh point (virtue), because living virtuously must be part of every man's vision for his life. Eli Machen wrote that people enter recovery motivated by need and vision (Laaser, 2009).

NEED

People motivated only by need will usually do just the minimum required for recovery. They seek recovery for four reasons:

1. Appeasement—to please others
2. Dependence—because they need others
3. Control—as a means to control their spouse
4. Manipulation—to influence outcomes

Seeking recovery for those reasons makes a person more vulnerable to failure. Since they are not doing it for themselves, the work of recovery eventually becomes boring and tedious and eventually they drop out.

VISION

People motivated by vision have a clear mental picture of a successful future that is attainable. They see a purpose for their lives. Vision compels them and gives them hope, strength, and energy. There are three fruits of vision:

1. Determination—being willing to do whatever it takes to recover because there is a bigger purpose for one's life

2. Commitment—making a sincerely heartfelt decision not to stray from recovery

3. Passion—one can see that a positive end is attainable. (As a result there is great output of energy and inspiration.)

Change is motivated by something deeper: a heart that sincerely desires it. With a genuine heart, success is possible. People who have a genuine desire to change will envision the goal and set their hearts on finishing.

In *The Purpose Driven Life* (2002), Rick Warren wrote "Living on purpose is the only way to really live. Everything else is just existing." People in recovery need to develop a vision statement for their life in order to cultivate and maintain vision. This also helps them to stay strong in recovery. Below are some questions that help men develop a vision statement.

1. What is God's purpose for you?

2. How do you see yourself as a leader, provider, and protector?

3. What would you like to do with your life?

4. What do you not want to do?

5. What do you want to build in your life?

6. What things, people, or ideas in life are most important to you?

7. What is success to you?

8. What are the desires of your heart?

9. What are your greatest strengths?

10. What motivates you?

11. What is the center of your life?

12. What are you going to live for?

13. What kind of person do you want to be?

14. What do you want your life to contribute?

15. What do you want your life to communicate?

16. At the end of it all, when you stand before Christ, what things in your life are going to matter?

One's type of life determines his character, character determines appetite, and appetite determines vision. In other words, who are you? What is in your heart? What are you hungry for? Are you looking for those things that will truly satisfy that hunger? (Modified from Laaser, 2009).

Developing the Program

Finally, therapists work with each person addicted to pornography to develop a customized 7-point recovery plan that works. In each therapy session, the 7-point plan is reviewed to ensure that the addicted individual is following it. If the person has remained sober, reviewing the plan regularly can help him identify why he has been successful. If he has fallen, reviewing the plan can help him see where he has strayed from the plan. It has been my experience that those who fall usually have neglected one or more points of the plan. Getting back on track helps them regain their sobriety.

The ultimate goal of counseling is to heal the deep wounds and change the addicted person's unhealthy core beliefs to these following new healthy ones:

1. I am loveable.

2. If people really knew me, they would love me more.

3. I can count on others and God to meet my needs.

4. God and healthy relationships are my greatest need and source of comfort.

With these new beliefs, there is no need to turn to pornography or sex to self-medicate. Triggers that once led to pornography use have lost their power, and there is a greater sense of purpose in life and optimism toward the future!

Note: When selecting a therapist, it's important to choose one who is certified in the diagnosis and treatment of sexual addiction. Such therapists truly understand pornography/sexual addiction and are best qualified to treat it.

Help for Marriages and Wives

Counseling is needed to heal wounds the addiction has inflicted on a couple's marriage. Remember, pornography use is a form of adultery that breaks the marital vows and must now be healed.

Many wives may be reading this wondering what to do about their pain. They have been deeply wounded by their husbands' addiction, feel hurt and betrayed, and many experience trauma. These women need help too. Help for marriages and wives will be discussed in the next chapter, Healing for Couples.

When Josh entered therapy for his addiction, he had no idea how wounds from his past affected his attraction to pornography. His parents divorced when he was ten. On the outside it seemed like an amicable divorce, but it hurt Josh deeply. He often blamed himself for his parents' breakup. As his parents struggled with the divorce, Josh felt neglected and unloved. He felt abandoned when his father moved out. But being a good child, he never complained or expressed his pain. Like other kids who lived through divorce, he tried to make the best of it and enjoy life as much as possible. Josh learned how much the pain of his parents' divorce led him to develop the five faulty core beliefs. When he discovered pornography, it made him feel good both physically and emotionally, easing the pain of divorce and giving him a sense of intimacy. In therapy Josh learned to forgive his parents. He also focused on letting go of shame and came to understand his true value, dignity, and goodness. He learned to identify his triggers and danger zones and deal with them more effectively so that he would not act out. Josh worked on healthier relationships with his parents, family, friends, and Karen, and this also helped him change his core beliefs to healthy ones and develop a healthy vision for his future. In addition, his therapist collaborated with Josh's spiritual director to develop a healthy, intimate relationship with God. More about this will be covered in our next point, A Spiritual Plan.

- Point Review: Five choices were the key to Josh's success with this point:
    1. Working with a therapist to identify and heal the wounds that led to his pornography use and addiction
    2. Developing healthy ways to deal with his triggers and danger zones
    3. Letting go of the shame associated with his parents' divorce and his addiction
    4. Developing a vision for a healthy and happy life with Karen
    5. Changing his faulty core beliefs to healthy ones

Point 5: A Spiritual Plan

Spirituality plays a crucial role in recovery. We often hear about this in 12-step recovery groups where people talk about "turning to God as you understand Him" or "turning to your Higher Power." However, here we are referring to the one triune God who created us and loves us immensely. It's important for persons with addictions to realize they are never alone in recovery. God is always with them and ready to help. In 1 Corinthians 10:13 we read, "No temptation has overtaken you that is not common to man. God is faithful, and he will not let you be tempted beyond your strength, but with the temptation will also provide the way of escape, that you may be able to endure it."

As I've stated several times, many addicted persons believe that no one, even God, could ever forgive or love them. They believe they are unredeemable, which keeps them in their shame and despair, preventing any healing or recovery. They need to know they are loved by God unconditionally. They need to understand God's mercy and compassion for them as wounded children. It has been my experience that when the addicted person understands that he has an Abba (Daddy), God, whom he can run to in his pain and experience love and affection, his motivation for healing and recovery reaches a whole new level! Our Catholic faith offers many ways that individuals with addictions can understand and experience God's love.

As I discussed in chapter nine, the sacraments are very important for healing and recovery, especially Confession and the Eucharist. In Confession a priest has the opportunity to share God's mercy with the addicted person, allowing the individual to physically hear that God loves and forgives him. The person also needs to understand that "God so loved the world that he gave his only-begotten Son, that whoever believes in him should not perish but have eternal life" (John 3:16), and that the Eucharist truly is the Body, Blood, Soul, and Divinity of Christ. Knowing Christ died for him and that he can receive Christ every day can be especially healing for the person addicted to pornography. Receiving these sacraments often, even if the addicted individual still falls occasionally, can greatly aid in the recovery process. They are reminders of God's love and God's promise to never give up on him, and that God wants to help him in recovery.

Many people suffering from addiction go to Confession and receive the Eucharist weekly for months and still act out regularly because they are not in a comprehensive recovery program or they are not fully committed. Addiction won't magically go away with Confession and the Eucharist. The sacraments can give them the strength and grace necessary to successfully work through their recovery program, but they first must fully commit to their recovery program.

In addition to the sacraments, I recommend that addicted persons work with the assistance of a spiritual director who can help them develop healthy, intimate relationships with God. Many suffering from addiction see God as an angry taskmaster waiting to punish them, and not as a loving Father who is both just and merciful. Spiritual directors can be priests, deacons, religious, and even laypeople. In my practice I often collaborate with addicted persons' spiritual directors to help them develop healthy relationships with God, forgive those who hurt or betrayed them, and let go of shame. When selecting a spiritual director, it's important to choose one who is trained in spiritual direction and is faithful to *all* the teachings of the Catholic Church. To avoid some serious pitfalls when choosing a spiritual director, I would recommend Dan Burke's *Navigating the Interior Life: Spiritual Direction and the Journey to God* (Emmaus Road, 2012).

Daily prayer and Scripture reading are powerful in recovery and crucial for developing an intimate relationship with God. This can include mental prayer, also known as conversational prayer, Scripture study, Rosary, novenas, and holy hours. The key to developing a relationship with God is to simply start talking to Him and listen to what He says in your heart. A spiritual director can help in developing your relationship with God.

In addition to prayer, fasting is helpful in recovery. When we fast, we deny ourselves certain luxuries. Whenever we miss those luxuries it can be a reminder that we need to stay focused on God. We can also offer up these sufferings for others who are struggling with pornography addiction. Thus, there is a practical use for our suffering. When you fast, it should not be made known to others, but only to the "Father who sees in secret." Fasting doesn't have to be a big endeavor. Abstain from little luxuries and conveniences. For example, refrain from adding sugar to your coffee, use the stairs instead of the elevator, skip deserts, one day a week eat smaller meals, etc.

Sacramentals can also aid in developing a closer relationship with the Lord. Blessing oneself with holy water before and after prayer, carrying a rosary, having a crucifix and/or icons in every room of the house, wearing medals or the brown scapular, and using holy cards in prayer are wonderful reminders of God's love for us. Keeping blessed salt and St. Benedict medals near your computer can help in warding off temptation from the evil one. While not to be used superstitiously, sacramentals can aid in recovery by offering tangible reminders of God's love and care.

Catholic men's groups and 12-step support groups can also help those with addictions grow closer to the Lord and turn to Him for help and strength. In these groups addicted persons learn from others who have strong, healthy relationships with God, which can inspire them to want to turn to God and have a deep and intimate relationship with Him too.

God provides many resources for healing through our Catholic faith. Most people I've worked with suffering from addiction carry deep family-of-origin wounds. To aid in the healing process I point them to the Holy Family. Many have deep mother wounds, resulting from mothers who were abusive, addicted, rejecting, abandoning, cold, or critical. For these people I recommend developing a deep devotion to the Blessed Mother as a gentle, loving, affectionate, spiritual mother who has been with them all their lives. Others have deep father wounds, resulting from fathers who may have been abusive, addicted, rejecting, abandoning, cold, or critical. For them I recommend developing a deep devotion to St. Joseph as a loving, affirming, and protective spiritual father who has been with them all their lives. Addicted persons whose parents have divorced could turn to the Holy Family as an intact, stable, loving family. This has helped many who struggle with addictions forgive their parents.

Finally, there clearly is a spiritual battle associated with addiction, and the enemy always targets the weakest point. For many men, sexuality is their weakest point. Jesus refers to Satan in Scripture as the "father of lies" (John 8:44). This is very true! His lies and false promises lead men to use lust, pornography, and masturbation to ease their emotional pain. Satan is also referred to in Scripture as the "accuser" (Revelation 12:10). Once a man is addicted, Satan accuses him of being a sick pervert who is unworthy to be loved. He fills men with shame that leads to despair. As addicted individuals grow in their faith, they can learn to identify Satan's lies and false accusations. With God's help they can heal their wounds, grow in confidence, face these spiritual attacks, and win the battle. This helps bring an end to the lust, pornography, and masturbation.

When Josh began his recovery he was afraid to go back to church, believing he could never be forgiven and that God had stopped loving him. With the gentle encouragement of his therapist, Josh went to Confession, which was a cathartic experience for him. Josh feared he would receive ridicule and condemnation from the priest, but instead he experienced love and compassion. It moved him to tears knowing that God still loved him, forgave him, and welcomed him back into the Church. Josh was also moved when he was able to receive the Eucharist again.

Josh began seeing his pastor monthly for spiritual direction. The spiritual director collaborated with Josh's therapist and, together, they helped Josh develop a new understanding of God as a loving Father who is both merciful and just. Josh came to embrace the fact that he was an adopted son of God. Since Josh didn't want to hurt his newfound relationship with God, he worked hard not to use women through lust, pornography, or masturbation. He chose to love women as the Father's cherished daughters.

Josh's 12-step group encouraged him to deepen his relationship with God. He found good role models for living a healthy Christian life in his parish men's group. He also began praying with Karen daily for healing in his life and their relationship. As he grew in his faith, Josh was also able to identify Satan's lies and false accusations and dismiss them. All of this gave Josh the strength and determination to recover from his pornography addiction.

- Point Review: Six choices were the key to Josh's success with this point:
    1. Returning to the Sacraments of Reconciliation and the Eucharist
    2. Working with a spiritual director to develop a healthy, intimate relationship with God

3. Understanding God's immense love for him

4. Joining a 12-step group and a parish men's ministry that provided good role models and encouraged him to grow in his faith

5. Praying with Karen daily for healing

6. Recognizing the spiritual battle and not giving in to Satan's lies and accusations

Point 6: Education

To succeed in recovery, one must be educated and truly understand the dangers of pornography, its addictiveness, and the recovery process. When men enter recovery, I immediately give them a list of books, websites, CDs, and DVDs on pornography and sexual addiction. Also, men need to learn about the pornography industry and how it hurts women, and often this is shocking to men. When an addicted person fills his heart and mind with the truth about pornography, it becomes very difficult for him to fall into using it. Using these resources encourages men in recovery, as they realize they are not alone in their struggle and that there is a way out of addiction.

Education in recovery is not just for the addiction. As men uncover the deep wounds that led them into pornography use, they are encouraged to learn about their wounds and the healing process. For example, if a man is a survivor of child abuse, he is encouraged to read books about it, watch DVDs, and attend conferences on the healing of child abuse wounds. If a man uses pornography to cope with extreme work, family, or financial stress, he is encouraged to educate himself on healthier ways of dealing with stress. Fortunately, there are many great books, workbooks, CDs, DVDs, and conferences for all of the emotional wounds that can lead to pornography addiction. Please see the appendix.

Education also includes studying Scripture and the Catholic faith. As the addicted individual learns more about the faith and his sense of value and dignity are strengthened, he can let go of shame and has greater incentive to succeed in recovery. Spiritual direction and Catholic men's groups are helpful here. In addition, he can take classes either in a classroom or online to learn more about what the Church teaches on these subjects and why.

Eliminating lust, pornography, and masturbation and healing the deep emotional wounds associated with them are key to recovery, but they are only half of the story. The other half is learning about healthy relationships and sexuality. Most of the men I've treated for pornography/sex addiction learned about sexuality and relationships from the Internet, which left them with distinctly unhealthy views. They need to throw out their old notions and start from scratch. Studying Pope St. John Paul II's written works, *The Theology of the Body* and *Love and Responsibility*, will help tremendously. *The Theology of the Body* focuses on God's beautiful plan for healthy sexuality while *Love and Responsibility* focuses on healthy relationships. These teachings can be studied using the resources provided by the Theology of the Body Institute. Listed in the appendix are many other great Catholic and Christian resources on this subject.

Gaining knowledge about pornography addiction, recovery, Catholicism, and healthy sexuality and relationships is tremendously helpful for the person struggling with pornography addiction; however, it doesn't end there. It has been said that the best way to truly learn anything is to teach it. Thus, any information an addicted person gains that helps him in his recovery must be shared with others. For many years, those addicted have been part of the problem. By teaching others about the dangers of pornography, the addiction, and the recovery process, they become part of the solution to the pornography epidemic! It starts with talking to their own family and friends. Some men give talks to parish men's groups and youth groups. There are even more visible ways to educate the public. One men's organization, The King's Men, goes on a monthly "No More Porn Tour." Once a month these men picket outside a local porn shop, carrying signs that say "Porn Hurts Women" and "Real Men Don't Use Porn." They have received a tremendously favorable response from the public and their demonstrations have deeply hurt the profits of the porn shop. In addition to the addicted person sharing helpful information with others, it is especially important for parents to share this information with their kids.

When Josh entered recovery, he was eager to learn all he could about pornography addiction and recovery. He read several books on it and viewed some DVDs, which gave him a much better sense of the recovery process. He also read books on Adult Children of Divorce. This helped him understand how his parents' divorce affected him and how he could heal those wounds. Josh and Karen studied *The Theology of the Body* and *Love and Responsibility* to learn about healthy sexuality and relationships. That helped them both grow in intimacy. Knowing that Josh was committed to having a healthy relationship with Karen helped her increase her trust in Josh. As Josh let go of his shame and grew in self-confidence, he shared his struggle with addiction with the men in his parish men's group. He was able to educate them on the dangers of pornography and how to protect themselves and their families. After one meeting a man came up to Josh and admitted that he too struggled with pornography addiction, and Josh referred him to a therapist who could help him recover. It made Josh feel good to know he could help others find freedom from pornography!

- Point Review: Four choices were the key to Josh's success with this point:
    1. Understanding that his pornography use was symptomatic of deeper problems
    2. Reading books, viewing DVDs, and attending conferences on pornography addiction, adult children of divorce, healthy sexuality, and relationships
    3. Studying *The Theology of the Body* and *Love and Responsibility* with Karen
    4. Sharing with his men's ministry group about his struggle with pornography addiction and his recovery

Point 7: Virtue

The final point in the Integrity Restored Recovery Program is virtue. This is so important in recovery. Vice is conquered through virtue. In developing this program I understood that virtue was a crucial element; however, none of the programs I reviewed promoted it. When men strive to live virtuous lives, they naturally won't want any vice to interfere. It also allows them to be the leaders, providers, and protectors that God calls them to be. This should be part of a man's vision for life.

The Catechism defines virtue as "an habitual and firm disposition to do the good. It allows the person not only to perform good acts, but to give the best of himself. The virtuous person tends toward the good with all his sensory and spiritual powers; he pursues the good and chooses it in concrete actions" (1803). This is the true measure of manhood and the life to which one should strive. It enables a man to present the best version of himself.

I use the image of a funeral to illustrate the importance of a virtuous life. When a man dies and people eulogize him, what do they usually say? Do they say, "Here was a millionaire who lived in a mansion and drove an expensive car?" One hopes not. One hopes they would say, "Here was a kind man, a generous man, a faithful man, a humble man." People ultimately judge others not by their wealth or accomplishments but by how virtuously they live their lives.

The Catechism lists two categories of virtues: Human (or Cardinal) and Theological.

> Human Virtues are firm attitudes, stable dispositions, habitual perfections of intellect and will that govern our actions, order our passions, and guide our conduct according to reason and faith. They make possible ease, self-mastery, and joy in leading a morally good life. The virtuous man is he who freely practices the good. The moral virtues are acquired by human effort. They are the fruit and seed of morally good acts; they dispose all the powers of the human being for communion with

divine love. Four virtues play a pivotal role and accordingly are called "cardinal"; all the others are grouped around them. They are: prudence, justice, fortitude, and temperance. (1804–1805)

The Human Virtues are rooted in the theological virtues, which adapt man's faculties for participation in the divine nature [cf. 2 Pet 1:4]: for the theological virtues relate directly to God. They dispose Christians to live in a relationship with the Holy Trinity. They have the One and Triune God for their origin, motive, and object. (1812)

The Theological Virtues are the foundation of Christian moral activity; they animate it and give it its special character. They inform and give life to all the moral virtues. They are infused by God into the souls of the faithful to make them capable of acting as his children and of meriting eternal life. They are the pledge of the presence and action of the Holy Spirit in the faculties of the human being. There are three theological virtues: faith, hope, and charity [cf. 1 Cor 13:13]. (1813)

There are many other virtues in addition to the Human and Theological virtues. They are often referred to as character strengths and include:

Trustworthiness	Obedience	Patience
Loyalty	Self-control	Manliness
Patience	Cheerfulness	Leadership
Respect	Thriftiness	Goodness
Helpfulness	Chastity	Forgiveness
Service	Courage	Gratitude
Friendliness	Cleanliness	Perseverance
Courteousness	Reverence	Fairness
Good Sportsmanship	Humility	
Kindness	Generosity	

When working with people suffering from addiction, I give them an exercise to grow in virtue. Each week they choose two virtues, and each day they find some way to put those virtues into practice. For example, if a man is working on the virtue of service, he might make a point to hold a door open for someone or help with another's chores without being asked. Every day the men record in a journal the ways they practiced virtue. This helps them see how they are growing in virtue. After a while, they notice that they are living more virtuous lives without much struggle, and others begin to notice it as well. Many wives comment on how much their husbands have grown and healed. They feel they can once again trust them.

Initially, recovery is about getting away from the pornography drug. However, as a man progresses in his recovery, there should be a transformation. Instead of just moving away from pornography, they begin to focus their energies on moving toward living a virtuous life. In chapter three I introduced the importance of a man fulfilling his God-given mission and duty of being a leader, provider, and protector. Striving for a virtuous life will help him succeed in that mission. Conversely, focusing on being the best leader, provider, and protector he can be will help a man live a virtuous life. Embracing this mission gives a man greater purpose and fulfillment, creating excitement about life without vice and without pornography. This makes recovery easier and more successful since he is striving to become the man God created him to be.

While Josh found growing in virtue to be challenging, he knew it would help him become a man of God and the leader, provider, and protector that Karen needed him to be. He made this part of his Vision for Life and he made living virtuously a daily goal. Some virtues, such as cleanliness and respect, were easy for him to practice. Other virtues, such as patience and forgiveness, were more difficult. Virtues such as faith and hope he simply committed to prayer every day, and although he didn't notice any changes in himself, Karen did. She commented that he was calmer, more patient, attentive, and things that once made him angry didn't seem to bother him as much anymore. Knowing that he was striving to be a virtuous man also increased Karen's respect for Josh. She admired his hard work and progress, and felt she could trust him more to be open and honest with her.

Focusing on his Vision for Life and living virtuously got Josh excited about life. He knew he was on the path to living a healthy and happy life. This encouraged him to set goals for his education, career, and future with Karen. In his 12-step group and men's ministry group, he encouraged other men to live virtuously. As a result of all this work, Josh was finally able to envision himself married to Karen with children in a happy life together! He didn't want anything to stand in the way of achieving these goals, especially pornography.

- Point Review: Four choices were the key to Josh's success with this point.
    1. Making living virtuously part of his Vision for Life
    2. Striving daily to practice virtue
    3. Becoming the leader, provider, and protector that God is calling him to be
    4. Encouraging other men to live virtuous lives

The Importance of the Points

Recall that I called this a 7-point program and not a 7-step program because each point is of equal importance and all are worked simultaneously, each addressing an important facet of recovery. Many of the men I've worked with have used some of the points (i.e. prayer and sacraments, group meetings, online programs); however, they were not successful because they were not using all the points. Keeping a daily journal helps men stay on track with all the points. I have found that when men are committed to working all the points of the program, they are able to recover from their pornography addiction and go on to live healthy, happy lives.

Obstacles to Recovery

There are many reasons why people who struggle with pornography addiction fail to seek help or are unsuccessful in recovery, the most common of which are denial, pride, shame, fear, and lack of commitment.

- *Denial.* Many men struggling with pornography deny that it is a problem. This is often due to societal influences. Many believe that all men view pornography and that it is a normal pursuit, or as we've said previously, they see it as a rite of passage into manhood. Our culture, saturated with pornographic images, reinforces those beliefs. The pornography industry, as well as the mass media, succeeded in making pornography more acceptable by renaming it "adult entertainment." Thus, it usually isn't until pornography has had a devastating effect on a man's life (e.g., divorce, job loss, financial ruin, or a sexually transmitted disease) that he may even consider he has a problem and needs help.

- *Pride.* A man might know he has an addiction to pornography, but pride keeps him from getting help. He believes that he is strong enough to overcome the addiction simply by avoidance and willpower. If he does seek help, he will only do what he feels is necessary instead of following his therapist's advice. This often leads to disastrous results. Instead of recovering from the addiction, it gets worse. People like this often drop out of treatment early and usually need to experience a true crisis, such as the threat of losing their job, marriage, or family before they are able to let go of their pride and fully commit to treatment.

- *Shame.* There are men who are addicted to pornography and know it, but avoid seeking help for fear of what others might think, which is also the sin of pride. They are filled with shame. Often these men hold respectable positions in their community, such as clergy, politicians, physicians, teachers, and coaches. They don't want anyone to learn about their problem,

240

so they suffer in silence, struggling to maintain the façade of a healthy person. However, this doesn't last for long. As the addiction consumes the man's life, the façade begins to crack and eventually something happens that makes the truth known to all. This could mean being caught viewing pornography by one's wife, being fired for viewing pornography at work, being seen at a local porn shop, or being arrested for soliciting a prostitute. When this happens, the shame is only magnified.

- *Fear.* Many men are afraid to seek help because they believe they are beyond help. They might be afraid they are not strong enough to overcome pornography use, or of the consequences they might have to face because of their addiction: an angry wife or parents, rejection by friends and family, or the loss of a job. These people need much support and encouragement. They need to realize that no one is a lost cause and most people would want to help them. With God's help anyone can recover from pornography addiction.

- *Lack of Commitment.* Some men fail at recovery simply because they are not committed to their program. They may be in recovery only to appease their wives or to look good to their family. While they may struggle with some denial, pride, and shame, ultimately they simply don't want to do the work required for recovery. These men often don't follow all seven points and offer many weak excuses for not doing so. They are generally not ready for recovery and soon drop out. To be successful in recovery one must want it more than anything and be willing to do whatever it takes to recover.

Encouragement

If you struggle with pornography use, I encourage you to seek help. You don't have to continue suffering. Freedom from pornography is possible. It will take time and effort, but you can be free. God is there to help you along with many wonderful therapists, support groups, clergy, friends, and family. Don't let denial, pride, shame, or fear stop you. God loves you and wants you to recover and has a wonderful plan for your life! For information on the Integrity Restored Recovery Program, log onto www.IntegrityRestored.com. Your road to freedom can begin today.

11

Healing for Couples

Pornography use has had devastating effects on many marriages. The marriage vows have been broken as well as trust. There are feelings of betrayal. The husbands' actions have deeply hurt their wives and, consequently, marital therapy is needed along with individual therapy. Although a wife is *never* responsible for her husband's pornography use, there often are many problems in the marriage that contribute to it. For example, a man may feel lonely because his wife is cold and distant, and turn to pornography to ease his loneliness. Likewise, he might use pornography as a way of punishing a wife who is always angry and critical. Here, the pornography use is really a symptom of deeper problems in the marriage.

Remember that pornography addiction in a marriage needs to be seen as a disease, not a moral failing. This disease affects a man, his wife, and their marriage, and therefore all three need to be treated. As a wife begins to understand that her husband's use of pornography was a weak attempt to ease the pain of deep emotional wounds, she can come to realize that it had nothing to do with her, her beauty, or her desirability as a woman. At this point, many wives develop great compassion for their husbands and want to help them in their recovery.

Many wives claim they want their marriage to return to where it was before pornography entered it, but this should not be the goal. The marriage was probably unhealthy from the start. The goal of therapy is to create a new and healthy marital relationship. The healing process starts by allowing the wife to freely express how deeply she has been hurt by pornography use. Her husband needs to truly understand her pain. There must also be full disclosure of all her husband's sexual activity outside the marriage, and although this is painful, it is freeing. The wife finally knows everything and the husband is no longer carrying any secrets. Through total openness and transparency, trust can be restored in the marriage.

Couples need to know that God wants to restore and bless broken marriages. Knowing that He has a marvelous plan for their marriage can give a couple hope in building a healthy, new marital relationship.

To truly recover from this addiction, couples need to find a licensed therapist who is trained in the diagnosis and treatment of sexual addiction as well as in marriage and family therapy. Such a therapist will have a deeper understanding of the addiction, how it affects marriages, and how to help individuals and couples recover.

The 7-Point Program for Couples

Earlier I discussed how the Integrity Restored Recovery Program is applied to those suffering from pornography addiction; here, I would like to show how many couples have found it a helpful roadmap for healing and restoration of their marriages. Spouses can understand the healing process and not feel helpless. I will discuss each point and how they apply to couples and spouses. Because most who are entrapped in pornography addiction are men, I refer to wives as spouses.

We now return to Tom and Janet's story to show how they were able to recover individually and as a couple from the wounds of pornography addiction in their marriage. To review their story in full, see pp. 7–8 from chapter one and interspersed throughout chapter five. For a brief review, Tom and Janet came into my office visibly distraught. Tom was filled with shame and Janet was very angry. They had been married for fifteen years, had four children, and Janet caught Tom viewing Internet pornography and masturbating late at night. She gave him an ultimatum to either get help to end his pornography use or she would leave him. He began counseling. This was their first step toward healing.

Point 1: Self-knowledge and Commitment

For addicted persons, self-knowledge means admitting they have a problem with pornography. For couples, self-knowledge means understanding that they both have been deeply wounded by the addiction and both are in need of help. This can help them take a team approach to recovery. It's also important to acknowledge how pornography use has affected them individually and as a couple—physically, emotionally, relationally, and financially.

They need to understand each other's triggers and how to help each other work through them. Tom often was triggered by work stress, anger, sadness, loneliness, and exhaustion. His danger zones were late at night, after a hard day at work, and when he felt lonely in their marriage. In recovery, Tom promised Janet that he would let her know when he was being triggered or was in a danger zone, and she promised to help him through these times. His honesty allowed her to start trusting him again. And because she was there to help him, he felt less lonely. However, everything didn't just sail smoothly along.

Janet often experienced bouts of anger, crying, fear, and even flashbacks of when she caught Tom viewing pornography. There were many late nights where she would rage at him for how he'd hurt her. These episodes were triggered whenever she would think about his betrayal, such as when she would see him using their home computer or his smartphone. Her danger zones were late at night, after a hard day, or being in the home office with the computer. In addition, when she felt fearful or insecure, she would try to control Tom's recovery by keeping track of his meetings and counseling appointments, and making sure he was reading his recovery books. To stop this behavior, she promised to talk to him when she was struggling and to let him be responsible for his recovery. If she felt a rage coming on, she would go out for a drive to cool off. Tom moved the computer out of the home office and into the kitchen where everyone could see him when he was online. To help alleviate Janet's triggers and fears, he got rid of his smartphone and purchased a phone that did not offer access to the Internet. His goal was to heal their marriage and show that he was trustworthy.

Together, Tom and Janet committed to help each other with both their individual healing and marital healing. This was challenging for Janet at times because of the pain and anger she felt from the betrayal, but she took it one day at a time and trusted that God would take care of her, Tom, and their marriage.

Point 2: Purifying Your Life

Tom came to understand what it meant to be called by God to be a leader, provider, and protector. He did his best to purify his life, to see women as God's daughters to be loved rather than sex objects to be ogled and used. Together, Tom and Janet worked to purify their lives of any pornography. They installed Covenant Eyes an all computers, tablets, and cell phones used by the family. As mentioned above, Tom traded in his smartphone for a phone that did not have Internet access. They blocked offensive programs and networks from their television and monitored all media that entered the home. It made them both feel good to know that their lives were protected. Working as a team also gave them a sense of control over their lives again.

Another way they were able to purify their lives was by agreeing to a ninety-day period of sexual abstinence. Anyone recovering from an addiction must go through a detox period. Because the brain of a person addicted to sex has grown accustomed to operating at such a high level of chemical stimulation, it needs time to return to operating at a normal level. To do this, an addicted person often has to abstain from any kind of sexual activity for an extended period of time. This includes use of pornography, masturbation, and sex with another person. The ninety-day period of abstinence was difficult for Tom; however, he had Janet, his accountability partners, his support group, and his therapist there to help him through it. In the end it did help Tom purify his heart, mind, and brain of the pornography.

The ninety-day period of abstinence was easier for Janet and very helpful to her. The thought of being sexually intimate with her husband who betrayed her was not something she was eager to do. It reminded her of his broken marital vows, and she needed time to heal and forgive. Janet slept in another bedroom and used this time to better understand Tom's addiction, forgive him, and work on her own healing. Those ninety days were like a spiritual retreat to Janet. She would go to her room at night and spend an hour in prayer for their personal healing and the healing of their marriage. This strengthened her love and compassion for Tom. At the end of the ninety days, Janet was more committed to working with Tom on their individual and marital healing.

Point 3: Support and Accountability

Support and accountability are also needed for spouses. Both need to surround themselves with people who understand their struggles and can help them in the healing and recovery process.

One of the hardest things Tom did in his recovery was to attend his first Sexaholics Anonymous (SA) meeting. He wasn't sure whom he'd meet there. Plus, it would mean admitting to others that he had an addiction. When he arrived he was surprised at the variety of people he met. Some, like him, struggled with pornography addiction. Others, struggling with more severe sexual addictions, used prostitutes, had affairs and even anonymous sexual encounters. At first Tom was taken aback by these men; however, as he got to know them he realized they were just as serious about overcoming their addictions. Several had achieved long-term sobriety. Tom was able to see the good in all of them and have compassion toward them. This also made it easier for Tom to let go of his shame. He exchanged phone numbers with some men at the meeting, which led to being accountability partners. These men received Tom's Covenant Eyes reports and were especially helpful during his initial ninety-day detox period. Tom eventually found a sponsor who helped him work through the twelve steps of SA.

Knowing that Tom had a good support group also helped Janet let go of her need to control Tom's recovery. If he missed a meeting, she knew one of his accountability partners would be calling him and keeping him accountable to his program. Seeing Tom's commitment to helping others was another sign of his commitment to recovery, which helped Janet's trust in him grow.

Janet also needed support. She needed to know that she was not alone in the healing process. She began attending COSA meetings for family members suffering from sex addiction, which was difficult for her because of the shame she felt being married to a man addicted to pornography. But she, too, found caring women who understood what she was going through. She could share from her heart and even cry with those women. It was a safe place to tell her story. Janet met women who had gone through similar experiences and recovered. It gave her hope to see that marriages could be healed and restored. She also accepted the truth that Tom's addiction to pornography had nothing to do with her beauty or desirability, and that he didn't want to replace her with younger women. Once she understood the drug that pornography is and how it's used to ease emotional pain, she could find the strength to forgive Tom. She still struggled with her own painful emotions, but she now could call other women in her group for support and encouragement. They helped her persevere and eventually Janet began having more good days than bad. The women in her COSA group gave her hope for a brighter future.

Tom and Janet also attended a Couples in Recovery group together, where they could see and talk to other couples who had recovered from the pain of addiction. They found a couple that was willing to mentor them through the healing process. Other couples in the group were wonderful role models as well. Through these meetings, Tom and Janet came to know how much they really loved each other, but they also came to know that their old marital relationship was never really healthy. Tom and Janet became excited about the positive future they were creating and they now had an opportunity to create a new and healthy marriage.

Point 4: Counseling

Counseling is crucial for married couples just as it is for the addicted person in recovery. Marital vows have been broken, trust has been violated, and marital healing is necessary. The healing process begins with the therapist hearing both sides of the story. This allows the therapist to get the couple on the same page and ready to heal individually and as a couple. Husbands need to share how they became addicted to pornography and how it has affected their lives. The addiction may have deep roots going back to childhood. Wives need to share how their husbands' addiction has affected them personally, their marriages, and their families. Recovery for Tom and Janet began in counseling.

Tom shared his story with Janet in counseling. He told her his pornography use began at ten years old when he and his friends found a *Playboy* magazine at a local construction site. By high school he was viewing porn on cable television, and after college he was going on binges and spending entire weekends viewing it. He explained how that led to phone sex and visiting massage parlors, and with the Internet taking off after they married, he was into viewing porn late at night after Janet and their kids were in bed.

It was very difficult for Janet to hear Tom share his entire story in counseling, but after seeing how far back his pornography use and addiction went, she realized that he was deeply wounded long before she met him. She was still very angry because of his dishonesty, but knowing that he did really love her, was truly sorry for his actions, and never meant to harm her, helped her let go of some of her anger and have more compassion for him. She promised to help him in his recovery.

But that wasn't enough. Tom needed to hear Janet's story so they could both heal as a couple. This is part of the counseling too.

Janet shared how much she loved Tom and often talked about how it was "love at first sight" when she met him. She saw him as a strong, confident, and responsible man. He had a deep faith, a lot of ambition, and a fun energy about him. After they were married and began their family, Janet believed she had the perfect life. Tom succeeded in his career, they had four healthy children, and everyone seemed content.

Then Janet related how things began to change. Tom became more distant, often worked late, and spent many hours alone at night in his home office. Because of "work," he missed many school events, kids' baseball and soccer games, and even some family gatherings. Janet shared how she felt ignored by him, how the deep, intimate conversations they used to have seemed to disappear, how their sex life dried up, and how she began to feel unattractive to him. After discovering Tom's pornography use, she expressed how deeply hurt and betrayed she felt, because this was cheating to her, these were extramarital affairs! She felt old and unattractive because Tom was masturbating to young and beautiful women. She felt her whole world come crashing down. She awoke to the fact that the man she had loved and trusted for so many years had a dark secret life she knew nothing about. Without warning, in a moment, he became a complete stranger. She didn't feel safe with him. She feared for their children. She was traumatized.

Although this was difficult for Tom to hear, he needed to understand how deeply his actions had affected Janet. It broke his heart when he realized how much he had hurt the one person he loved the most. Janet needed him to acknowledge her pain. Tom was profoundly moved, his eyes tearing up, and he sincerely apologized to Janet and vowed never to hurt her again. Knowing that his apology was sincere helped strengthen Janet's desire to heal their marriage. While there was still more to uncover and discuss, both Tom and Janet were on the same page and ready to heal individually and as a couple.

That's what counseling makes possible. A lot of tears were shed, yet it was necessary for healing, and by the end of the first session, Tom and Janet were exhausted but relieved. Tom no longer had to carry a deep, dark secret and Janet was able to let Tom know how hurt she was.

In subsequent therapy sessions Tom and Janet discovered the roots of his pornography addiction. Tom always believed he used pornography for entertainment and to relieve stress. He never thought he was self-medicating emotional pain. He thought he had a normal family life growing up, but delving into his past revealed considerable family dysfunction. Tom's maternal grandfather was physically abusive toward his mother, and when she was eleven he abandoned the family. The family struggled to survive financially, which deeply wounded Tom's mother and made it difficult for her to trust anyone. Tom never doubted her love for him, but she was always emotionally distant and unaffectionate toward him. Tom began to see how his pornography use may have been a way for him to ease the pain of never receiving affection from his mother. It was very difficult for him to even consider this because it somehow left him feeling disloyal toward his mother and that he was betraying her. Through therapy he came to understand that his mother was a good woman who loved her children very much, but her emotional wounds prevented her from showing it.

In individual therapy Tom worked on healing his wounds by forgiving his mother and grandfather. Knowing about Tom's history and family woundedness helped Janet immensely. When she realized how deeply wounded Tom and his whole family were, she was able to have more compassion toward him, and this helped her in healing their relationship.

The next step for Tom and Janet was to have a full disclosure session, which is where the addicted individual discloses the truth about *all* his sexual activity outside the marriage. His spouse then has the opportunity to ask questions. I usually ask the addicted person to write down in a journal the entire history of his pornography use and addiction. It can take a while to prepare for this, but the individual needs to let go of his shame and be willing to disclose *everything* to his spouse. He must also be prepared for her response, which could include rage. The wife must also be prepared to hear the full details of her husband's sexual activity, which can be very painful and temporarily intensify her pain. However, a disclosure session is necessary for both spouses. It is freeing for the addicted person because he no longer has to carry any dark secrets, and it's freeing for the wife because she finally knows everything. She no longer wonders what her husband has done. This is a true act of honesty by the person addicted to pornography, and helps heal the trust wound in the marriage. For men who attend 12-step support group meetings, working step one can help with the disclosure session. In step one, the person writes down the full history of his addiction, which he can read aloud in the disclosure session.

The disclosure session was both painful and relieving for Tom and Janet. Tom shared the history of his sexual activity outside their marriage including the pornography use, online chatting, and phone sex. Because his addiction spanned over twenty years, some of the details were a bit fuzzy for him, such as exactly how many times he actually viewed pornography, visited a porn shop, or chatted with women online. Phone records revealed how often he engaged in phone sex. He disclosed all the types of sexual behavior he engaged in, where he did it, when he would do it, how he would do it, and through his individual therapy, why he did it. While this was tremendously helpful to Janet, she wanted to know who Tom chatted with online and who he had phone sex with, which Tom could not fully answer because he chatted anonymously with woman in chat rooms and in phone sex. He didn't know their names or where they were located, but he did show Janet the chat rooms he used online and the phone sex numbers he used.

After the disclosure session, Tom and Janet didn't talk for two days. He struggled with the shame of his sexual behaviors. She struggled with her anger toward him. However, they both realized that the session was needed for them to move forward. As bad as Tom felt, he was relieved that all of his secrets were revealed, and Janet felt relieved that she finally knew the truth.

Having a greater understanding about the dangers of pornography, Tom's sexual behaviors, the roots of his addiction, and the recovery process helped Tom and Janet feel less powerless over their situation. They knew the "who, what, when, where, how, and why" of the addiction. This gave them hope that they could overcome the addiction, heal their wounds, and restore their relationship.

Tom's family-of-origin wounds weren't the only issues that played a role in his addiction. Another issue that emerged through therapy was Tom's career. He had been in sales for twenty years, and although he was a good producer for his company, he felt unappreciated. He was passed over several times for promotions. Furthermore, his career required him to travel a lot, and these business trips often were danger zones for him. Being alone in a hotel room was a strong trigger to go online and view pornography. As part of Tom's recovery, he and Janet agreed that he should look for a new job that didn't require as much travel. This could mean a complete career change for Tom with a cut in pay; however, they were willing to deal with that if it helped his recovery and their marriage.

They also had to deal with marital issues that led to Tom's pornography use. Like most wives, Janet had to understand that she was not responsible for his addiction; however, she also needed to recognize that there were problems in their marriage that led him to use pornography to self-medicate. Tom's main problem was loneliness. He was happy early in their marriage, but as they started having children and Janet began focusing all her attention on the children, he felt rejected and lonely. Pornography was his escape. In Tom's words, "The women in porn are always there for you. They give you their sole attention." That Janet wasn't present to Tom was difficult for her to hear. She always thought she was a good wife who made him a key part of her life. While she was still very angry with him, she took what he said to heart and they made a commitment to spend at least thirty minutes alone each night to devote to each other. They also decided to go on regular dates. They knew these decisions would ultimately help them with their marriage and strengthen their commitment to each other.

In addition to marital therapy, Janet needed individual therapy to heal from her own wounds. Discovering Tom's addiction was traumatic for her, leaving her feeling ugly and sexually unattractive. She was beautiful, but at forty and having had four kids she couldn't measure up to the women in porn. She felt rejected by Tom and replaced by younger women. At times she felt a deep rage toward him and the women in porn for leaving her feeling that way. She needed to heal these wounds.

Janet also felt deep fear, insecurity, and intense sadness because the past fifteen years of her marriage appeared to be a charade. She grieved over the marriage she thought she had but didn't. She felt both cheated and like a fool. She didn't know if she could ever trust her husband again. In her individual therapy, Janet was able to work through these wounds. Her first challenge was letting go of her anger and resentment in having to work on recovery. She thought, "Tom caused all this pain!

Why should I have to work!?" In her mind Tom received all the sympathy for being "sick." He seemed to get off scot-free while she was left to suffer. As she came to accept her situation, she realized that she needed healing for more than just the wounds he caused.

Through therapy, Janet learned how to forgive Tom and begin to trust again. She learned to be gentle with herself and with him. She had to trust in God and His care for her, and although it was a painful process, she knew it was healing her. Janet also discovered she brought her own family-of-origin wounds into the marriage. Her parents divorced when she was twelve, and while it appeared amicable on the outside, she suffered much because of it. Her father had an extramarital affair and fathered a child out of wedlock. Her mother never forgave him and would always criticize him. This experience wounded Janet's ability to trust men. She loved Tom, but always fearing he would leave her, she kept him at arm's-length emotionally. When the children came, she focused all her time and energy on them to avoid dealing with Tom. The betrayal of her father also made the betrayal of Tom's pornography use even more painful. Janet worked on forgiving her parents and asked Tom for forgiveness for neglecting him. Therapy allowed them to more clearly see how their individual wounds affected the marriage and made them more eager to delve into the past and discover wounds that needed healing. They recognized how this would lead to a healthier marriage.

As Tom and Janet experienced forgiveness and healing in their lives, they were able to start working on a vision for their marriage. They each wrote down what they believed a great marriage entailed, and then they combined their definitions into one they could share. They wanted their marriage to be Christ-centered where there was total trust and openness. They wanted to be able to talk to each other without fear. They wanted passion and romance in their marriage, and desired to be best friends who were always there for each other. As husband and wife, they knew their job was to get each other to heaven and they wanted their marriage to mirror the love of the Trinity. This got them excited about their marriage because it was something they could work on together as a couple. They became architects for their marriage and their vision was totally attainable.

Therapy is a challenging part of any recovery program. It means facing deep and painful wounds. Some people spend years doing everything possible to avoid dealing with their wounds; however, the wounds eventually surface and can lead to terrible consequences, including addictions. By uncovering them and working together on resolving them, couples find healing for themselves and their marriage. Through counseling, Tom and Janet were able to understand their woundedness and work together toward healing as individuals and as a couple. This increased their love and commitment to each other and their marriage, and although they wished they never had to deal with addiction in their marriage, they both admitted that recovery helped them create the healthy marriage they always wanted.

Point 5: Spiritual Plan

Bringing God into the healing process is so important for couples. They need to know that God has not forgotten them in their suffering and He has a wonderful plan to restore their marriage. I compare this to rebuilding a house. Sometimes a bad storm can damage a poorly built house down to its foundation, and in order to rebuild that house it must first be torn down. One must then sort through the rubble and pull out the good things that have not been damaged. These, along with new materials, are used to build a new house that is stronger, healthier, and able to withstand the storms of life.

That's exactly what we saw in counseling sessions with Tom and Janet. Their marriage is like a house. The old marriage was rocked to its foundations. Like a new house, the new marriage can be stronger, healthier and happier. To help a couple through the demolition and rebuilding process, they need to turn to God daily for hope and strength. Prayer and the sacraments are necessary. They gave Tom the strength to persevere in recovery and they helped Janet to forgive him. Tom and Janet made a commitment to attend weekly Mass and Confession together, and they each started meeting monthly with a spiritual director to help them grow in their relationships with God. They also committed to pray daily for each other and with each other. Although

255

this was difficult for Janet at first because of her anger, she started praying a decade of the Rosary with Tom each night for their marriage. As
they experienced more healing, they spent more time praying together.
Their prayer time became a sanctuary where they could grow in their
love for God and for each other.

In her individual daily prayer, Janet prayed that God would help
her see Tom as Jesus saw him, which helped soften her heart and forgive him. In his daily prayer, Tom asked the Lord to help him become
the husband and father Janet needed him to be, which gave him the
strength to be a true leader, provider, and protector in their marriage
and family.

Because of Tom's deep mother wound and Janet's deep father
wound, they both prayed to the Holy Family to intercede for them.
They came to view the Blessed Mother as a gentle, affectionate spiritual
mother and St. Joseph as a protective, affirming spiritual father. The
loneliness Tom experienced in childhood was replaced with knowing
that the Blessed Mother was there for him, and the abandonment Janet
experienced from her father was lessoned by knowing that St. Joseph
was always there and would help her heal this wound. Their devotion
to the Holy Family also helped Tom and Janet forgive their parents.

Their support groups helped Tom and Janet in their relationships
with God. They supported Tom and Janet as they grieved over the loss
of their old marriage and encouraged them not to lose hope in God's
plan for a better marriage. Seeing how God brought healing and restoration to other marriages that were rocked by pornography increased
their hope and trust that God would do the same for them.

Developing a deeper relationship with God took several months,
but as this relationship grew, they began to see Him as a loving Father
who never abandoned them. He was there to heal their wounds and
help them create a newer, healthier marriage. It required them to trust
God and each other, and it actually amazed them to see how God
could take a marriage that was on the brink of ending and turn it into a
new creation!

Point 6: Education

Knowledge is power. Most people enter recovery lost and frightened. They know very little about the addiction and are unsure of their future, which is particularly scary for couples. An important part of recovery is education. Couples need to learn about pornography addiction, how pornography affects the brain, what it does to wives and marriages, and what the recovery process entails. Knowing what they are dealing with reduces their fears and strengthens their confidence in their ability to recover.

Education begins in therapy. The therapist takes time to educate the couple and assigns them various resources to read, listen to, or watch, some for men, some for women, and some for the couple to use together. A full list of resources for couples is listed in the appendix. Support groups also provide educational literature, particularly on the twelve steps.

For Tom and Janet, I first recommended they read through my website: www.IntegrityRestored.com and my first book, *The Pornography Epidemic: A Catholic Approach*. I also recommended they read *In the Shadows of the Net: Breaking Free of Compulsive Online Behavior*. This gave them a basic understanding of the addiction and recovery process. I then recommended Tom read *Wired for Intimacy: How Pornography Hijacks the Male Brain*, and for Janet I recommended *Shattered Vows: Hope and Healing for Women Who Have Been Sexually Betrayed*. Because they were eager to learn as much as they could about this issue, they even read each other's books. Tom gained a much better understanding of how pornography use deeply hurts wives, which further strengthened his resolve never to hurt Janet that way again. Educating herself on how men get trapped in pornography addiction helped Janet to be able to forgive Tom and see him as a victim of a vicious industry that wants to enslave men and ruin marriages, all for profit.

To further their understanding even more on how the pornography industry hurts women, especially the weak and vulnerable, I recommended *Pornland: How Porn has Hijacked Our Sexuality*. After reading that, Tom never again wanted to support an industry that damages innocent women, and Janet was able to let go of her anger toward the women in pornography as she began to see them as true victims.

Couples also need to educate themselves about healthy relationships. Most couples discover in therapy that they never had a healthy relationship to begin with. They learn about caring and respecting one another, as well as forgiveness, trust, communication, romance, friendship, and teamwork. Using recommended resources can help them in this process. I recommended a Marriage Encounter weekend for Tom and Janet, which helped them improve their communication and grow in intimacy. I also recommended reading *The Five Love Languages* and *The Love Dare*, which gave them tangible ways to show their love for one another.

The same holds true for sexuality. Unfortunately most people do not receive a healthy sexual education, and what they receive at home and at school is limited at best. Most of what people learn about sex comes from "the street," and today it's often from pornography. In therapy I discussed with Tom and Janet what healthy sexuality is all about, referring often to Pope St. John Paul II's *The Theology of the Body*. I recommended conferences and resources provided by The Theology of the Body Institute.

This was a radical paradigm shift for both Janet and Tom. While it took several months for Janet to feel comfortable having sex with Tom again, knowing that they both had a clear understanding of healthy sexuality helped her move forward through this intimate area of their marriage. For years, Janet rarely enjoyed sex. She felt used by Tom and viewed sex as something she needed to endure as part of her "wifely duty." Now, for the first time, Janet began to really enjoy sex with her husband. Instead of feeling used, she felt that Tom was truly giving himself to her as a gift, and this also enabled her to respond in kind. They learned through the Church's teaching that every time they engaged in sexual intercourse they were renewing their marital vows. Sex became a celebration of their love for each other and for God.

Other areas of education included helping Tom learn how to deal with work stress, burnout, and finding a new career.

Point 7: Virtue

This point sets this program apart from all other programs and makes it uniquely Catholic. It's based on Positive Psychology and the writings of Pope St. John Paul II. Living a virtuous life has been found to be very healing for individuals and for couples. It helps with forgiveness and restoring trust and becoming the people God created us to be. As shown in chapter ten, there are many virtues and character strengths in which we can grow to become better individuals, spouses, couples, parents, families, and communities.

Several years ago, Tom Brokaw wrote an excellent book entitled *The Greatest Generation*. In this book he chronicled the men and women who fought in World War II, discussing how men would eagerly enlist in the military knowing they would be sent into battle and could die. Why would so many men do this? The answer is simple: duty. These men had a well-developed understanding of what was right and were willing to defend it. They never whined or complained. These men lived highly virtuous lives. Those who returned from the war alive and those who lost their lives were treated as heroes because they were willing to sacrifice everything for a greater good. The men who returned alive got married, went to work, and dutifully supported their families. At the end of their lives they were able to look back with much joy and satisfaction. Despite the many challenges and suffering they encountered, they were able to say they lived happy, fulfilling lives. These highly virtuous men knew it was their duty to be leaders, providers, and protectors. They became the men God created them to be. This is how living a virtuous life can benefit a person.

I gave Tom and Janet the virtue worksheet and they made the commitment to work on these together. The first week they chose honesty and forgiveness, and every evening they talked about how they were able to practice their virtues. As they worked on growing in virtue, they realized how much they needed to improve on it and how it could help them. Discussing the virtues improved their communication and emotional intimacy.

Tom's deep desire was to be the best husband and father he could be. He wanted to be a man that Janet and their children could be proud of. He wanted to be the leader, provider, and protector God was calling him to be. Working on virtue gave him a road map to achieve this and it became part of his Vision for Life and their Vision for Marriage. He now had a life goal, a mission. Growing in virtue also helped Janet see that he was trustworthy.

Janet wanted to be able to forgive and restore trust in Tom, and seeing him diligently work on living a virtuous life helped rebuild that trust. She also saw great strength in Tom that she never saw before, and this helped her tremendously to feel safer with him now than she ever did before. As Janet worked on growing in virtue, she also saw it as key to becoming a better person, wife, and mother. It helped her to have more empathy for others and to forgive those who hurt her, especially Tom.

The End Result

While I provided an overview of Tom and Janet's healing process, please realize that this took many months. Tom needed time to overcome his compulsive sexual behavior and Janet needed time to recover from her trauma, anger, sadness, and betrayal. She had to grieve the loss of the marriage she thought she had, embrace the marriage she did have, and work on creating the marriage she wanted to have. As they worked on their recovery, their love for each other grew. Tom was able to show his trustworthiness through his devotion to his recovery program, and by being totally open and honest with Janet, she in turn was able to forgive Tom and grow in trust. They reached a deeper level of intimacy than they had ever known as they worked on creating their new healthy marriage. Their love for the Lord also grew as they came to see how God could heal the most broken people and marriages and give them a new life together. Tom and Janet eventually began reaching out to other couples in recovery to help them see that healing and restoration of a broken marriage is possible. They wanted to show their thanks and gratitude to God and to all the people who helped them, by "paying it forward."

Obstacles to Recovery for Couples

Most couples truly want to recover from addiction and its harmful effects, but there are clear obstacles that can inhibit healing and restoration. While these obstacles can be deduced from all the above that we covered in the recovery process, I think it's important to spell out these distinct obstacles that can thwart a couple's recovery.

- *Lack of Empathy.* Spouses must have empathy for each other. Wives need to realize that their addicted husbands are victims of a terrible disease, that their pornography addiction is not simply a moral failing by bad people. Addicted people are good people trapped in their compulsive behaviors. Husbands need to acknowledge how deeply their addiction has hurt their wives. Empathy strengthens their resolve to recover and heal the marriage.

- *Lack of Forgiveness.* It is totally understandable that a wife would be angry with her husband because of his pornography use. He has betrayed her and broken their marital vows. Hers is a justified anger. Holding onto the anger, however, will not help the healing process. Initially it may provide a sense of power, but it eventually turns back on the angry spouse and consumes her like a cancer. True healing and restoration only occurs if anger is resolved. Husbands also need to let go of any anger they may be harboring, which may have played a key role in their addiction. Resolving anger through forgiveness is crucial for recovery.

- *Lack of Honesty and Transparency.* Betrayal of trust is the deepest wound caused by addiction and it must be restored in order to heal. This requires the addicted individual to be totally open and honest with their spouse. They must be able to account for their actions and whereabouts twenty-four hours a day. Any suspicion will thwart growth in trust. Husbands who are unwilling to have all their actions monitored will not recover from their addiction or heal their marriages.

- *Unwillingness to Identify and Resolve Root Causes of Addiction.* Because addiction is often the result of using substances to ease the pain of deep emotional wounds, it is imperative these wounds be identified and resolved for healthy recovery. Many people resist identifying root causes for fear of what they might find or have to face in resolving them. For example, it might mean admitting that one was abused or abandoned as a child. It takes courage to face these issues and resolve them, and with the help of a therapist and support group, one can find the courage needed to identify and resolve root causes of their addiction.

- *Untreated Trauma.* For many addicted to porn, their use of it was an attempt to cope with the pain of trauma, whether caused by abuse, rejection, abandonment, divorce, family addictions, or other means. Spouses may also struggle from the trauma because of their husbands' addiction. Trauma must be properly diagnosed and treated by a qualified therapist in order for healing and recovery to occur.

- *Unwillingness to Get Help.* Unfortunately there are husbands and wives who refuse to get help. Some addicted persons simply refuse to admit there is a problem and see nothing wrong with using pornography. For some husbands, their wives are the ones with the problem and should simply accept their pornography use. This is beyond narcissistic. Then there are wives who refuse to get help for their wounds. They believe they shouldn't have to do any work because their husband caused all the problems. These women tend to hold onto their anger and mistrust, which eventually leads them to become more bitter and resentful. Unless these spouses confront their issues and get help, their marriages are doomed and often in need of ultimatums to get their attention.

Hope for the Future

The healing process takes time and hard work, but I encourage couples not to be afraid of it. Remember that God has not forgotten you. He has a wonderful plan for your marriage, one of healing and restoration. You will have to work on healing individual and marital wounds, but it is worth all the effort. I like to compare the restoration of marriages to the restoration of Jerusalem in the Book of Nehemiah in the Old Testament. The work was slow, but the Israelites worked steadily. They did not let enemies thwart their progress. They persevered and eventually restored Jerusalem to an even greater glory. God will do the same for your marriage if you have faith and persevere!

12

God's Plan for Sexuality

Owen and Liz were in my office for a couple's session. They had been dating for four years and were engaged to be married when Liz discovered Owen's addiction to pornography. She felt very hurt and betrayed that Owen would keep such a secret from her. Liz still loved Owen and wanted to marry him; however, she didn't want to bring the addiction into their marriage. A large part of their recovery was learning about healthy sexuality. While they both agreed that pornography had warped Owen's view of it, they didn't realize they both had been seriously misinformed about *healthy* sexuality.

Owen and Liz met while they were in college. They were both raised in Catholic homes and attended Mass regularly, but neither of them received any sexual education at home. Instead, their views on sexuality were heavily influenced by the culture. Owen attended public schools and received sex education there, but it was not values based. He knew all about reproduction, yet little about relationships. The main focus seemed to be on having "responsible sex." In his words, what he took away from this was, "If you're going to have sex, use a condom." Liz attended Catholic schools. She had sex education that was values based but incomplete. She was also presented the Church's views on sexuality but was never given the reasons for the Church's teachings. Consequently, she thought the Church's teachings were developed by "a bunch of cranky old men who had serious hang-ups about sex." Naturally, this made it easy to reject the Church's teachings. Liz felt that it was okay to have sex outside of marriage as long as "you really love the person you have sex with." She also saw nothing wrong with contraception.

American culture strongly shaped their views on sexuality. In the media many unwed couples are depicted in sexual relationships. Owen and Liz came to see this as normal and even healthy. Most of their single friends were sexually active and many who were dating were living together. In fact, living together and being sexually active was seen as a natural step toward getting married; moreover, the culture had them believing that a good way to judge the health of a relationship was by evaluating how satisfying the sex was. It's not hard to see why it was easy for Owen and Liz to become sexually active soon after they began dating. They were even planning on moving in together before she discovered his addiction. But after her discovery she called off the engagement and ended all sexual activity with him.

Neither Owen nor Liz had any qualms with using contraception when they were sexually active. They saw it as being responsible toward each other and society. They appeared to see nothing wrong with any form of sexuality or any sexual acts, with the exception of incest and sex with children. They wanted to appear sophisticated and open-minded when it came to sexuality, and so they even attended the commitment ceremony of two lesbian friends. However, it was revealed later that they actually were uncomfortable with much of the sexuality they saw in society.

Because of his poor sex education, most of what Owen learned about sex came from pornography, particularly Internet pornography. By now you well know the thought process: women love being sexually dominated by men, love the type of sex portrayed in pornography, and can't get enough of it. Own became interested in deviant forms of sex, including bondage. He didn't know what healthy sex was much less how to have a healthy sex life.

Liz loved Owen and enjoyed being sexual with him; however, she couldn't help feeling that somehow sex kept him from making a firm commitment to their relationship. Sometimes she felt that Owen was just using her. She put up with it because she believed that "men offer a relationship to get sex and women offer sex to get a relationship." This was the advice she often got from popular women's magazines. Liz thought that sex was the key element needed to get a husband, and while she enjoyed intercourse, she also engaged in sexual acts that felt degrading to her. This included performing oral sex on Owen, receiving anal sex, and participating in role-playing games where she was sexually dominated by Owen. She tolerated it because she felt it was needed to get a husband. She admitted this made her angry at times and she wished that she could dominate Owen sexually just to see how he liked it!

Despite being heavily influenced by the culture, Liz somehow sensed there was a problem with their sex life. To understand how Owen, Liz, and millions of other Americans got to this place, please review "How We Got Here" in chapter one (pp. 26–28).

Where, precisely, are we? We have crossed a new threshold to a perverted view of sex and relationships as the new norm. Birth control pills allow people to have sex at any time without responsibility or consequences or moral concerns. All cultural and religious values regarding sex have been replaced with narcissistic, hedonistic, and relativistic views (Reclaim, 2013). Sex is all about me (narcissistic). The primary purpose of sex is pleasure (hedonistic). This personal pleasure excludes being open to new life or even being in love. It's all about achieving the perfect orgasm or having as much sex with as many partners as possible. It doesn't exclude experimenting with deviant forms of sexuality that are risky and even deadly. This hedonistic attitude in sexuality can be seen on websites where people place personal ads for sex, as well as in online chatting, sexting, and social media for sexual pleasure. No one is wrong (relativistic) and just about any kind of sex is accepted including, group sex, swinging, homosexuality, bondage, domination, fetishes, bestiality, necrophilia, and rape role-playing sex. The Internet is full of pornographic websites that cater to those desires. There are no more rules. It's a free-for-all. To see how relativism has replaced morality in sexuality, see www.AshleyMadison.com, which promotes extramarital affairs for people who are not happy in their marriages. Their motto is *Life is short. Have an Affair.*

If anyone objects to the new norm, they are being prudish, judgmental, and closed-minded. However, the long-term effects of this newfound sexual freedom are devastating: an exponential increase in divorce, broken families, sexually transmitted diseases, unplanned pregnancies, teen pregnancies, abortion, and wounded hearts. Many of the new "liberated" women feel used and tossed aside.

The sexual narcissism, hedonism, and relativism of our culture have injured people's ability to have healthy relationships. The influence of radical feminism has led women to reject their God-given feminine traits, such as warmth, nurturance, sensitivity, and receptivity. They have replaced these with anger and aggression. Men, having discarded their God-given drive to be leaders, providers, and protectors, have been emasculated and weakened. It's as if men and women have switched roles. The number of young people who want to make the commitment to marriage and to raising children keeps falling. Marriage and children are seen as confining. Happiness is seen as the ability to come and go as one pleases and to do whatever one pleases.

Like many of their young peers, Owen and Liz bought into this modern, liberated view of sexuality. It was supposed to be healthy and contribute to a happy relationship. The exact opposite happened! Owen ended up addicted to pornography and Liz ended up feeling used and betrayed. After a long discussion of how cultural views toward sexuality have actually become unhealthy over the past fifty years, Owen and Liz were eager to learn exactly what healthy sexuality was.

The True Purpose of Sex

As Catholics, we need to turn to the God who created sexuality to understand sexuality. Who better to turn to for answers? Scripture and Church Tradition tell us a lot about God's plan for sexuality, but one of the best sources of information that I will refer to throughout this chapter is St. John Paul II's *The Theology of the Body*. According to Christopher West (2004), *The Theology of the Body* is "the study of how God reveals his mystery through the human body." Through our bodies and our sexuality, God reveals His great love for us and His plan for all humanity!

Created in God's Image

To understand this plan, we need to go back to the beginning in Scripture. In Genesis 1:26–28 we read, "Then God said, 'Let us make man in our image, after our likeness; and let them have dominion over the fish of the sea, and over the birds of the air, and over the cattle, and over all the earth, and over every creeping thing that creeps upon the earth.' So God created man in his own image, in the image of God he created him; male and female he created them. And God blessed them, and God said to them, 'Be fruitful and multiply, and fill the earth and subdue it; and have dominion over the fish of the sea and over the birds of the air and over every living thing that moves upon the earth.'"

In this passage, "our image" refers to the Trinity. God loves us so much that He created us in His image. He also instructs us to "be fruitful and multiply." As we will later see, in addition to procreation, this also refers to God's love because it is always giving. Love expands and multiplies. Furthermore, our value and dignity is so great that He places us above all other creatures giving us dominion over all. This is confirmation of how we are "wondrously made" (Psalms 139:14)!

Created in God's image also means we were created to reflect the love of the Trinity. To do this, God created mankind as male and female. In Genesis 2:18–25 we read:

> Then the Lord God said, "It is not good that the man should be alone; I will make him a helper fit for him." So out of the ground the Lord God formed every beast of the field and every bird of the air, and brought them to the man to see what he would call them; and whatever the man called every living creature, that was its name. The man gave names to all cattle, and to the birds of the

269

air, and to every beast of the field; but for the man there was not found a helper fit for him. So the Lord God caused a deep sleep to fall upon the man, and while he slept took one of his ribs and closed up its place with flesh; and the rib which the Lord God had taken from the man he made into a woman and brought her to the man. Then the man said, "This at last is bone of my bones and flesh of my flesh; she shall be called Woman, because she was taken out of Man." Therefore a man leaves his father and his mother and clings to his wife, and they become one flesh. And the man and his wife were both naked, and were not ashamed.

A Communion of Love

God is love. He not only loves us, but He is a communion of three Persons in the Trinity, which is an eternal exchange of love. According to John Paul II, a communion is a "common union" of persons who mutually give of themselves to each other in love and service. The Father begets the Son by giving Himself to and for the Son. The Son receives that love and returns it. The love they share is the Holy Spirit, which proceeds from the Father and Son. God created us to share in that love. He didn't need to create us, but love is ever giving and it desires to expand its own communion. Thus, God created us as male and female so we could reflect that beautiful exchange of love found in the Trinity. When a husband and wife engage in sexual intercourse, they reflect the deep intimate love of the Father and Son. This love can create new life in the form of children, which reflects the Holy Spirit, who proceeds from the love of the Father and the Son. Just as the Father and Son are one with the Holy Spirit, a husband and wife become one in sexual union and from that they become one with their children (West, 2004).

In addition to reflecting the love of the Trinity, sexual love also reflects the love of God for humanity. Christ's outpouring of Himself as a sacrifice for the Church is a new outpouring of the Trinity's love. The Church receives this love and attempts to return it by loving God and neighbor.

God the Bridegroom

Throughout Scripture God often uses the analogy of spousal love to describe His love for us. This is vividly portrayed in the Song of Solomon. God has a deep desire to be one with all humanity, and is frequently referred to as the "Bridegroom" with the Church as His bride (cf. John 3:29; Mark 2:19; Revelation 22:17; Ephesians 5:29; CCC 796). He is the Giver and the Church is the receiver. God wants to impregnate us with His divine love. This ever-giving love leads us to want to love God in return, and out of this comes new life. This is why the Church views sex as holy. It is a celebration of love between a husband and wife, and a celebration of God's love for all humanity. It is a foretaste of the incredibly intimate relationship we will have with God in heaven. Sex is "unitive" because it unites a husband and wife physically, emotionally, and spiritually. It is "procreative" because it can create new life. This is the same type of love God has with humanity. It is unitive because it unites us to God, and procreative because through God's love He creates new life (West, 2004).

Nakedness without Shame

Understanding the verse "And the man and his wife were both naked, and were not ashamed" (Genesis 2:25) is key to understanding God's original plan for humanity. After the Fall, Adam and Eve wore fig leaves because they experienced shame. According to John Paul II, prior to the Fall they had perfect love for each other. It was a free, sincere, and total gift of self. Sexual desire wasn't experienced as a drive for self-gratification. "They saw God's love inscribed in their naked bodies—and that's exactly what they desired—to love as God loves in and through their bodies. And there is no (shame) fear in love" (West, 2004). "[P]erfect love casts out fear" (1 John 4:18). In a healthy marriage, a couple can be physically and emotionally naked with each other without shame because they know they are loved unconditionally and don't fear being violated by the other. This is the way God loves the Church. Because He loves us totally and unconditionally we need not fear Him.

Nuptial Love

Prior to the Fall, Adam and Eve were "naked without shame" and were able to freely give themselves to one another. This is the nuptial meaning of love. Each person becomes a total gift that allows them to truly know each other, physically, mentally, emotionally, and spiritually. This type of knowing leads to generation: "Adam knew Eve his wife and she conceived" (Genesis 4:1). Thus, parenthood completely reveals the mystery of sexuality. When God commanded humanity to "be fruitful and multiply," He didn't simply mean to propagate our species. He is calling us to love in His image. This fulfills the very meaning of our being and existence, and brings us as bride (the Church/God's people) back to God as bridegroom. As the bridegroom, God gave Himself freely to humanity. As His bride, humanity freely receives Him. Man and woman reflect this exchange of love in their own marital self-giving, which is unitive and procreative.

The Effects of Sin

With sin came lust, the selfish desire to use another person for sexual pleasure. It is a deep violation of one's body and one's dignity. After the fall, Adam and Eve experienced shame. They realized how vulnerable they were to being violated by lust, and to protect themselves they wore fig leaves. Pornography violates God's plan for humanity because it promotes lust—using others for selfish pleasure. Christ emphasizes in the Sermon on the Mount, "You have heard that it was said, 'You shall not commit adultery.' But I say to you that everyone who looks at a woman lustfully has already committed adultery with her in his heart" (Matthew 5:27–28). He has violated her. This also applies to looking lustfully at one's wife. It violates God's plan for sexuality because lust can never be unitive or procreative, is entirely selfish, and never reflects the love of the Trinity that God so desires us to participate in. Pornography promotes lust as a way to increase or intensify sexuality; however, it can only lead to frustration and despair because it prevents man from experiencing the true meaning of sexuality—the total gift of self. This is true depravity.

The Real Gift

Christopher West (2004) notes, "Only a person who is free from the compulsion of lust is capable of being a true 'gift' to another. The 'freedom of the gift,' then, is the freedom to *bless*, which is the freedom from the compulsion to *grasp* and *possess*. It is the freedom that allowed the first couple to be naked without shame." Thus, by avoiding lust, man and woman can freely love as gifts to one another. They can be naked without shame. Through their unitive and procreative love, they can reflect the love of the Trinity and the love of God for all humanity. With each experience of sexual intercourse they renew their wedding vows. It is a foretaste of the great wedding celebration we will experience in heaven with God.

Healthy Sex

Now that we know the purpose of sex, one may ask, "What does a healthy sex life look like?" Sex is meant to be a wonderfully pleasurable experience for a married couple.

As a true gift of self it begins with submission. In Ephesians 5:21–24 we read, "Be subject to one another out of reverence for Christ. Wives, be subject to your husbands, as to the Lord. For the husband is the head of the wife as Christ is the head of the Church, his body, and is himself its Savior. As the Church is subject to Christ, so let wives also be subject in everything to their husbands." Many wives struggle with these verses because it defies the modern belief in equality between spouses. It portrays wives being subordinate and inferior to their husbands. However, if we read on, St. Paul is really talking about spouses mutually submitting to each other.

In Ephesians 5:25–33 we read,

> Husbands, love your wives, as Christ loved the Church and gave himself up for her, that he might sanctify her, having cleansed her by the washing of water with the word, that he might present the church to himself in splendor, without spot or wrinkle or any such thing, that she might be holy and without blemish. Even so husbands should love their wives as their own bodies. He who loves his wife loves himself. For no man ever hates his own flesh, but nourishes and cherishes it, as Christ does the Church, because we are members of his body. "For this reason a man shall leave his father and mother and be joined to his wife, and the two shall become one flesh." This is a great mystery, and I mean in reference to Christ and the Church; however, let each one of you love his wife as himself, and let the wife see that she respects her husband.

In these verses St. Paul actually challenges men more than women. Christopher West (2004) explains marital submission like this: "Wives, put yourself *under* (sub) the *mission* of your husband." What is the husband's mission? To love his wife as Christ loved the Church. What did Christ do for the Church? He died for it! For a husband, this is a serious form of submission because in order to submit he must die to himself and serve his wife. In directing men to love their wives as themselves, St. Paul is admonishing them to treat them as equals. A man who loves his wife as much as he loves himself doesn't love her more or less than himself. She is an equal.

In Luke 22:25–27 we read, "And he said to them, 'The kings of the Gentiles exercise lordship over them; and those in authority over them are called benefactors. But not so with you; rather let the greatest among you become as the youngest, and the leader as one who serves. For which is the greater, one who sits at table, or one who serves? Is it not the one who sits at table? But I am among you as one who serves." Being the head of the marriage and family doesn't mean that a husband lords his power over his wife. It means he lovingly serves her as leader, provider, and protector.

In order to have a healthy sex life, husbands and wives must both submit to and serve one another. They must love each other totally and freely give themselves to each other as a gift. Does this sound familiar? It's how God loves the Church!

When a couple gives of themselves to each other in sex, there is no lust. Neither uses the other for selfish pleasure. They participate in God's great love and plan for humanity. This love is free, total, faithful, and fruitful (West, 2004). These four principals are required for healthy sex, and as you will see, they also overlap with each other.

- *Free.* Just as Christ gives His body freely, spouses must give themselves freely to one another. There is no coercion to have sex. They can be naked without shame with each other. There is no fear of being violated in any way. They are safe with each other.

- *Total.* Christ gave Himself totally for the Church, even unto death! God wants spouses to have the same kind of love for each other. To love totally means to give without reservation, condition, selfishness, or violation. Sex is not used to control or manipulate. Overlapping with freedom, a person who feels safe with their spouse can give of themselves totally.

- *Faithful.* Most couples readily understand this principal. Christ is always faithful to His word. Couples must also have this fidelity to each other, and it is why the Church requires that couples be married before having sex. When a couple makes their wedding vows, they are saying, "I reserve myself for you only for the rest of my life." This is a true act of love. One can only give of himself as a total gift to one other person. A person cannot live a healthy life with a divided heart. By freely committing to be faithful to one's spouse for life, a person can freely and totally give of himself to his spouse. This commitment to one person also makes sexuality such a precious gift. It is reserved for the one person you will spend the rest of your life with.

- *Fruitful.* God's love is ever life-giving. It continually expands and multiplies. To participate in the love of the Trinity and God's love for humanity, the love between a husband and wife must be fruitful. When a couple is open to new life in their marriage, they are open to the love of God and all His gifts. Refusing to be fruitful means refusing God's love and blessings. This is why sex must be procreative as well as unitive, and is also why the Church is against contraception, which we will discuss more later.

Those four principles are not only required for healthy sex, they are also necessary for a healthy marital relationship. If you listen closely to what is said during a Catholic wedding ceremony, you will find that they are all addressed. The priest or deacon will ask the couple if they have freely chosen to be married, if they are willing to give of themselves totally to each other, and be faithful to one another for life. Finally, he will ask if they will openly accept children as gifts from God. Because a couple commits to these principles at their wedding ceremony, every time they have sex they renew their wedding vows. Couples who are aware of this find that sex is free, total, faithful, and fruitful, and it actually strengthens their love for each other and helps them maintain a healthy marriage and family.

It is easier to be chaste in marriage when a couple practices healthy sex. This means they not only reserve sex for their spouses, but they also have a clear understanding of the powerful meaning of sex and want to maintain it in their lives. For single people, understanding this helps them refrain from sexual activity until they are married. They want to preserve their sexuality as a gift for their future spouses, which will help ensure healthy marriages for them. People who are celibate for the kingdom understand that God will give them the grace to love freely, totally, faithfully, and fruitfully in a broader, nonsexual way. This is their fore-taste of the incredible love we will experience with God in heaven.

Sexual Activity

When the secular world speaks about healthy sex, they often refer to sexual activity in the bedroom. As you can see, God's plan for sexuality goes far beyond the basic mechanics of sex—there is deeper meaning and purpose, a richer and even mystical meaning. Thus, sex for a couple can be a rich and even mystical experience, and this strengthens their love and their marriage.

Many people believe the Church answers every question about sexual activity with a giant NO. The reality is that the Church says little about sexual activity. The basic rules are that sex should be free, total, faithful, and fruitful. Contraception should not be used and semen must ultimately be deposited in the vagina. In addition, couples should not engage in sexual acts that are risky or dangerous. This leaves a lot to the imagination! The Church is not against sex. It wants people to enjoy sex; however, it must be healthy sex.

There are some types of sexual activity to which the Church has some objections. These include the following:

- *Pornography.* As I've stated throughout this book, pornography is a mortal sin. It leads people to selfishly use others. Even if the performers and users of pornography are "consenting adults," everyone involved is still exploited for profit.

- *Masturbation.* God created sex to be a unitive and procreative expression of love between a husband and wife. Masturbation to orgasm for both men and women is neither unitive nor pro-creative. It is a selfish pursuit that cannot reflect the love of the Trinity or the love of God for humanity. Whether a person uses pornography or simply fantasizes during masturbation, the person is still objectifying others and using them for selfish pleasure. Some couples use masturbation as a form of stimulation or foreplay prior to intercourse. This may be necessary for sexual activity, and the Church allows this as long as ejaculation occurs in the vagina. Masturbation to orgasm is condoned for women whose husbands have climaxed before them during intercourse. However, couples should strive to climax together in intercourse. The Church does not condone mutual masturbation to orgasm simply for personal pleasure and as the culmination of sexual activity.

- *Contraception.* Married love is supposed to reflect the love of the Trinity and the love of God for humanity. This love is always directed toward new life. On the human level this openness to new life solidifies a marriage. It says, "I love you and God so much that I give all of myself without reservation." This is a true and total gift of self that prepares couples to raise children. When a couple separates sex from procreation they are saying, "I may love you and God, but not enough to give of myself totally." In this instance, sex even among spouses who love each other really becomes a selfish pursuit. Contraception has participated in leading our culture to believe that love and commitment are no longer needed for sex, which, as we have clearly witnessed, has turned sex into little more than recreational activity. We often see this in teens and young adults who go out on weekends looking for "hookup sex." This view ignores God's beautiful plan for sexuality and humanity. However, while sex must be open to new life, not every act of sexual intercourse needs to result in conception. I will speak more about this later.

- *Oral Sex.* As we discussed in chapter five, couples may partake in oral or manual genital stimulation as a form of foreplay; however, engaging in "oral sex" as the culmination of sexual activity is a grave matter of mortal sin. Furthermore, in my clinical experience, I have found that many women do not enjoy this, and while they may do it to please their husbands, they actually find it degrading. If during sexual intercourse the husband reaches a climax before his wife does, he may seek other forms of stimulation to bring his wife to "natural gratification." Pope John Paul II says that "if a woman does not obtain natural gratification from the sexual act there is a danger that her experience of it will be qualitatively inferior, will not involve her fully as a person" (*Love and Responsibility,* 273).

- *Anal Sex.* Some couples actually enjoy this form of sex. However, because it is not open to new life, anal sex cannot be performed to orgasm. Remember, ejaculation must occur in the vagina. I personally do not recommend anal sex. Contrary to popular opinion, the anus was never designed to be a sex organ and serious physical injury can occur from anal sex. In addition, many women do not enjoy this type of sex as it can be very painful. In my clinical experience, women who agree to participate in anal sex do so only to please their husbands. They feel it is degrading and that their husbands are simply using them as sex toys.

- *Homosexuality.* While society has declared homosexuality a "normal variation in human sexuality," the Church disagrees. The Church understands that God created two sexes for more than just procreating. There is an incredible complementarity between men and women. Like two pieces of a puzzle, they fit together perfectly—physically, emotionally, and spiritually. The love between a man and woman is meant to reflect the love of the Trinity and the love of God for humanity. God's relationship with His people has always been portrayed as a marriage between a man and a woman, with God as the bridegroom and the Church as His bride. Because this love is seen as a relationship between two sexes, it cannot be reflected in same-sex relationships. This may be why such relationships typically don't last long. The procreative aspect of the two sexes also reflects the life-giving love of God. Because same-sex couples cannot procreate as God intended, they cannot reflect God's love. This unitive and procreative love is also necessary for healthy families. The Church and current research recognize that the healthiest environment to raise children is with a mother and a father who are in a loving, committed marriage (USCCB, n.d.; The Family Research Council, n.d.). Unfortunately, many Christians, even entire denominations, have chosen to disregard God's plan for sexuality and have accepted homosexuality.

God created everyone with a natural sense of the proper order of nature. People may claim to be free-thinking and open-minded, but when it comes to human sexuality, most would admit that homosexuality is neither natural nor God's plan for humanity. This may be why many people are uncomfortable around people who live active homosexual lifestyles.

While the Church views *homosexuality* as a disorder, it clearly states that *homosexual persons* are still beloved children of God who deserve our love and respect. We may disagree with their lifestyle, but the Church does not condone insults, ridicule, or violence against them. The Church admonishes those with same-sex attractions to live holy lives of chaste celibacy, even though it can be very difficult for them. In their nonsexual love and service to others, they can reflect God's love and experience it personally. We need to love and support those who choose to live such heroic lives (CCC 2357–59).

Natural Family Planning

Many people who have heard about Natural Family Planning (NFP) are afraid to use it. They fear it is not as effective as contraception because they confuse it with the old "rhythm method," which can be ineffective. When properly used, NFP is over 98% effective (Creighton Model, 2006). Condoms aren't as effective because they are often improperly used and can break (NFP & More, n.d.). While the contraceptive pill, Norplant, and IUD have similar effectiveness, they fill a woman's body with hormones, which can have harmful side effects. NFP prevents a woman from having to take hormonal contraceptives, which can have many harmful side effects. Another benefit of NFP is that it requires a couple to work together in planning their sexual activity, and this actually improves their communication and intimacy. Many women can resent having to use artificial birth control because they feel they are left solely responsible for family planning and dealing with the side effects of contraceptives, while their husbands are reaping all the benefits.

It's true that couples cannot have sex whenever they desire by using NFP, but this is actually beneficial to them as individuals and as a couple because it requires them to exercise self-control. There are fertile days for women during a month when they cannot have sexual intercourse without the possibility of conceiving. During those days they are encouraged to work on their emotional intimacy, which can be done by going on dates, talking about their relationship, planning their future, working on projects together, and other such mutual activities. Many have found that these moments actually help strengthen their marriages.

While NFP often is used to avoid conception, it can be used to plan conception. NFP helps a couple understand the woman's fertility cycle, and knowing when she is most fertile can help a couple plan intercourse for the greatest possibility of conceiving. NFP can also help detect physical problems, such as hormonal imbalances, that can impede conception or contribute to miscarriages.

Some Catholics refuse to use NFP because they view it as a sinful form of contraception that uses a woman's fertility cycle to purposely remove the procreative aspect from every act of intercourse. They believe that all acts of sexual intercourse must be open to the conception of a new life. The Church, however, disagrees. While couples need to be open to new life in their marriages, they also need to be responsible in planning their family. There may be physical, emotional, or financial issues that make conception imprudent, and therefore it may be wiser to wait to conceive. God created a woman's body to be fertile only during a certain time of the month, and thus conception—naturally—will not occur with every act of intercourse. Couples use NFP in conformity with the way that God naturally made women, and thus exercise prudence in planning for children (CCC 2370).

The Spiritual Battle

While our culture has contributed much to the breakdown of sexual morality, we need to acknowledge the vast spiritual attack fueling it. If our sexuality reflects the love of the Trinity and God's love for humanity, what better way for Satan to attack God and us than to attack sexuality? By perverting it he defiles God's entire plan for humanity. If we are unable to reflect God's love or fully cooperate in His plan for humanity, we cannot become the people God created us to be. Instead of being total gifts to each other as God is to His Church, we use sex in very narcissistic, hedonistic, and relativistic ways. Conversely, by choosing to use our sexuality as God planned, we are thwarting Satan's attack in our lives. By helping others understand God's plan for healthy sexuality, we are helping others win this spiritual battle. If we simply give into the cultural view of sexuality, Satan wins the battle (West, 2004). Ultimately, we know that at the end of time God reigns victorious over Satan. Satan knows this, but until then he wants to gain as many human casualties as possible. We can reduce his casualties by refusing to accept society's view of sexuality and by clinging to God's view.

The Gift of Sexuality

Sexuality is a wonderful gift from God and a gift we give to our spouse. It is the one thing that is so precious that it is reserved for one person we choose to love for the rest of our lives in marriage. It is not something that is to be randomly given to multiple people, and in my experience, when people finally understand this, they protect their sexuality and refuse to give it away to just anyone. They decide to save it for the time when God can truly bless them in their sexuality and marriage. This is what happened with Owen and Liz.

Back to Owen and Liz

It took a while for Owen and Liz to fully grasp God's plan for sexuality, but when they finally understood it, they decided to wait until they were married to be sexually active again. I refer to this as a "renewed virginity." Although they still planned on getting married, they chose not to set a wedding date or plan their wedding for six months, and cancelled their plans to move in together before marriage. They wanted to use that time to restart their relationship and make it a healthy one. They both wanted their sexuality to be a gift they would give to one another in marriage alone.

Not being sexual enabled them to have a healthy relationship where they could truly get to know one another, improve their communication, and deepen their intimacy in non-sexual ways. Sure, it was difficult for them at times, but making the sacrifice to be pure strengthened their relationship and love for one another.

Liz was happier because she could finally stop taking birth control pills that her mother insisted she take as a "precaution" ever since she was sixteen. She resented having to be the only "responsible" one in their relationship and having to deal with the side effects of hormonal contraceptives, and she feared the possible long-term effects. Liz finally felt like Owen was an equal partner in their relationship and even admitted that she was enjoying this "old fashioned" courtship. She was being respected and treated like a lady.

Owen was happier because he now knew what Liz really wanted in their relationship, and he wanted to be that man she desired and needed in her life. He focused on winning her heart and her trust again by living a virtuous life. They not only fell more deeply in love romantically, they also became best friends. They could tell each other anything. Just the fact that Owen was no longer carrying any secrets about his sexual activity helped tremendously.

Initially it was difficult for Owen and Liz to tell their friends about their decisions. Many thought they were crazy and had become prudes, as most of their engaged and married friends lived together before marriage in order to "test the waters to ensure a successful marriage." Yet many of their married friends were getting divorced. Owen and Liz could see that "testing the waters" by living together and being sexual prior to marriage was not a good way to find the right spouse. They could see that sex outside of marriage was really hurting relationships and keeping couples from getting to know each other emotionally and spiritually. Owen and Liz related how their friends actually admired them for their self-control, and they even suspected that some of their friends seemed jealous of what they had together, especially those whose relationships had broken up.

Owen and Liz grew in their relationship and began to see the many ways God was blessing them. They returned to the Mass and the sacraments. Instead of a "destination wedding" in the Caribbean, they chose to have a church wedding at their parish. They also joined a young adult Bible study group and began to pray together.

Final Thoughts

Following God's plan for sexuality is not easy in today's culture, but when it's understood and embraced, couples begin to see how the world's view of sexuality actually enslaves people in pain and misery. In contrast, God provides a plan for a healthy, happy life that includes great sex! It does require faith, self-control, humility, deference, generosity, commitment, and a willingness to sacrifice. It may seem unconventional by today's standards, but believe me, it's the path to true sexual freedom!

In this chapter I have provided an overview of God's plan for sexuality, but there is much more to learn. For more in-depth information, I recommend studying Pope St. John Paul II's *The Theology of the Body* and *Love and Responsibility*. Two great books to complement those are *Theology of the Body for Beginners* (2004) and *Good News about Sex and Marriage* (2004), both by Christopher West. The Theology of the Body Institute also offers excellent resources on marriage and sexuality at www.tobinstitute.org.

13

Protecting Children from Pornography

I n chapter six we looked at the harmful effects of pornography
on children (pp. 121–124). In this chapter let's discuss effective
strategies to help parents protect their children from pornography.
Teachers, clergy, and youth workers can also use these strategies. Most
adults would agree that pornography is harmful to children. I don't
know of any good parent who would allow their children to view it.
They want to protect their children from it.

Because the average age a child first encounters Internet pornography today is eleven, I divide kids into two age groups—those under
the age of eleven and those eleven and older. Children under the age of
eleven must be *protected* from pornography so that they never encounter it. This chapter presents strategies to accomplish that. Children
eleven and older must be *taught to reject* pornography. The next chapter
will discuss ways to train those eleven and older to reject it.

Strategies for Protecting Children

1. Don't be naïve. As you have read throughout this book, everyone is at risk for being exposed to pornography. Unfortunately,
   there are parents who believe that children are too young to be
   affected by pornography. Research and common sense speak
   differently. Parents must educate themselves on the dangers of
   pornography so they can effectively protect their children.

2. Educate yourself on computer technology and the Internet. Children today have never known a world without the Internet. Technology is an integral part of their lives. If parents are going to protect their children, they need to know what technology kids are using and how they are using it. Spend time with your kids on the computer and observe them using various electronic gadgets. You will learn a lot!

3. Monitor all media that enters your home. Pornographic material can enter the home in many ways, and children today are more affected by mass media than ever before. Parents need to be aware of what media their children are exposed to and monitor it carefully.

   - Television. Every year children spend thousands of hours watching television. However, over the past forty years the number of sexual references in television has risen exponentially. Even "family shows" now contain sexual references. It's as if the censors in Hollywood simply gave up and went home. As parents, you need to decide which shows and networks are appropriate for your children and which ones are not. You may need to block certain shows or entire networks to protect your children, as well as limiting the amount of time your children view television. I recommend no more than two hours a day. Parents should also avoid using the TV as a babysitter.

     In addition to monitoring what children watch, parents need to set a good example with their own television viewing, which means not viewing anything offensive, including trashy sitcoms, violent police dramas, risqué reality shows, soap operas, etc. I also don't recommend channel surfing, which obviously can lead to viewing inappropriate or offensive shows. If children are around, even viewing it for only a minute or two can have an impact on them. Channel surfing is also a bad habit that children pick up by observing their parents. Thus, it's best for parents to simply get into the habit of not channel surfing. Most cable and satellite television systems have guide channels where one can find out what's on TV without having to channel surf.

- Movies. Even G-rated movies today can have sexual references. Hollywood seems to believe that unless a movie has some sexual content, it won't sell. Research has shown that there is an 87% chance that a typical movie will have some sexual content (Kaiser, 2001), and so parents need to monitor the movies their children view at home and in the movie theater. Fortunately, the Catholic News Service rates movies for offensive content so that parents can ensure their children don't view anything inappropriate. See www. CatholicNews.com/Movies.

  As with television, parents need to set a good example with the movies they view. This means not viewing any films with a rating of PG-13 or above.

- Mail/Catalogs. While email has replaced much of the "snail mail" we receive, there is still plenty of junk mail that ends up in our mailboxes. This includes advertisements and catalogs, many of which include racy lingerie ads that are inappropriate for children to see. Many children enjoy getting the mail from the mailbox for their parents, but I advise against this. Parents need to be the ones who get the mail and sort out anything inappropriate. Offensive material should be shredded immediately and offensive catalogs should be sent back to the retailer. Those retailers should also be notified to remove your name and address from their mailing list.

- Newspapers and Magazines. Many people don't realize how offensive a newspaper can be; however, a quick look at the ads will show how much sex is used to sell products. This is most noticeable around Christmas and St. Valentine's Day when newspapers are full of racy lingerie ads. Many newspapers also have "personals" sections where provocative ads for escort services are listed. Magazines must also be monitored, especially men's magazines, provocative women's magazines, and Hollywood tabloids. When most people think about pornography in magazines, they think of *Playboy* and *Penthouse*, but popular men's magazines can also be pornographic. For example, *Details*, a popular men's style magazine, is known for having photos of scantily clad women. The publisher of *Sports Illustrated* Swimsuit Issue may claim it celebrates physical fitness in women, but any intelligent person knows it is a marketing ploy that uses sex to sell subscriptions. Provocative women's magazines, such as *Cosmopolitan,* are just as pornographic. In addition to risqué photography they include pornographic stories and articles. These types of magazines must never enter the home. Even if parents think they have hidden these magazines well, I guarantee that curious kids will eventually find them!

• Internet. While monitoring the Internet is a no-brainer for most parents, many are clueless as to how to protect their kids from Internet pornography. Many computers offer free parent controls to help protect kids. However, I have found many of these systems to be weak and easy to circumvent. Remember, children are often more technologically savvy than their parents, so parents need to research various filtering systems to identify the one(s) that will work best for them. Again, I recommend the filtering service offered by www.CovenantEyes.com, and for additional information on how to protect children from Internet pornography, I recommend *Unfiltered: A Parent Workshop Kit* by Covenant Eyes (2013). This kit contains a DVD, Workshop Guide, and Parent How-To Guide, and can be purchased at www.covenanteyes.com.

- Music. The music industry also believes "sex sells." The lyrics of popular songs have become increasingly sexually explicit. Pop, heavy metal, rap, hip-hop and R&B music are filled with foul language and sexually explicit verses, and anyone who has grown up with MTV knows how sexual music videos can be. To be successful today, it appears that a performer need not have much talent. A hot body is more important. The sexualization of music has been going on for decades. Years ago when I was in college I worked cleaning an elementary school that hosted a summer camp for children. On rainy days the kids would play inside, and one day the kids were allowed to bring in their favorite record albums. I was shocked to see eight-year-old girls listening to Madonna's music and dancing in provocative ways. The camp counselors saw nothing wrong with this, and one can only imagine what the mother who purchased the album for her daughter was thinking. This happened back in 1987. We all know that things have gotten much worse since then. Parents need to be careful about what enters their children's ears. Today many kids are downloading a lot of inappropriate music onto iPods, MP3 players, computers, and cell phones. Parents need to weed this out and also clean up their own music. Kids are just as technologically savvy at finding your music library! The radio is also a danger, especially when a parent driving may not be paying too much attention to it. Instead of listening to popular music, which can be very offensive, I recommend families listen to classical and jazz music. While pop, hip-hop, rap, R&B, and heavy metal can agitate children, classical music calms them.

- Video Games. Many parents are worried about the violence in video games, but they are unaware that these games can also be very pornographic. Before parents allow their children to play any video game, they should play it themselves to see if it is appropriate. Parents shouldn't depend on ratings alone. Several websites review video games for parents and can help identify which games are appropriate for children and which ones are not. An excellent website to help parents evaluate video games is www. FamilyFriendlyVideoGames.com.

Parents also need to beware of video gaming systems such as Xbox, Wii, and PlayStation. Since many of these games are accessed through the Internet, children can accidently access Internet pornography while searching for games.

Many young parents today grew up with video games and continue to play them. It is a part of their culture. As with all other forms of entertainment media, they need to set a good example for their children. Sexually explicit and violent video games should be shunned.

4. Keep the computer in a public area of the home. This is a common piece of advice that many people hear, but few follow. If the computer is a desktop computer, it's easy to keep it in the kitchen where everyone can see it. However, many people today are trading in their desktop computers for laptops because the portability of laptop computers makes it easy to use them in any room of the house. Parents need to consciously enforce the rule that no one is to use the computer in an isolated area, a rule that must apply to parents too. I recommend that all computers be used in the kitchen and they all must be easily observed by others.

5. Monitor what children are doing online away from home and at public access computers. Beyond supervising all Internet activity at home on computers, cell phones, tablets, videogame systems, etc., parents must also be aware of children's online activity away from home. This means ensuring that their friends' parents are also vigilant about monitoring Internet activity in their homes when your children are visiting, and

that they use proper filtering and accountability software. So many parents have told me that their child encountered Internet pornography while using the computer at a friend's house. If friends' parents don't take these precautions, the child should not be allowed to visit that friend's house. Internet use is now common among children in elementary schools and libraries. Parents need to ensure that school computers have proper filters and that teachers are monitoring all computer use. Parents should also investigate whether their local public library uses filters on computers in the children's section. Unfortunately, because the American Library Association is against filters on all library computers, many libraries do not use them, even in children's sections. If a library does not use filters or refuses to install them, parents need to supervise their children's computer use at the library or forbid them to use those computers.

6. Never leave your child alone with the Internet. As I stated previously, to do so is no different than leaving your child alone with a perfect stranger! Parents should always be present when children are using any device that has access to the Internet, including computers of any type, cell phones, tablets, eReaders, iPods, MP3 players, and video game systems. Children usually don't understand the dangers of the Internet and they need to be taught it is not a toy. Parents can explain to their children that the Internet is like a sharp tool that requires adult supervision to prevent them from getting hurt.

7. Never let your child use your cell phone as a toy. Often when I am out shopping or running errands I see parents giving their six-year-old child their cell phone to entertain and keep the child quiet. This is extremely dangerous for children. The children could be stumbling upon pornography on the phones as their parents are occupied with shopping. While this may appear to be a stretch of the imagination, parents can never be too vigilant about protecting their children. Letting children use a cell phone to entertain them is also like leaving

them with a perfect stranger. One can never know what they might encounter.

8. Limit screen time. This includes the television, computer, tablet, eReader, cell phone, iPod, MP3 Player, and video game systems. Unfortunately, many parents use these devices as babysitters. According to Norman Herr (2007) of California State University at Northridge, young children spend approximately twenty-eight hours a week watching television while parents spend only 3.5 minutes per week having meaningful conversation with them. We need to change this. I recommend no more than two hours of screen time per day for children. Parents need to focus more on spending more quality and quantity time with children. This may be difficult, especially for working parents; however, the sacrifices parents make to spend time with their children will pay great dividends. It will result in stronger and healthier family relationships and happier children.

9. Children should not have cell phones with Internet access. Because more parents are working we have more latchkey kids today. Parents are buying their children cell phones to stay in touch with them. Children as young as seven now possess cell phones. While cell phones for children are a good safety measure, they can be dangerous, especially if they have Internet access. I recommend the Firefly Phone at www.fireflymobile.com. This phone is designed for kids without offering Internet access. It's easy to use and allows parents to keep in touch with them.

10. Parents should restrict and monitor social media. Today, texting and email are an integral part of our culture, helping families stay in touch. Teachers and coaches often use them to communicate with kids. Parents need to monitor all emails and text messages that their children send and receive to ensure there is no inappropriate content. Texting should be limited so children don't overuse it. Children should not have Facebook

accounts or participate in any chat rooms, which are common places for predators to lurk seeking out victims. Pornographers also use these forms of social media to lure kids into viewing pornography.

11. Subscribe to an Internet filtering and accountability service. These are two different but necessary services. A filtering service attempts to block all inappropriate and offensive content so that Internet users cannot access them in the first place—an imperative service to have for children using the Internet. An accountability service doesn't block any content, but it does monitor all Internet use so that if an inappropriate website is accessed, parents can receive an email notifying them of it. This is needed because even the best filtering services can be circumvented, and an accountability service can warn parents if the filter has been breached. Once again, the Internet filtering and accountability services I recommend are from CovenantEyes. com. More information on this is provided in the appendix. While Internet filtering and accountability are powerful tools for protecting children, I cannot stress enough the need for parents to always supervise their children's use of technology. A child should never be left alone with the Internet.

12. Parents must monitor their own use of technology. Parents teach by example, and even when you think your child is not paying attention, in the back of his mind he is taking copious notes. If a child discovers his father's "stash" of pornography on a computer, tablet, or cell phone, he will think it's okay to view pornography. Parents must show their children they are concerned about Internet safety for themselves as well. This means that parents must not isolate themselves with the Internet. They should set good examples by showing that their own Internet use can be seen by everyone. Also, they should not set a bad example by idly surfing the web. Children will copy parents and could end up viewing pornography.

Additional Safeguards

Parents must teach children to respect their own bodies and other people's bodies. This starts by teaching them about modesty in dress. Certain body parts should always be covered because they are holy and God wants us to keep them clean, safe, and healthy. These parts include anything covered by a bathing suit. Children must also learn to dress appropriately according to their situation. For example, a person would not wear a bathing suit to school or church. Teaching children to dress appropriately out of respect for God, themselves, and others helps them to understand the meaning and value of modesty.

In addition, children should be taught that any body part covered by a bathing suit should not be touched by another person, with the exception of a doctor during a check-up or a parent while bathing a child. This is also done out of respect. Parents need to be careful not to present this information in a way that leaves children thinking their body parts are "bad" or "dirty." Children should be encouraged to tell their parents if someone has touched their private parts. Acting sexually or using sexual language at an early age may be a sign that the child has been exposed to pornography or has been sexually abused. A trained therapist should be consulted in this situation.

Teaching children to respect their own bodies and the bodies of other people will strengthen their confidence and self-esteem. If they do encounter pornography, they will see it for what it really is, a violation of people's dignity. They will immediately want to reject it.

What if my child has been exposed to pornography?

Teaching children to respect their bodies and other people's bodies also means encouraging them to tell their parents if they ever see someone who is not properly clothed, whether in person or in pornography. If your child informs you that he has been inadvertently exposed to pornography, never blame or shame the child or make him feel bad about it in any way. Thank and commend him for telling you. Calmly ask your child what he saw and how it affected him. This will help determine how traumatic the experience was to him. Explain to your child that the people he saw are being disrespectful to themselves, others, and God. You and your child can then say a prayer for those people. After that find out where your child saw the pornography or people and make sure he never encounters it again! For example, if he discovered it on the home computer, appropriate steps should be taken to protect the child when online. If he viewed Internet pornography at a friend's house, talk to that friend's parents to ensure that they will prevent it from happening again. If the parents are uncooperative, then your child should not be allowed to visit that house again. Encountering violent pornography can be traumatic for a child. If your child appears frightened, anxious, or has nightmares as a result of being exposed to violent pornography, professional help should be sought.

What if my child has been purposely viewing pornography?

Unfortunately, some children are being exposed to pornography at very young ages. Out of curiosity or shock, they may go on to seek out pornography over and over again. If you discover that your child has been viewing pornography, don't overreact. Remember, the child may not be able to understand what he is viewing or the gravity of the situation. Calmly speak to your child to find out how he was first exposed to pornography. Was it by accident or did someone introduce him to it? If it was another person, who was it? Where did he see it, home or somewhere else? Ask your child how the pornography affected him. Was it scary, funny, shocking, and so on? When talking to your child, it's important not to blame or shame him. Calmly explain that viewing pornography is wrong because the people in it are not using their bodies as God intended. This is an opportune time to talk about modesty and respect for the body. Then make sure all the safeguards are in place to ensure your child isn't exposed to pornography again. If it appears that your child may have been traumatized by it, it's time to consult a therapist who is trained to work with children.

What if I suspect my child has been viewing pornography?

One of the best ways to see if your child has been viewing Internet pornography at home is to use Internet filtering and accountability software, such as Covenant Eyes. This will allow you to see where your child is going on the Internet. There are other signs to look for, such as the child acting in very sexual ways. He may mimic sexual behaviors with other children or use sexually explicit language. Some children may even sexually molest other children. For many young children viewing pornography can be traumatic, which may be the case if he seems frightened, anxious, loses his appetite, has difficulty sleeping, or has nightmares. In addition to being exposed to pornography, these behaviors are also symptoms of possible sexual abuse. Predators often use pornography to lure innocent victims. If you see any of these symptoms in your child, seek professional help immediately.

Teaching Children about Healthy Sexuality

While children might not be able to fully understand sexuality, they will have questions about it. Often these are basic questions about reproduction (Where do babies come from?), physical development (Why do women have breasts and men have beards?), or lifestyles (Why does Billy have two mommies?). Answers to these questions should be honest, age-appropriate, and adhere to Church teaching. Sex should not be presented as something bad or dirty. Parents need to explain that it is a wonderful and holy gift from God that is reserved for married people. To help parents answer children's questions, the Archdiocese of New York has created a *Parent Guide to Human Sexuality*. This is a series of three booklets to address the questions of children ages five to ten, nine to fourteen, and thirteen to nineteen. The booklets answer questions in age-appropriate ways and conform to Church teaching. Information on these resources can be found at www.flrl.org/Chastity.htm.

Healthy Parent-Child Relationships

Families are always on the go in today's fast paced world. There's swimming lessons, dance recitals, piano lessons, basketball practice, soccer games, school plays, church activities, etc. All this activity is pulling families apart. When I work with struggling families I often ask them how many nights a week they sit down to have dinner together. Most are lucky if they can share one meal together. This must change. While supporting your children by attending their extracurricular events is important, children crave personal attention from parents that can only come from spending one-on-one time together. This lets children know that their parents truly care about them and everything going on in their lives. When children feel this type of love, it's easy for them to talk with their parents. They won't be afraid to tell their parents when something bad has happened to them, such as viewing pornography.

LifeBalance Coach Leo Weidner recommends having a "Kid's Day" with each child every week. On a Kid's Day, time is set aside where you can spend one-on-one time with your child that should last at least twenty minutes. You and your child should engage in a fun activity that your child enjoys. When planning a Kid's Day, remember to plan it when it works best for the child, because he needs to be in the right mood and frame of mind. Your child can also help plan the Kid's day by choosing the activity. This is a great time to talk about what is going on in your child's life, and most importantly, it's a time for you to listen and show that you are truly interested in every facet of your child's life. It's also a time to tell your child how proud you are of him and to give positive affirmation. Talk about all the good things he does and his special gifts and talents. Kid's Day should not be a time to focus on criticizing or correcting the child. If a correction needs to be made, I recommend using a 7:1 ratio. For every one correction give seven positive affirmations. Your child will walk away from these times feeling loved, valued, and special! He will look forward to spending this time with you. Best of all, he will want to talk to you, and if you're a good listener, he will want to listen to you, too (Kastleman, 2007).

Most parents believe that it's the special events of life that their children will remember—trips to Disney World, birthdays, and holidays. These have their place, but spending regular one-on-one time with children will allow them to see their entire childhood as a special memory!

The Big Question

Leo Weidner also recommends parents ask their child the "Big Question" when they get together for Kid's Day. That question is:

"How can I be a better father/mother to you?" Your child may be surprised at first to hear this question coming from you, but he will then feel special. It shows him that you really care about him and his opinion (Kastleman, 2007). Some of their suggestions may be a bit unreasonable, like going to bed later or having ice cream every day. But other suggestions are priceless, like reading more stories together, playing more games together, or just spending more time together. Regardless of their responses, your children will walk away with a greater love and respect for you.

Balance in Life

To have a healthy family, all members must strive for balance. In today's world everyone seems to be moving at a breakneck pace. I believe it's great for kids to be involved in extracurricular activities because it gives them opportunities to develop their gifts and talents and learn many valuable life lessons. However, many kids today are overcommitted and in too many activities. The result is burnout and feeling overwhelmed. Parents can also be overcommitted in their careers and personal lives, which keeps them on the move with little time for family. Consequently, families are disconnected. One way to determine if your family is overcommitted and disconnected is to ask, "How many nights a week do we sit down as a family to eat dinner?" If the answer is only one or two, your family may be overcommitted and disconnected.

Why are kids so overcommitted today? I believe it's due to parental peer pressure. Parents want to be good parents. When they see other parents enrolling their kids in multiple activities, they may believe that to be good parents they must do the same. They may feel guilty about "depriving their children" if they don't follow suit. They might also fear what other parents will think of them if their kids aren't in as many activities as other kids. Parents need to avoid comparing themselves to other parents. Going with the flow of other parents doesn't necessarily make one a good parent.

Balance in family life ensures that extracurricular activities don't take precedence. It's healthy for kids to be involved in activities, but this should not prevent a family from having dinner together at least four nights a week. They should also not interfere with Kid's Days. When kids feel connected to their parents and siblings, they won't feel that they're missing out on anything by not participating in as many activities as their friends.

Some of the warning signs of kids being overcommitted can be seen by their moods. They might be overcommitted if they seem anxious and overwhelmed by their schedules. They might protest about all their activities, or become depressed and feel they can't keep up with their hectic pace, so parents must be willing to pull back when their kids are overcommitted. I generally recommend no more than two activities during a season, such as a sport and a club. Kids also need a break from time to time, which means no extracurricular activities at all. This gives them time to rest and prepare for the next season's activities. Kids who are not overcommitted are happier and healthier and don't feel so pressured to perform or overachieve.

Spiritual Development

Parents need to provide for their children's spiritual formation. Many parents believe that by sending their kids to Catholic schools or parish religious education programs they will grow up to be faithful Catholics. However, evidence points to the contrary as more Catholic young adults don't practice their faith today than ever before. Parents need to take time to teach their children the faith. Kids may not be able to understand Pope St. John Paul II's *The Theology of the Body*, but they can understand God's immense love for them and that they are fearfully and wonderfully made.

Attending Mass together as a family is crucial. Unfortunately many families are unable to do this, often because of Sunday morning sporting events. I recommend parents not enroll their children in any sports league that practice or hold games on Sunday morning. Children need to know that Sunday is the Lord's Day.

The family should also pray together every day. At meal times, kids can say grace and take turns thanking God for the blessings in their lives, or pray for someone who is ill or going through a difficult time. Parents can gather the kids for a family Rosary in the evening. For younger children, simply praying one decade of the Rosary is fine. Also, children love reading Bible stories or the lives of the saints. Grade school children can take turns reading to the rest of the family. Parents need to show their enthusiasm for the faith. If you are excited about it, your children will get excited about it too.

Raising Healthy Kids

All of these guidelines are meant to help parents raise healthy kids. I admit a lot of this is common sense parenting, but in today's hectic world, parenting can seem like a series of fires to extinguish. Thinking about how they are parenting and what is really best for their children can help parents develop healthy, intimate relationships with their kids, and ensure good communication between them and their children. Parents who know about all their kid's activities, friends, and school life, as well as their thoughts and feelings, can identify possible dangers in their kids' lives. They can then take the appropriate steps to protect their children.

A Final Warning and Hope

Parents need to remember that pornographers are no different than drug dealers. They don't care about anyone but themselves. They know that pornography is highly addictive and their goal is to get as many people as possible addicted to pornography so they can make as much money as possible. Any smart drug (pornography) dealer knows that if he can get a child addicted to his drug, he will have a customer for life, regardless of how damaging pornography is to young children.

Pornographers relentlessly pursue new customers and will try every way possible to infiltrate their lives. They are at the forefront in using new technology to distribute their wares and they know that kids are the greatest users of new technology. Parents should never underestimate how devious pornographers are in luring in kids. Every effort needs to be taken to protect children from these evil fiends.

Fortunately, we can protect our children. Positive steps can be taken to ensure that pornography doesn't enter our homes. If children are exposed to pornography, the issue can be addressed so that the damage is minimal and healing can occur. Raising healthy families will contribute immensely to protecting children. Communication improves when children feel loved, valued, and connected to their parents. This allows parents to know everything about their children's lives and to quickly identify dangers to protect them from.

14

Helping Teens Reject Pornography

The risk of teens becoming addicted to pornography is extremely high today. Their broad use of technology, adolescent sexual development/puberty, and curiosity about sexuality can be a dangerous combination. In chapter six we discussed in detail those dangers and the effects pornography has had on teenagers (pp. 124–139). I introduced you to Eric, a sixteen-year-old teenager, and his parents.

Eric and his parents are like many people I've treated. No teen sets out to become addicted to pornography, and every parent believes they are doing everything possible to protect their teenager. The reality is that pornography is a silent cancer. It comes into people's lives without warning and slowly grows unnoticed until one day a person realizes it has totally consumed him. The addiction has taken over the teen's life and leaves him feeling helpless and hopeless.

Teenagers' natural sense of invincibility can lead them to disregard many of life's dangers, which is why they often engage in very dangerous, thrill-seeking behaviors. The results can be devastating, and this is just as true with pornography use. The pornography industry and mass media have left teens believing that pornography is harmless, and if it is addictive, it certainly won't happen to them. However, in my research, my practice, and my conversations with other therapists and parents, I am finding more teens are being treated for pornography addiction today than ever before.

Because of the harmful long-term effects pornography has on teenagers, their parents, teachers, coaches, youth workers, and clergy need to work together to help protect them from this terrible drug. In the last chapter I stressed the need to protect children up to the age of eleven from pornography. After age eleven, we need to educate kids on the dangers of pornography so that they will reject it. Parents might successfully protect their kids at home, but it's almost guaranteed their teens will encounter pornography outside the home, and thus education is the best protection. While the strategies listed below are mainly directed toward the parents of teens, any adult who works with minors can use them.

Strategies to Help Teens Reject Pornography

1. *Educate teens on the dangers of pornography.* Teenagers should be fully aware of the addictiveness of pornography. It's not enough for teens to be simply told not to use pornography; they need to know *why* they shouldn't use it. Current scientific evidence should be presented to show that pornography is no different than a hard drug, such as cocaine. They need to know that it can ruin their lives because:
    a. They can easily become addicted to it.
    b. They will not learn about healthy sexuality and relationships from pornography.
    c. It is a very selfish pursuit that only leads men to use women for sexual pleasure.
    d. It is disrespectful to all involved.

Too often when warning teens about the dangers of pornography, parents first present religious or moral reasons. However, teenagers affected by secular culture rarely accept this reasoning. It is best to present the scientific evidence before the religious or moral.

2. *Warn teenagers about pornographers.* Teens need to know that pornographers are drug dealers purposely targeting them to become addicted. The comparison can he made between pornographers today and tobacco companies of the 1950s–1970s, which developed advertisements to entice minors to start smoking. Like the "Marlboro Man," porn stars today are presented as role models for young people. Teens can be shown all the ways that pornographers try to infiltrate their lives through modern technology, such as video games and social media.

3. *Schools need to get involved in the fight.* Educating teenagers on the dangers of pornography should be part of every school drug and alcohol awareness program. Programs specifically on Pornography Awareness should be developed for middle school and high school students.

4. *Encourage teens to talk to their parents if they are struggling with pornography.* Teens need to know that if they do struggle with pornography use, they can talk to their parents without fear of being blamed, shamed, humiliated, or made to feel bad in any way. Parents need to assure their teenagers they will be there to help with love and compassion. Open communication is the key to helping teens who have become addicted.

5. *Carefully monitor all media that enters the home.* As with children, parents need to protect teens by screening television shows, networks, movies, mail, catalogs, magazines, newspapers, music, video games, etc. Pay attention to videogame ratings, and choose only age appropriate games. I don't recommend any game with a higher rating than "T" for teens. I also recommend that parents play the games with their kids. This helps them understand the game and see if there is anything offensive in it. However, with teenagers it's important to discuss with them how pornography has infiltrated the mass media and why it is important to keep it out of the home. If some offensive material does enter your home, instead of getting upset, calmly discuss

this with your teen. Talk about why it is offensive and should be kept out of the home.

6. *All Internet use should be done in a public area of the home.* Teens should not be allowed to isolate themselves with the Internet, whether on the computer, cell phone, iPad, tablet, eReader, iPod, or video gaming system. This can be difficult to enforce, especially when a teenager wants a quiet place to do his homework. To remedy this, set up a special place in the home where teens can quietly work, yet be in full view of everyone. The dining room is often a good place for this.

7. *Limit screen time.* As with children, parents need to limit the amount of screen time their teenager has. This includes spending time with the television, computer, cell phone, iPod, MP3 player, tablet, eReader, and video gaming system. I recommend that these devices be used for no more than a total of two hours per day for entertainment purposes. The computer and Internet may be used for longer periods of time for school work. Using these electronic gadgets at night is often a problem for teens and is where many end up viewing pornography or engaging in inappropriate social media use. I recommend at 9:00 p.m. every night parents collect all gadgets, turn them off, and lock them up for the night. In addition to protecting teens from harmful media, this will allow them to unwind and relax before going to bed. Many teens claim that surfing the web, using social media, or playing video games before bed relaxes them; however, this actually overstimulates their brain. A teenager might feel more relaxed, but he will not get a proper restful night's sleep, which can make it more difficult for him to get up in the morning and fully pay attention in school.

8. *Monitor all Internet use.* For children I recommended an Internet filtering system; however, I don't recommend this for teens. This is because filtering systems often block content that is needed for schoolwork. For example, a teenager writing a

paper on breast cancer might not be able to access the information needed because the filtering system identified the word "breast" in the search engine request. In addition, tech-savvy teens can often find ways to get around filtering systems to view pornography. For teenagers, I recommend an Internet accountability service, which does not block any content but monitors all Internet use and sends an email report to parents when inappropriate content is accessed. This gives teenagers full access to the Internet with the knowledge that Mom and Dad will know if they are using it improperly. This is a good deterrent. It also helps them get into the habit of not going to inappropriate websites in the first place. As I recommended in the last chapter, parents should purchase *Unfiltered: A Parent Workshop Kit* by Covenant Eyes (2013), a kit that includes a DVD, Workshop Guide, and Parent How-To Guide. The kit can be purchased at www.covenanteyes.com

9. *Monitor all social media use.* Social media is integral to teen culture today. It's the way they communicate with each other and is how many parents, teachers, and coaches communicate with them. Social media includes email, text messaging, instant messaging, chat rooms, discussion boards, blogs, Facebook, Myspace, Twitter, YouTube, Instagram, Face Time, and SnapChat. Newer forms of social media are coming out every day and teens are usually the first to use them. For this reason, parents need to monitor how their teens are using social media. You need to make sure your teen friends you on Facebook and Myspace. You need to monitor all of their emails, texts, and tweets. Subscribe to their blogs and YouTube pages. Parents should have access to any form of social media their teen uses. Many teens object to this level of monitoring and view it as a violation of their privacy. They feel their parents don't trust them. It's important to explain to your teen that it's not so much them that you don't trust as much as it is the pornographers and sexual predators. You want to make sure they don't

creep into your teen's social media outlets and lure them in. You can also ensure they are not the victim or perpetrator of cyber bullying. Teens also need to realize that no form of social media is 100% secure. There are a lot of hackers out there who can break into a person's email, Facebook page, Twitter account, and other social media and cause untold damage. Some teens will create secret Facebook pages and email accounts to avoid being monitored by their parents, which is often done so they can sext. In my experience, teens are unable to keep these sites secret for long because their parents eventually discover them. In these cases I recommend parents talk with their teens about how hurt and betrayed they feel because of their teen's deceit. The consequence of this should be a tighter restriction on the use of technology. For example, no more emails or texts, and the Internet can only be used for school work. Any emails or texts from teachers, coaches, or friends can be sent to a parent. The ultimate goal of monitoring is to protect your teen from pornography and criminals.

10. *Discuss the dangers of sexting.* Sexting has become a major problem among teenagers, who often engage in it because they view it as fun, exciting, and a way to become popular. Many girls participate in it believing it is needed to get and keep a boyfriend. Explain to your teenager the legal ramifications of sexting, as many teens don't realize that sexting by minors is a form of child pornography and they could be convicted for creating, distributing, or possessing child pornography. Also explain that once photos are sent via email or posted on social media sites, they are out there forever. Even if they are deleted or a service such as Snapchat is used, someone out there could be collecting those photos and posting them elsewhere. Furthermore, teens need to be aware that colleges and employers can gain access to their Facebook pages without their permission. Thus, any inappropriate photos or posts could endanger their chances of getting into a college or getting a good job. Finally,

teens need to know that sexting ultimately allows others to use them for selfish sexual pleasure and will not help them develop healthy relationships.

11. *Monitor where your teen hangs out and with whom.* During the teenage years, friendships are just as or more important to teens as family relationships. During these years it's important to know who your teenager's friends are and to even get to know their parents. Make sure your teen is spending time with good kids who are not likely to get into trouble with drugs, alcohol, pornography, or sex. These kids usually come from healthy families where parents are involved in their lives and the kids are involved in healthy pursuits, such as sports, art, and music. If your teenager is getting involved in the wrong crowd, share your concerns with him and direct him toward the right crowd by getting him involved in healthy extracurricular activities.

12. *Stay involved in your teen's life.* Many parents are actively involved in their children's lives when they are young, but then they back off when their kids become teenagers. Parents often don't realize that even though their kids may complain about them, they still need their parents in their lives. One of the best ways to stay involved in your teen's life is to offer to help out with his extracurricular activities. You can also work on projects together around the house or do volunteer work together in your community. This will keep the lines of communication open between you and your teenager because you will have things to talk about.

13. *Teach teenagers about healthy sexuality.* Unfortunately, many teens receive inadequate sexual education at home and at school. In many homes sex is considered a taboo subject and never discussed, which is dangerous for a teenager who is naturally curious about sex. Their only resort is to learn from pornography and the mass media where they receive unhealthy messages, and the effects are devastating. Parents and educators

need to make it a point to teach teens about healthy sexuality. Here is where Pope St. John Paul II's *The Theology of the Body* and *Love and Responsibility* are helpful in explaining to teens the true meaning of sex as God intended it. With this understanding they will realize that pornography desecrates God beautiful plan for sexuality and humanity and see how selfish and degrading pornography is to all involved.

The Archdiocese of New York's *Parent Guide to Human Sexuality* provides parents with specific knowledge of the Catholic Church's teachings regarding human sexuality, and ways they can educate their children in the faith in a developmentally appropriate way with specific references to Church teachings from the Bible, the *Catechism of the Catholic Church*, *The Truth and Meaning of Human Sexuality* (Pontifical Council of the Family), *Catechetical Formation in Chaste Living* (United States Council of Catholic Bishops), and other prominent Church documents. Our goal is to empower parents and encourage them to joyfully embrace an active role in their children's lives, especially when it comes to speaking about topics of human sexuality, which many parents feel ill-equipped to do. By providing parents and teens with concise and accurate information about their faith, we are promoting a culture of informed, faithful Catholics who have the knowledge to live out and defend their faith. To purchase copies of the *Parent Guide to Human Sexuality*, please contact the Archdiocese of New York Family Life Office.

14. *Teach teens about healthy relationships.* Pornography is harming young people's ability to have healthy relationships. Many young people are entering into relationships for the sole purpose of having sex. Many also struggle with communication because of their excessive use of pornography and technology. In fact, the most common way couples break up today is via text message. We need to teach our teenagers how to have healthy relationships, how to respect one another, communicate well,

and relate to one another without the use of technology. Parents need to both teach and model good relationship skills for their teenager.

15. *Present the Church's teaching on pornography.* After you have presented the scientific facts about pornography's effects, your teen should be ready to hear what the Church has to say about pornography. He will then realize what the Catholic Church teaches is supported by scientific research and vice-versa. This is also a wonderful opportunity to evangelize. You can help your teenager understand that God wants him to stay away from pornography because He wants your teen to live a happy and healthy life. When God or a parent says no to anything in a teen's life, it is for the teen's own good, whether or not the teen realizes it or not.

These strategies may seem overwhelming, but when mothers and fathers work together as a team, protecting teens is not such a daunting task. The main focus is education. As with drugs, alcohol, and tobacco, teens need to be given the correct information about pornography so they can make the right choices. Be aware that your teenager will stumble and fall at times. Don't overreact when this happens. Use it as a teaching opportunity and discuss his actions without condemning him or being "preachy." Help him understand the consequences of his actions and how to avoid making the same mistake in the future.

Parents need a healthy relationship with their teen that fosters honesty, respect, trust, and communication. Here are some tips on how to achieve this.

Balance in Life

More than children and parents, teens today can find themselves overcommitted. Beyond the myriad of extracurricular activities they're involved in, there are part-time jobs as well. School is also more demanding. Honors and Advanced Placement courses take up much time and effort. As teens become juniors and seniors in high school, they become more concerned with SATs and college applications. Stress levels for teens today are extremely high, with more teens struggling with depression and anxiety disorders as a result. Parents need to monitor their teenager's activities to ensure they are not overcommitted. Warning signs of overcommitment are:

- Your teen is involved in several sports and activities at once.
- He seems overly anxious or depressed.
- He is not getting enough sleep.
- His grades have dropped.
- He complains about his schedule.
- There is little time for a social life.
- The family only has dinner together once or twice a week.
- He is unable to attend Sunday Mass because of extracurricular activities.

I recommend discussing the need for balance and the dangers of being overcommitted with your teenager. Brainstorm together on how balance can be achieved. You can then suggest that your teen be involved in no more than two activities during a season, such as one sport and one club. By keeping balance in your teenager's life, you will help him avoid much of the stress and anxiety that many teens self-medicate with pornography.

On my Soapbox about Traveling Teams

Traveling sports teams are very popular among teenage athletes. Unlike sports teams, they provide the opportunity to play more games against more teams, which gives them more practice in honing their skills. However, with these benefits come serious drawbacks. Traveling teams can consume a family's life. Weekends are consumed with the playing of two to four games, distances families need to travel to and from these games consume much time, and often the family is unable to attend Sunday Mass because of weekend games. Add to that all the after-school and weekend practices and the increased likelihood of sports injuries due to the increased physical strain. In addition, if only one child is on a traveling team, family time is focused on that child, which can leave other children feeling neglected. While traveling teams can be a time for family bonding if all kids are involved, it has been my experience that they divide families and impede healthy family life. The results are obvious: teens are overcommitted and family time is monopolized by the sport.

I am not against youth sports. I believe they teach teenagers many valuable life lessons and they keep teens physically fit. However, they should not consume family life. There are many sports leagues where teenagers can have fun playing sports that don't consume their life or family life, including school teams, and community CYO, PAL, and YMCA leagues.

Parents should beware if their motives for having their teenager on a traveling team are unhealthy. Many parents get their child involved in traveling teams because they believe it could lead to a sports scholarship to college. While this could happen, the odds for most teens are remote. Some parents involve their teens in traveling teams because they always wanted to be a great teenage athlete themselves but never made it, so they live vicariously through their teenager instead. Still others do it because of parent peer pressure. They see other parents involving their teens in traveling teams and believe they must do the same to be good parents. Teenagers should only be involved in traveling sports teams if they enjoy it, it doesn't overcommit them, and it doesn't compromise family life.

Kid's Days for Teens

In the last chapter I recommended spending at least twenty minutes a week alone with each of your children. This one-on-one time is crucial for developing a healthy relationship with each child. Having a Kid's Day can be difficult with teens. For teenagers, peer relationships are often more important than family, and as a result they would rather spend more time with their friends. They still, however, need to have healthy relationships with their parents, especially with their fathers.

A good way to stay involved in your teenager's life is to be involved in their activities. Volunteer to help out with their sports teams and clubs. Initially, they may not like this because for most teens their parents are a big embarrassment. Don't let this deter you. While I would not recommend admitting to your teen that your involvement is to keep an eye on them, you can assure them that you don't intend to be a "helicopter parent" constantly hovering over them.

I recommend that fathers have breakfast with their teen at least once a month. Because of their busy academic, extracurricular, and social lives, finding one-on-one time with teens can be difficult, but a breakfast can easily be fit into most schedules. Once or twice a month, take your teenager out to a local diner for breakfast—preferably one that serves huge portions. Teens will like this since most have insatiable appetites. This will become a special time for you and your teenager, and if you are already active in his life, there will be plenty to talk about. This is also a great time to ask the "big question." Teens need to know that you are committed to being the best parent you can be. It's another way to show them just how much you love them.

Staying active in your teenager's life will help you identify if he is struggling with overcommitment, depression, anxiety, stress, loneliness, or any other issue that might lead him to use pornography. If he is struggling with pornography, he will feel comfortable enough to come to you for help.

What if I suspect my teenager is struggling with pornography?

There are several warning signs that your teenager might already be using pornography. If you suspect any of them, action should be taken immediately to help him. Common warning signs include:

- Discovering porn on your teen's computer, cell phone, iPad, tablet, iPod, etc.

- Isolates himself with the computer, cell phone, iPad, tablet, iPod, or gaming system

- Tries to hide or lie about his online activities
- Makes jokes about pornography
- Makes sexual references in conversation
- Engages in sexting
- Sudden drop in grades
- Dropping out of extracurricular activities
- Neglects responsibilities
- No longer is interested in spending time with family or friends
- Change in mood: angry, sullen, moody, depressed, or anxious
- Disrespect for family rules

If you notice any of these symptoms, consult a mental health professional who is trained in the diagnosis and treatment of sexual addiction. It is also important to thoroughly check your teenager's electronic gadgets for Internet pornography use. Best Buy's *Geek Squad* and Staples' *Easy Tech* staff can help with this. Immediately install Internet accountability software such as the one provided by Covenant Eyes on all electronic devices your teenager may use that has access to the Internet.

The most important thing you can do when discovering your teenager has been viewing pornography is not to overreact. A teenager should not be condemned, blamed, shamed, or humiliated. He probably already feels horrible about it, so you don't want to make things worse. Even though society tells them that viewing pornography is okay, I believe that, deep down, teenagers know it's wrong. They need love, compassion, and understanding, not condemnation. Calmly talk to him about the dangers of pornography and then consult a mental health professional to assess whether your teenager might be addicted. Let your teenager know that you will do everything possible to help him. And encourage him to go to confession and seek spiritual guidance.

Dating

Many kids want to begin dating during the teenage years, which is a concern for many parents. Although they want their kids to learn how to have healthy relationships with the opposite sex, they also know all the trouble teenagers can get into. Many parents ask me, "What is the appropriate age for a teenager to begin dating?" My answer is, "It depends." I believe that teenagers should not begin to date until they are at least sixteen. However, if parents believe their teenager is not mature enough to date, the teenager should wait until age eighteen. It's the parents' job to assess when their teenager is ready to date.

If you have decided your teenager is ready to date, their first date should be with a parent. A mother should take her son out on a date and a father should take his daughter. On these dates, parents teach their kids how to act on a date. Sons learn to act like gentlemen and daughters learn to act like ladies. In addition to teaching their teenager how to treat others, parents need to model for their kids how to have a healthy relationship. They will then know how to treat their dates with respect. They will also be able to discern who not to go out with. For example, if a girl goes out on a date with a boy who doesn't treat her like a lady, she will know not to go out with him again.

Parents, clergy, educators, and youth workers need to work together to dispel the myths about dating to which many teens subscribe. For example, the "third date rule" is very popular among teens and young adults, where they believe by the third date a couple should have sex to determine if they should continue dating. If the sex is good, they continue. If the sex is bad, they break up. They have bought into the myth that the way to evaluate the quality of a relationship is by the quality of the sex, which leads teens to believe the lie that having sex outside of marriage is okay.

When teenagers have a proper understanding of God's plan for relationships, sexuality, and humanity overall, they will be able to make the right choices when it comes to their own relationships. They won't be swayed by peer pressure or the constant messages our culture presents. Their peers may initially label them as "prudes," but they will ultimately garner their respect for standing up for what is right.

A Final Warning and Hope

It is up to parents and teens alike to be aware of the dangers of pornography and our culture that glorifies using others for selfish pleasure and profit. The pornography industry and mass media want a world without sexual morality so they can reap as much profit as possible, and they are targeting teens to achieve this. This can only lead to personal and cultural destruction. When teens understand how they are being used by the media, and how following current sexual mores can hurt them, they can make the informed decision not to fall into these traps. Education is the best preventive measure for teenagers!

God has given them a blueprint for healthy relationships and healthy sexuality. No matter how deeply a teenager might become entrenched in pornography addiction, help is available. Recovery and freedom from pornography is possible!

15

New Life in Recovery

What is life in recovery like? A life in recovery is a life of integrity restored.

To help illustrate what this life in recovery looks like, I want to provide the salient points of the principles and strategies in this distinctly Catholic recovery program. Note that this can be applied to both married couples and single men.

Men and women in recovery continue to work on the seven points of the Integrity Restored Program and stay committed to the recovery process. Here's what their new life in recovery looks like:

- *Self-knowledge and Commitment.* Despite all the healing, growth, and change a man has experienced, he keeps his recovery journal and often goes back to read it. He never wants to forget how pornography use hurt him, his family, and especially his wife. He doesn't hide a secret life. He is transparent and enjoys a tremendous amount of freedom. He remains aware of his woundedness and need for continued healing. He knows his triggers and danger zones and is committed to using effective strategies to keep from falling into pornography use. He has developed healthy habits to deal with stress, anger, loneliness, and any other difficult emotion. He communicates with his spouse and accountability partners when he is struggling emotionally. He has gained the trust of his spouse and others.

His wife is committed to her own healing. Working together in the healing process has drawn them together in a stronger bond of intimacy where they enjoy being partners in the process.

- *Purifying Your Life.* Any place where the man and his family would have access to the Internet, including all electronic devices, is now monitored through Covenant Eyes (or some similar accountability program), and so is all media that enters the home. He avoids situations and places that lead to a fall. He has purified his heart and mind and is careful to guard his eyes. Daily he asks the Lord to help him see every woman as a precious child of God who deserves to be loved and respected, and he has made it a point to teach his sons to do the same.

- *Support and Accountability.* A man with new life in recovery is no longer plagued by the compulsion to view pornography, but he still maintains a strong support and accountability network. He attends weekly SA meetings and is an accountability partner for other men. He meets with his sponsor monthly and with his accountability partner frequently. He attends a weekly men's ministry group at his parish or a weekly Couples in Recovery meeting. He and his wife mentor other couples struggling with pornography addiction. With new and healthy intimate relationships formed through his accountability partners, he rarely feels lonely anymore.

- *Counseling.* The couple has experienced much healing in their lives, but they know they still need more. A man meets with his therapist biweekly to continue working on his family-of-origin wounds, and he keeps a journal to monitor his emotions and how he deals with them. He continues to work on forgiving the people who hurt him and growing in self-confidence. The couple meets monthly with a therapist for marital counseling if needed, and continue to work on creating the healthy marriage they've always wanted. They remain authentic with each other and are no longer afraid to tell each other when they are hurting, sad, afraid, or angry. They know their spouse is always there with love and acceptance. As their marriage has improved, so has their relationship with their kids. They are able to model for their kids a healthy, loving marriage. They are excited about the future and have developed a clear vision for the marriage they want to have. They know they don't have to be stuck in the wounds of the past and can now decide how they want their relationship to be. They marvel at how God has been able to restore their marriage and make it better than before.

- *Spiritual Plan.* The man will work closely with his spiritual director to build his relationship with God. He knows that God loves him unconditionally. His knowledge is reinforced in his relationships with his wife, family, sponsor, accountability partner, Couples in Recovery group, and men's ministry group. Having experienced God's incredible love, he does not want anything to come between him and God, especially sin, and so he attends Confession regularly. He and his wife make it a point to pray together every night and know that as they strengthen their relationship with God they are also strengthening their relationship with each other.

- *Education.* Having educated himself on overcoming his compulsive pornography use through books, DVDs, conferences, group meetings, and counseling sessions, the man now focuses on becoming the man God created him to be. He educates himself on healthy masculinity, marriage, family life, virtue, and spirituality. Instead of seeing himself trapped in addiction, he sees a world of freedom and opportunity. He has a healthy vision for his life that is attainable. He wants to share this knowledge with others. He educates his kids on the dangers of pornography and speaks to other men about it. He mentors his teenage sons through his words and actions to be virtuous men of God.

- *Virtue.* He knows that growing in virtue is the most important part of his continued recovery. He knows that God has called him to be a leader, provider, and protector of his marriage, family, parish, and community at large. To successfully fulfill this duty, he knows he must focus on living a virtuous life. He continues to use his virtues worksheet and journal to grow in virtue and avoid pornography and any other vice. This provides him with renewed strength for the battle.

Related Strategies

Related to the seven points are several principles and strategies that identify a life in recovery. Following them helps those addicted to pornography to remain sober and achieve the healthy life they have always wanted.

Being Gentle and Patient with One's Self

Being successful in recovery means being gentle and patient with one's self, especially early in the process. Recovery takes time. There will be falls along the way. Because of the many pornographic images trapped in an addicted person's head, it's easy to fall into viewing pornography, fantasizing, or masturbation. However, a fall is not a backslide. With a fall, a man lets his guard down temporarily and falls into acting out. He quickly gets back up, analyzes what led to the fall and utilizes the necessary safeguards to prevent it from happening again. In this situation the fall becomes a learning experience to help him improve his recovery program and ensure greater success in the future. Conversely, a backslide is when a man falls back into acting out and gives up on recovery. He no longer has any interest in achieving and remaining sober. Getting upset with a fall can lead to despair and more falls. By being gentle and patient, an addicted person can look at a fall rationally and not let it affect him adversely.

Abandoning Shame

A successful man in recovery lets go of the shame that kept him trapped in his addiction. He clearly understands how shame perpetuates unhealthy core beliefs. Shame is not from God. It is a tool Satan uses to enslave people in addiction. The man in recovery also understands the difference between guilt and shame. Guilt is the emotion that tells us when we have sinned and must make amends, which is good. Shame is the emotion that makes us believe we are terrible people because of our sins. It makes us want to hide from others, which leads to more isolation and shame and right back into the addiction. Obviously this is bad. The man in recovery values guilt and avoids shame. He knows that when he falls, he must confess it to a priest, spouse, sponsor, accountability partners, and support group members. With their love and support, he can quickly get back on the road to recovery.

Commitment to a Healthy Life

Unless a person properly cares for himself, he can end up feeling *B.L.A.S.T.ed.* Recall that this stands for:

Bored or Burnt Out

Lonely

Angry, Apathetic, Afraid, or Alone

Sad, Stressed, or Selfish

Tired

Being BLASTed can lead to the compulsion to self-medicate with pornography or any other vice. One way to effectively deal with being BLASTed, or to avoid it altogether, is to daily work on proper self-care. This means making sure one gets plenty of sleep, eats a healthy diet, exercises regularly, maintains healthy relationships, sets healthy boundaries, limits stress, and so on. All of this adds up to living a healthy lifestyle, which can eliminate the need to self-medicate with anything.

Setting Healthy Boundaries

Related to living a healthier lifestyle is setting healthy boundaries. Boundaries protect us from both internal and external influences that can affect our lives in negative ways. Internal boundaries influence the habits we form. Healthy internal boundaries can include working out at the gym regularly, going to bed by 10:00 p.m. every night, and refraining from eating junk foods. Maintaining healthy internal boundaries can help in developing habits for a healthier life. External boundaries are needed for healthy relationships, work, and social activities. Examples of healthy external boundaries could include limiting contact with selfish or angry people, working only forty hours a week, and refusing to take on unnecessary responsibilities. Setting healthy boundaries means being able to say no to self and to others. Some people may find this difficult for fear of disappointing others. When you have clear boundaries, however, people eventually learn to accept and respect them, and this reduces much stress and ensures a healthier life.

Keeping Priorities Straight

A person in recovery is always aware of his priorities and makes sure they are in proper order. To have a happy and healthy life, one's priorities must be as follows:

1. God
2. Marriage
3. Children
4. Career
5. Friends/Extended Family
6. Self

Obviously God must come first in every person's life. None of us would be here if it weren't for God's will and immense love. We often forget about God or give Him little credit for our lives because of the secularization of culture, but we must never forget that He is the Creator and we are His creations. All credit goes to God for all the blessings in our lives, our gifts and talents, our achievements. Even our struggles should be considered a blessing from God, for He wills or allows them in order to serve a greater purpose in our lives, even though we may not see or understand it (cf. Job 2:10). Every day it's important to thank God for everything in our lives. This requires humility and much faith to have absolute trust in God with every area of our life. Society might look down on those who place God first, but God certainly doesn't. Eventually such a person becomes an inspiration to others for having such strong faith. We were all created to worship God. This is an innate need. However, our secularized culture has denied people from meeting this need in a healthy way, and instead they worship money, sex, power, fame, material possession, and other enticements. By humbly placing God first we can be an example to others on how to live healthy lives. It's also an effective way to evangelize. How we live can be a powerful witness to the Gospel.

The next priority is marriage. I have found that many men place their careers ahead of their marriage and women do the same with their children. People often forget that we eventually retire from our careers, and children grow up and move out. However, marriage is for life. When we marry, we physically, mentally, emotionally, and spiritually become one with our spouse, so caring for our spouse is akin to caring for ourselves. A man who protects and nurtures his marital relationship experiences the joy of giving out of love for his wife, which in turn helps him receive her love. This deepens their intimacy and keeps him from feeling lonely. Having someone to talk to also helps him deal with life's stressors in a much healthier way. When a man is completely honest and authentic with his wife, he can easily overcome any trigger that could lead to a fall. He knows he has an ally in his wife who will be there to support and help him through any difficult situation. Thus, the successful man in recovery makes time to be with his wife, ensuring they have daily "alone time" together where they can nurture their relationship. He takes her out on dates and regularly tells her how much he loves and appreciates her. Modeling a healthy marital relationship is a wonderful gift for one's children. When they are adults and seeking spouses, they will know what to look for in a healthy spouse, which will help ensure that they will have healthy and happy marriages.

The third priority is children. It is easy for men to get wrapped up in their career, all in the name of providing for their children. While supporting the family is important, it should not consume a man's life to the point where he spends little time with his kids. They need a strong healthy relationship with their father in order to grow up healthy. This is also important for recovery. As with his wife, focusing on his children can fill a man with the joy of giving to his children. This gets him outside of himself and combats selfishness. In return he receives his children's love and respect. The successful man in recovery has dinner with his family regularly, is active in his kids' education and extracurricular activities, and makes sure he schedules one-on-one time with each of his kids. He protects his younger children from pornography and educates the older ones to reject it. Doing this gives a man more incentive to succeed in recovery because it requires him to be a leader, provider, and protector. He also models effective fathering, which will help his kids when they are parents.

The fourth priority is career. A successful man in recovery knows it is his job to provide for his family. Thus, he puts forth his best effort at work not only to meet but exceed his expectations. He understands his potential and strives to reach it. He is honest at work, putting in a full day without slacking or cheating anyone. While he's a hard worker, he's not a workaholic. He understands that God, marriage, and children come before his career. If he is in a career that consumes most of his time, he looks for a new one that allows him to keep his priorities in order.

The fifth priority is extended family and friends. Extended family is very important and can be a good source of support. Grandparents can provide wise advice for having a happy marriage and raising healthy kids. Aunts and uncles can be like second parents. Cousins can be like siblings to one's children. Holidays are always more special when spent with extended family. However, it's important to have healthy boundaries in these relationships. Parents and in-laws who are controlling and overbearing can cause strife in a family. A man in recovery ensures that extended family doesn't encroach on his immediate family life and makes sure they know his priorities.

Friends are also important, especially if one does not have a large extended family. Some men turn to pornography to ease the pain of loneliness for lack of friends. For these men, developing healthy friendships with other men is crucial for their recovery. Here is where Catholic men's ministries can help. However, just as with extended family, friendships must not overshadow immediate family relationships. A successful man in recovery maintains healthy friendships, yet he keeps them in the proper order of his priorities.

The sixth priority is self. This is a challenge because our society encourages people to be narcissistic. All over the media we hear about "getting one's needs met" and having "me time." People are led to believe that focusing on one's self is the key to happiness. This is an illusion. True happiness comes from emptying one's self and serving others. A successful man in recovery understands this and places all others before himself, realizing to do this he must care for himself physically, mentally, emotionally and spiritually. He cannot give of himself if he is not healthy. Thus, he exercises daily, eats a proper diet, gets adequate sleep, fosters healthy relationships, works on his spiritual life, maintains balance in life, and keeps his priorities straight.

Men who are single, whether lay, priests, or religious must also keep their priorities in order. For the single layman, his priorities might look like this:

1. God
2. Family and Friends
3. Career
4. Self

For a priest or religious, his priorities might look like this:

1. God
2. Vocation

3. Family and Friends
4. Self

Regardless of one's state in life, it's important to recognize that God must be one's first priority and self must be last. This is the key to a happy and healthy life.

Embracing the Mission

Maintaining the seven points of recovery, keeping one's priorities straight, and living a healthy, balanced life need not be difficult. All it takes is understanding one's mission. Throughout this book I have discussed the importance of men being leaders, providers, and protectors. This is the mission to which God has called all men. It is their duty. Women are leaders, providers, and protectors in their own way, but their primary mission is to be nurturers and helpmates. The man who embraces his role as leader, provider, and protector has a clear sense of his purpose. It permeates everything he does and gives him a great sense of satisfaction and fulfillment in life. To embrace this calling requires a man to strive to live a virtuous life. Here is how it applies to a married man and father:

- *Leader.* The successful man in recovery knows he must be a leader in his marriage, family, career, church, and community. He strives to live a virtuous life, and in doing so leads by example. Every day he makes sure he is doing everything necessary for his recovery. He keeps his priorities straight. He works with his wife to make healthy decisions for his marriage and his family. At work he strives to be an honest, hard-working employee. He is fair to the people who work under him and sets a good example for them. He is not afraid to take control in a crisis situation and make difficult decisions. For his kids, he models a healthy marital and fatherly relationship. As a spiritual leader in the home, he models a strong faith in God by actively practicing his faith with his family. He treats all people with love and respect, especially women. He places the needs of others ahead of his own needs.

- *Provider.* The successful man in recovery works hard to provide for his family's physical needs. He strives to succeed in his career so he can provide them with financial security. He also provides for their emotional and spiritual needs by being actively involved in their lives and their faith. This requires that he make his wife and children priorities over his career. He provides his family with a safe home. He makes sure his children get a proper education and passes on his Catholic faith to them. He teaches his children to be virtuous and to keep healthy priorities.

- *Protector.* The successful man in recovery protects his family from harmful influences of the culture, especially in the media. He monitors all media that enters the home. He protects his young children from pornography and educates his teenagers on the dangers of pornography. He also provides them with a safe home ensuring that no physical harm comes to them. Outside the home, he makes sure his family is safe from predators of any kind. This includes bullies in his kids' schools. He ensures that his wife is respected by others and defends her honor.

Maintaining sobriety becomes easier when a man fully embraces this God-given mission. By striving to live a virtuous life, he gains a clear vision of how he is supposed to live out this mission. He must be a leader, provider, and protector wherever he goes in life. This guides the way he looks at the world. For example, he'll see all women as children of God and worthy of his respect. He chooses to guard his eyes when he's out in public rather than ogle young women. He avoids pornography, as this attacks the dignity of all women as well as his own.

He focuses more specifically on being a leader, provider, and protector in his vocation. While I apply this to married men in this summary, it also applies to men who are priests, religious and single. A man can be a leader, provider, and protector in whatever state of life he is called—in one's family, parish, and community. For example, a single man needs to be a leader, provider, and protector among his friends, family, and colleagues. If he is dating, this applies to the relationship with his girlfriend. A priest must be a leader, provider, and protector as a spiritual father in his ministry.

Finally, a man strives to be a leader, provider, and protector in his career. Careers are very important to men and are where they find much of their identity. This requires a man to achieve success in a virtuous way. He is honest and hard-working, which often lead to promotions and greater opportunities in one's career.

Never Out of the Woods

Once a man has achieved a few months of sobriety, his greatest fear is having a relapse. Becoming complacent or overconfident in recovery is dangerous and can lead to letting one's guard down and leading to relapse. A successful man in recovery is never out of the woods. To avoid a relapse, a man must never forget what his life was like in the addiction. He must never forget the guilt and shame he lived with, how his actions hurt his wife, all the special moments with his kids he missed, how it hindered his career, and how it separated him from God. He constantly maintains all seven points of his recovery program. He keeps his priorities straight, and strives to live a balanced, healthy life. If he ever does struggle with temptation to view pornography or act out sexually, he immediately talks to his wife, accountability partners, and sponsor. He understands his weaknesses and makes sure they don't get the best of him. For the successful man in recovery, this is a lifelong quest. Even if he rarely experiences any temptations, he constantly maintains his recovery program.

Living a Life of Gratitude

In recovery it's all too easy to focus on what was lost as a result of the addiction. Instead, a man should focus on the many blessings in his life. Positive psychology has found that people who live lives of gratitude are happier and healthier, that there actually is value in "counting one's blessings." Thus, it's important to daily thank God for all the good things in one's life. For example, thanking God daily for the success one has achieved thus far in recovery can fill an addicted person with hope for a brighter future and give him strength to continue in recovery. Being thankful can also help a person let go of shame and self-hatred by helping him realize how much God loves him.

Changing Core Beliefs

Addicted people often live their lives by five core beliefs (adapted from Carnes 2001):

1. I am unworthy of being loved.
2. If people really knew me, they would reject me.
3. I cannot trust anyone, including God, to meet my needs.
4. I must find something that I can control that will meet my needs.
5. Pornography/Sex is my greatest need and source of comfort.

However, the successful man in recovery understands and changes these faulty core beliefs. Through the unconditional love and acceptance he has received from his therapist, support group, accountability partners, sponsor, wife, family, and God, he has come to understand his true value and dignity. Now he lives his life by four new core beliefs:

1. I am loveable.
2. If people really knew me, they would love me more.
3. I can trust God and others to meet my needs.
4. God and healthy relationships are my greatest need and source of comfort.

With these new core beliefs, he can enjoy healthy relationships and finally receive the intimacy he always needed. He is able to forgive those who hurt him that led him to developing unhealthy core beliefs.

There is no need to self-medicate with pornography, and if he ever does feel tempted he reminds himself of his new core beliefs and seeks to meet his needs in a healthy way.

Renewed Confidence

Altogether, the successful man in recovery has a renewed confidence and enthusiasm for life. He enjoys the present and looks forward to the future. He no longer lives in hopelessness and despair, nor does he live his life in fear or shame. Through his faith he is able to see himself as a new creation in Christ. He is able to make short-term, mid-term, and long-term plans for his life, and accomplish them. He is not trapped in the past. While he may not be proud of the things he has done, he does not allow his past to dictate his present or future. He uses his past mistakes as learning experiences to ensure he doesn't make the same mistakes.

This renewed confidence helps him in several areas of life. First, it helps him live a virtuous life and be the leader, provider, and protector that God created him to be. He understands his God-given gifts and talents and is unafraid to use them. Second, he is no longer a pushover. He loves and respects others, yet he refuses to be exploited. Third, it improves relationships in every area of his life. In his marriage, his wife is impressed with the way he is now able to be an effective head of the family. She can count on him to always be there for her and their children. She can now trust him more fully. In his career, he has the confidence to go above and beyond the call of duty. This effort is recognized by his employer and can result in pay raises and promotions. The people who work under him respect him more because he strives to help them advance in their careers. In his parish and community, he is recognized as an effective leader and enjoys a respect he never had before.

Although this renewed confidence comes with many benefits, the successful man in recovery maintains his humility, understanding that everything he has and all of his accomplishments are because of God. He is man enough to give God the full credit.

NEW LIFE IN RECOVERY

Paying it Forward

As a man achieves success in recovery he often finds the need to help others who suffer from addiction, wanting them to experience the new life and freedom he has achieved. Just as God blessed him with so many good people, he now wants to be one of those blessings for others who are struggling with their own addictions. Thus, he helps by offering to be an accountability partner or sponsor for them, or he may also take a leadership role in his support group. Some recovering from their addiction are so moved by the joy of helping others that they attend graduate school to study psychology so they can become addictions therapists.

Paying it forward gives those recovering from addiction the joy of giving back, and it also helps them continue their own recovery. It has been said to truly learn a subject one must teach it. As addicted persons teach others about recovery, they reinforce it in themselves, and this makes recovery even more successful and long-lasting. This is the secret to a successful long-term recovery for many addicted persons.

Hope for the Future

While recovery is work, the payoff is worth it. Recovery is not white-knuckling it through temptations to prevent acting out. It means working with other people so that you are never alone in recovery. It means resolving the root causes of your addiction, changing core beliefs, and living a healthier life. It means growing closer to God, healing and restoring relationships, enjoying the present, and looking forward to a bright future. While you are never out of the woods, and recovery will have to be a lifestyle for you, it's one that is full of joy and hope. When compared to the lifestyle of one who remains active in his addiction, the recovery lifestyle means freedom!

If you are struggling with pornography use, I urge you to seek help. There is no need to continue living enslaved to pornography with hopelessness and despair. God has a wonderful plan for your life! In Jeremiah 29:11 we read, "For I know the plans I have for you, says the Lord, plans for welfare and not for evil, to give you a future and a hope." This applies to addicted individuals and their loved ones. Like the Israelites in the Book of Nehemiah, God wants to bring restoration into your life. However, you cannot do it alone. You need the help of others who understand the struggle and the recovery process. Fortunately, God has provided many compassionate people willing to help.

For the wife of an addicted husband, don't lose hope. Remember that an addiction is not a moral failing. It's a disease. No one sets out to become addicted. It is usually the result of years of self-medicating deep emotional wounds. It has nothing to do with your beauty or desirability as a woman. Your husband doesn't want to replace you with the women in porn. Most of all, he never wanted to hurt you, and more than anyone else, he needs your love and support as he works through the recovery process. At the same time, you need to heal from the pain of betrayal you have experienced as a result of the addiction. I urge you to seek counseling and support for your healing. God has given you many caring people who understand your pain and want to help you heal. Things may seem bleak right now, but I assure you that God has a wonderful plan for your marriage. He wants to give you a healthy and happy marriage. This is what innumerable couples have experienced. With God all things are possible!

For more information on the pornography epidemic, pornography addiction, protecting families, and where those suffering from addiction and their loved ones can find help, log onto www.IntegrityRestored.com. There you will find valuable information, videos, checklists, and resources for recovery. You can also find out about my *Fighting Porn in Our Culture . . . and Winning!* conferences. The healing process can begin today!

May God bless you in your journey to healing and wholeness!
Peter C. Kleponis, PhD

Bibliography

ABC News. (2013). Survey: Kids access porn sites at 6, start flirting online at 8. Retrieved on June 5, 2014 from http://archive.news10.net/news/national/245195/5/Survey-Kids-access-porn-sites-at-6-start-flirting-online-at-8

Adschiew, B. (2000, June 24). A Web Workers. *NBC Nightly News.*

American Psychological Association (2007). *APA task force on the sexualization of girls.* Retrieved on November 1, 2010 from http://www.apa.org/pi/women/programs/girls/report-full.pdf

APA task force on the sexualization of girls (2007). Retrieved on May 15, 2013 from www.apa.org/pi/women/programs/girls/report.aspx.

Associated Press. (2000, July 28). Dow chemical fires 50 over offensive E-Mail. CNET News. http://news.cnet.com/news/0-1007-200-2372621.html

Balderrama, A. (2007). Generation Y: Too demanding at work? Retrieved August 1, 2009 from http://www.careerbuilder.com/Article/CB-778-The-Workplace- Generation-Y-Too-Demanding-at-Work/

Benedict XVI, Pope (2006). *Deus Caritas Est,* Washington, DC: USCCB.

Black, S. (2013). The porn circuit; Understand your brain and break porn habits in 90 days. Owosso, MI: CovenantEyes. Retrieved May 15, 2013 from http://www.covenanteyes.com/science-of-porn-addiction-ebook

Bonino, S, Ciairano, S., Rabaglietti, E., Cattelino, E. (2006). Use of pornography and self-reported engagement in sexual violence among adolescents, in *European Journal of Developmental Psychology,* 3, pp. 265–88.

Bridges, A. J., Wosnitzer, R., Scharrer, E., Sun, C., & Liberman, R. (2010). Aggression and sexual behavior in best-selling pornography videos: A content analysis update violence against women. Retrieved on June 5, 2014 from http://vaw.sagepub.com/content/16/10/1065

Carnes, P. (1989). *Contrary to love: Helping the sexual addict.* Center City, MN: Hazelden Foundation.

Carnes, P. (1991). *Don't call it love: Recovery from sexual addiction.* New York, NY: Bantam Books.

Carnes, P., Delmonico, D. L., & Griffin, E. (2007). *In the shadows of the net: Breaking free of compulsive online sexual behavior.* Center City, MN: Hazelden Foundation.

Carnes, P. (2001). *Out of the shadows: Understanding sexual addiction.* Center City, MN: Hazelden Foundation.

Carroll et al. (2008). D. Zillman and J. Bryant. Pornography's impact on sexual satisfaction. *Journal of Applied Social Psychology* 18, no. 5 (1988): 438–53.

Centers for Disease Control (2011). STDs in adolescents and young adults in *2011 sexually transmitted disease surveillance.* Retrieved on May 26, 2013 from http://www.cdc.gov/std/stats11/adol.htm

Collins, L. A. (2000). "Dow Chemical Fires 50 Over E-Mail." http://news.excite.com/news/ap/000727/18/dow-chemical-e-mail July 27, 2000.

Covenant Eyes (2011). Porn U: Protecting purity at college. Retrieved on March 24, 2013 from http://www.covenanteyes.com/2011/09/16/porn-u-protecting-purity-at-college/

Covenant Eyes, (2013). *Unfiltered: A parent workshop kit.* Owosso, MI: Covenant Eyes.

Creighton Model, (2006). The Creighton model fertility care system. Retrieved on August 20, 2013 from http://www.creightonmodel.com

Delmonico, D. L. (2000). *Internet sex screening test.* Pittsburgh, PA: Duquesne University.

Dines, G. (2010). *Pornland: How porn has hijacked out sexuality.* Boston: Beacon Press.

Dixon, K. (2005). Weighing the costs of presenteeism. *Chief Executive*, June 2005.

Doran K. & Price, J. "Movies and marriage: Do some films harm marital happiness?" in progress, 2009.

Eberstadt, M. & Layden, M. A. (2010). *The social costs of pornography: A statement of findings and recommendations.* Princeton, NJ: The Witherspoon Institute.

Family Safe Media (2010). Pornography statistics. Retrieved on January 1, 2011 from http://familysafemedia.com/pornography_statistics.html

Ferree, M. (2002). *No stones: Women redeemed from sexual shame*. Fairfax, VA: Xulon.

Finn, R. W. (2007). *Blessed are the pure in heart: A pastoral letter on the dignity of the human person and the dangers of pornography*. New Haven, CT: Knights of Columbus, Catholic Information Service.

Fitzgibbons, R. P. (2010). *The sexual utilitarian philosophy*. West Conshohocken, PA: The Institute for Marital Healing.

Gilkerson, L. (2012). Why young women are now being drawn to pornography. Retrieved on April 17, 2013 from http://www.covenanteyes.com/2012/07/27/why-young-women-are-now-being-drawn-to-pornography

Giordano & Ross, 2012; Flood, 2009; Lauzus et al, 2007; Wade et al, 2005. Stop Porn Culture. Retrieved on June 5, 2005 from http://stopornculture.org/about/about-the-issue/facts-and-figures-2/

Goodenough, P. (2003). Online porn driving sexually aggressive children. Retrieved on May 22, 2013 from CNSNews.com

Gray, D. (2013). BLAST Acronym. Adapted from *Reclaim Sexual Health*. n.p. Kaukauna, WI: Elizabeth Ministry International & Candeo. Retrieved on February 19, 2013 from http://reclaimsexualhealth.com

Herr, N. (2007). Television and health. *The source book for teaching science*. Northridge, CA: California State University. Retrieved on September 4, 2013 from http://www.csun.edu/science/health/docs/tv&health.html

Hewitt, J. (1998). *The myth of self-esteem*. New York: St Martin's Press.

Hilton, D. L. & Watts, C. (2011). Pornography addiction: a neuroscience perspective. *Surgical Neurology International*. n.p. Available from http://www.surgicalneurologyint.com/text.asp?2011/2/1/19/76977

Huffington Post (2011). University of Chicago Student launches casual sex website, UChicago hookups. Retrieved on April 4, 2013 from http://www.huffingtonpost.com/2011/03/17/university-of-chicago-stu_1_n_837205.html

Huffington Post (2012). Porn & Relationships: Men's pornography use tied to lower self-esteem in female partners. Retrieved on June 5, 2014 from http://www.huffingtonpost.com/2012/06/01/porn-relationships-men-female-partner-self-esteem_n_1562821.html?ref=women

Huffington Post (2012). Women really hate porn? An interview with Carlin Ross. Retrieved on June 5, 2014 from http://www.huffingtonpost.com/jincey-lumpkin/carlin-ross_b_1278032.html

Huffington Post (2013). Porn sites get more visitors each month than Netflix, Amazon and Twitter combined. Retrieved on June 5, 2014 from http://www.huffingtonpost.com/2013/05/03/internet-porn-stats_n_3187682.html

Hughs, D. R. (1997). Interview with Ann Burgess, professor of nursing, University of Pennsylvania, 15 January 1997. Pornography—victims and perpetrators, *Symposium on media violence &pornography, proceedings resource book and research guide, ed. D. Scott (1984).*

Jennings, D. R. (2013). The average life expectancy of a porn star. Retrieved on March 29, 2013 from http://danielrjennings.org/TheAverageLifeExpectancyOfAPornStar.html

Joiner, L. M. (2008). *Congregants' responses to clergy pornography addiction.* PhD dissertation, Lubbock, TX: Texas Tech University.

Kaiser, (2001). Sex on tv: Content and Context. *The Henry J. Kaiser Foundation Report*, 5 February 2001.

Kastleman, M. B. (2007). *The drug of the new millennium: The brain science behind Internet pornography use.* Provo, UT: PowerThink Publishing.

Kavanaugh, S. J. (1997). *Protecting children from cyberspace.* Springfield, VA: Behavioral Psychotherapy Center.

Kleponis, P. C. (2012). *The pornography epidemic: A Catholic approach.* Oldsmar, FL: Simon Peter Press.

Laaser, M. (2004), *Healing the wounds of sexual addiction.* Grand Rapids, MI: Zondervan.

Laaser, M. (2009), *Freedom begins here: Counselor toolkit workbook.* Siloam Springs, AR: Gray Communications, Inc.

Layden, M. A. (2004). "The science behind pornography addiction," U.S. senate committee on commerce, science, & transportation, November 18, 2004. Retrieved on April 30, 2013 from http://www.ccv.org/wp-content/uploads/2010/04/Judith_Reisman_Senate_Testimony-2004.11.18.pdf

Le, J. (2012, June). The digital divide: How the online behavior of teens is getting past parents. McAfee.com. Retrieved on December 9, 2013 from http://www.mcafee.com/us/resources/misc/digital-divide-study.pdf

Love and Responsibility Foundation (2002). *John Paul II on love and responsibility: Summer 2000 edition.* New York: Author.

Loverde, Bishop Paul S. (2006). *Love undefiled: A pastoral letter on the evils of pornography.* Arlington, VA: Diocese of Arlington.

Luben, Shelly (2010). *Truth behind the fantasy of porn: The greatest illusion on earth.* Seattle: CreateSpace Publishing/Amazon.

Mark (2007). Pornography, sex addiction, and the workplace. Retrieved on March 24, 2013 from http://sexual-sanity.com/2007/04/sex-addiction-and-the-work-place

Medical Daily (2013). Disturbing new survey reveals how porn is damaging relationships. Retrieved on June 5, 2014 from http://www.medicaldaily.com/disturbing-new-survey-reveals-how-porn-damaging-relationships-244335

Mitchell, K. D., Finkelhor, D., and Wolak, J. (2003). The exposure of youth to unwanted sexual material on the Internet: A national survey of risk, impact and prevention, *Youth and Society* 34, no. 3. pp. 330–58.; Mitchell, K.D., Finkelhor, D., and Wolak, J. (2003), Victimization of youth on the Internet, *The victimization of children: Emerging issues.* Binghamton, NY: Haworth Maltreatment & Trauma Press.

NFP & More, (n.d.) Comparing effectiveness rates. Retrieved on June 5, 2014 from http://ccli.org/nfp/effectiveness/compare-methods.php

Paintbottle (2013). Everyone you know watches porn. Retrieved on June 5, 2014 from http://www.huffingtonpost.com/2013/05/03/internet-porn-stats_n_3187682.html

Paolucci-Oddone, E., Genuis, M., & Violato, C. (2000). A meta-analysis on the published research on the effects of pornography. In Violato, C., Paolucci-Oddone, E., & Genuis, M. (2000). *The changing family and child development.* Aldershot, England: Ashgate Publishing.

Paul, P. (2004, January 19). The porn factor. *Time.*

Peter, J. and Valkenburg, P. M. (2007). Adolescents' exposure to a sexualized media environment and their notions of women as sex objects, *Sex Roles*, 56. February 2007, pp. 381–95.

Phillips, K. A. (2001). Body dysmorphic disorder in men. *BMJ Journal.* n.p. Retrieved on February 17, 2013 from http://www.ncbi.nlm.nih.gov/pmc/articles/PMC1121529/

Pickett, D., & Fuller, J. R. (2003, April 27). Teens shifting balance of power. *Chicago Sun-Times.* Retrieved August 1, 2009 from http://www.bus.iastate.edu/news /2003/042703.asp

Pyle, R. (2011, September 2). City reveals names of employees tapped for viewing porn. *Avalanche-Journal*, n.p. Retrieved on March 24, 2013 from http://lubbockonline.com/crime-and-courts/2011-09-02

Reclaim (2013). Rescue our youth from the porn trap: Parent primer. Kaukauna, WI: Elizabeth Ministry International.

Reiss, M. (2006). What happens when everyone's a winner? Some ask whether feel-good trophies are actually good for children. *The Boston Globe.* Retrieved August 8, 2009 from http://www.boston.com/news/local/articles /2006/02/23/ what_happens_when_everyones_a_winner/

Remley, A. (1988). From obedience to independence. *Psychology Today*, 22(10), 56–59.

Renaud, C. (2011). *Dirty Girls Come Clean*. Chicago: Moody Publishers.

Sex Tracker (2012). Facts and Figures. Stop Porn Culture. Retrieved on June 5, 2014 from http://stoppornculture.org/about/about-the-issue/facts-and-figures-2/

Sprigg, P. & Dailey T. (2004). Getting it straight: What research shows about homosexuality. Washington DC: Family Research Council.

Stack, S., Wasserman, I., and Kern, R. (2004, March). Adult social bonds and use of Internet pornography. *Social Science Quarterly*, 85, no. 1: 75–88.

Steffens, B. & Means, M. (2009). *Your sexually addicted spouse: How partners can cope and heal*. Far Hills, NJ: New Horizons Press.

Struthers, W. M. (2009). *Wired for intimacy: How pornography hijacks the male brain*. Downers Grove, IL: Intervarsity Press.

Tennant, P. (2010, November 7). Ex-pastor accused of taking $83K from parish. *Eagle Tribune*. Retrieved on June 5, 2014 from http://www.eagletribune.com/haverhill/x603547561/Ex-pastor-accused-of-taking-83K-from-parish

The Family Research Council (n.d.). Benefits of family for children and adults. The Family Research Council. Retrieved on June 5, 2014 from http://www.familyfacts.org/briefs/6/benefits-of-family-for-children-and-adults

The Independent (2013, September 22). Pornography addiction leads to same brain activity as alcoholism or drug abuse, study shows. *The Independent*. Retrieved on June 5, 2014 from http://www.independent.co.uk/life-style/health-and-families/health-news/pornography-addiction-   leads-to-same-brain-activity-as-alcoholism-or-drug-abuse-study-shows-8832708.html

The leadership survey: Pastors viewing Internet pornography (2001). *Leadership Journal*, 22, no. 1. 87–89.

The trophy kids go to work. (2008, October 21). *The Wall Street Journal (Eastern Edition)*, p. D1. ProQuest Document ID:1579698661.

Twelve Steps of Sexaholics Anonymous. Retrieved on July 27, 3013 from http://www.sa.org/steps.php

Twenge, J. M., & Campbell, W. K. (2003). Isn't it fun to get all the respect we're going to deserve?: Narcissism, social rejection, and aggression. *Personality and Social Psychology Bulletin*, 29(2), 261–272. doi: 10.1177/0146167202239051.

Twenge, J. M. (2006). *Generation me: Why today's young americans are more confident, assertive, entitled—and more miserable than ever*. New York: Free Press.

Twenge, J. M., Konrath, S., Foster, J. D., Campbell, W. K. & Bushman, B. J. (2008). Egos inflating over time: A cross-temporal meta-analysis of the narcissistic personality inventory. *Journal of Personality*, 76(4), 875–902. Doi: 10.1111/j.1467–6494. 2008.00507.x.

Twenge, J. M., & Campbell, W. K. (2009). *The narcissism epidemic: Living in the age of entitlement.* New York: Free Press.

USCCB (n.d.). Why children need married Parents. United States Conference of Catholic Bishops. Retrieved on June 5, 2014 from http://www.usccb.org/issues-and-action/marriage-and-family/children/children.cfm

United States Department of Justice (1996). Post hearing memorandum of points ad authorities, at *ACLU v. Reno*, 292 F. Supp. 824. Washington, DC.

Ward, L. M. & Friedman, K. (2006). Using TV as a guide: Associations between television viewing and adolescents' sexual attitudes and behaviors, *Journal of Research on Adolescents*. 16, no. 1. March 2006, pp. 133–56.

Warren, R. (2002). *The purpose driven life.* Grand Rapids, MI: Zondervan.

Washington Times (2009, September 29). Exclusive: Porn surfing rampant at U.S. Science Foundation. *Washington Times*. Retrieved on June 5, 2014 from http://www.washingtontimes.com/news/2009/sep/29/workers-porn-surfing-rampant-at-federal-agency/?page=all

Websense Inc., (2000). *Survey on Internet Misuse in the Workplace.* March 2000, 1–6.

Weiss, D. (2000). *Informal survey of 58 pastors at the National Coalition for the Protection of Children and Families*, Cincinnati: OH.

Weiss, R. (2014, January 20). Is male porn use ruining sex? Are men becoming totally out of sync with real-world romantic relationships? *Psychology Today*. Retrieved on June 5, 2014 from http://www.psychologytoday.com/blog/love-and-sex-in-the-digital-age/201401/is-male-porn-use-ruining-sex

West, C. (2004). Good news about sex and marriage. Cincinnati: Franciscan Media.

West, C. (2004). *The theology of the body for beginners: A basic introduction to John Paul II's sexual revolution.* West Chester, PA: Ascension Press.

Wilson, G. (2012, January 17). Why do I find porn more exciting than a partner? Neuroscience reveals how Internet porn can trump real sex. *Psychology Today*. Retrieved on February 26, 2013 from http://www.psychologytoday.com/blog/cupids-poisoned-arrow/201201/why-do-i-find-porn-more-exciting-partner

Winograd, D. (2013, November 11). CEOs gone wild: Executives watching porn is a leading cause of corporate malware. *Time*. Retrieved on June 5, 2014 from http://newsfeed.time.com/2013/11/11/ceos-gone-wild-executives-watching-porn-is-a-leading-cause-of-corporate-malware/?utm_ content=buffer23819&utm_source=buffer&utm_medium=twitter&utm_campaign=Buffer.

Wojtyla, K. (1993). *Love and responsibility*, trans. H.T. Willets. San Francisco: Ignatius.

Wolack, J., Mitchell, K. J., & Finkelhorn, D. (2006). Online victimization of youth: Five years later. Retrieved on May 22, 2013 from www.unh.edu/ccrc/pdf/CV138.pdf

Young-Eisendrath, P. (2008). *The self-esteem trap: Raising confident, compassionate kids in an age of self-importance*. New York: Little Brown.

Zillman, D. (2000). Influence of unrestrained access to erotica on adolescents' and young adults' dispositions toward sexuality. *Journal of Adolescent Health*, 27S(2), 41–44.

Appendix: Recommended Resources

Below are resources I recommend for those who want to protect themselves and their families from pornography. I have also included resources to help those who struggle with pornography addiction.

Books

THE PORNOGRAPHY EPIDEMIC

- *Every Man's Battle* and *Every Young Man's Battle*
  by Stephen Arterburn, Fred Stoeker, and Mike Yorkey

- *Preparing Your Son for Every Man's Battle*
  by Stephen Arterburn

- *Getting Off: Pornography and the End of Masculinity*
  by Robert Jensen

- *Pornified: How Pornography Is Damaging Our Lives, Our Relationships, and Our Families*
  by Pamela Paul

- *Pornland: How Porn has Hijacked Our Sexuality*
  by Gail Dines

- *The Drug of the New Millennium: The Brain Science Behind Internet Pornography*
  by Mark B. Kastleman

- *The Pornography Epidemic: A Catholic Approach*
  by Peter C. Kleponis, PhD

- *Wired for Intimacy: How Pornography Hijacks the Male Brain*
  by William M. Struthers

PORNOGRAPHY ADDICTION & RECOVERY

- *Breaking Free: 12 Steps to Sexual Purity*
  by Stephen Wood

- *Clean: A Proven Plan for Men Committed to Sexual Integrity*
  by Douglas Weiss

- *Delivered: True Stories of Men and Women Who Turned from Porn to Purity*
  by Matt Fradd

- *Don't Call It Love: Recovery from Sexual Addiction*
  by Patrick Carnes, PhD

- *Facing the Shadow*
  by Patrick Carnes, PhD

- *Faithful and True: Sexual Integrity in a Fallen World*
  by Mark Laaser and Eli Machen

- *Healing the Wounds of Sexual Addiction*
  by Mark Laaser

- *In the Shadows of the Net*
  by Patrick Carnes PhD, David L. Delmonico PhD,
  Elizabeth Griffin, MA, and Joseph M. Moriarity

- *L.I.F.E. Guide for Men*
  by Mark Laaser

- *Out of the Shadows*
  by Patrick Carnes, PhD

- *Pure Eyes*
  by Craig Gross and Steven Luff

- *The Pornography Epidemic: A Catholic Approach*
  by Peter C. Kleponis, PhD

- *The Pornography Trap:*
  Setting Pastors and Laypersons Free from Sexual Addiction
  by Mark Laaser, PhD and Ralph H. Earle Jr.

- *The Porn Trap: The Essential Guide to*
  Overcoming Problems Caused by Pornography
  by Wendy and Larry Maltz

- *Treating Pornography Addiction:*
  The Essential Tools for Recovery
  by Kevin B. Skinner, PhD

RECOVERY FOR WOMEN

- *Dirty Girls Come Clean*
  by Crystal Renaud

- *L.I.F.E. Guide for Women*
  by Marnie C. Ferree

- *No Stones: Women Redeemed from Sexual Shame*
  by Marnie C. Ferree

- *No Stones: Women Redeemed from Sexual Addiction*
  by Marnie C. Ferree and Mark Laaser, PhD

HELP FOR WIVES

- *Every Heart Restored: A Wife's Guide to*
  Healing in the Wake of a Husband's Sexual Sin
  by Fred Stoeker, Brenda Stoeker, and Mike Yorkey

- *Facing Heartbreak:*
  Steps to Recovery for Partners of Sex Addicts
  by Stefanie Carnes, Mari A. Lee, and
  Anthony D. Rodriguez

- *Hope After Betrayal:*
  Healing When Sexual Addiction Invades Your Marriage
  by Meg Wilson

- *A L.I.F.E. Guide for Spouses*
  by Melissa Haas

- *Shattered Vows: Hope and Healing for*
  Women Who Have Been Sexually Betrayed
  by Debra Laaser

- *The Pornography Epidemic: A Catholic Approach*
  by Peter C. Kleponis, PhD

- *When His Secret Sin Breaks Your Heart:*
  Letters to Hurting Wives
  by Kathy Gallagher

- *Your Sexually Addicted Spouse:*
  How Partners Can Cope and Heal
  by Barbara Steffens and Marsha Means

AUTHENTIC MANHOOD

- *Be a Man!*
  by Fr. Larry Richards

- *Becoming a Man of Valor*
  by Mark Laaser, PhD

- *Boys to Men*
  by Tim Gray and Curtis Martin

- *Man to Man, Dad to Dad: Catholic Faith and Fatherhood*
  Edited by Brian Caulfield

MARRIAGE

- *Open Hearts: Renewing Relationships with*
  Recovery, Romance & Reality
  by Patrick Carnes, PhD, Debra Laaser, and Mark Laaser, PhD

- *Seven Desires: Looking Past What Separates Us to Learn What Connects Us*
  by Mark Laaser, PhD and Debra Laaser

- *The 5 Love Languages: The Secret to Love that Lasts*
  by Gary D. Chapman

HEALTHY SEXUALITY

- *Good News about Sex and Marriage*
  by Christopher West

- *Holy Sex! A Catholic Guide to Toe-Curling, Mind-Blowing, Infallible Loving*
  by Greg K. Popcak, PhD

- *Parent Guide to Human Sexuality Edited*
  by the Archdiocese of New York

- *Theology of the Body Explained*
  by Christopher West

- *Theology of the Body for Beginners*
  by Christopher West

Websites

THE PORNOGRAPHY EPIDEMIC

- www.theporneffect.blogspot.com: a website created by Matt Fradd to educate Catholics on the dangers of pornography

- www.IntegrityRestored.com: a website created by Peter C. Kleponis that is designed for Catholic men and teens struggling with pornography use

- www.moralityinmedia.org: the leading national organization opposing pornography and indecency through public education and the application of the law

PORNOGRAPHY ADDICTION AND RECOVERY

- www.nyfamilylife.org/chastity/truefreedom/: a website sponsored by the Archdiocese of New York that provides resources for overcoming pornography use

- www.freedomeveryday.org: a site sponsored by L.I.F.E. Ministries (Living In Freedom Everyday), a sexual addiction recovery ministry

- www.IntegrityRestored.com: a website created by Peter C. Kleponis that is designed for Catholic men and teens struggling with pornography use

- www.pornnomore.com: a Catholic website of information, prayers, and witness talks for those struggling with pornography

- www.settingcaptivesfree.com: a Christian website addressing a number of addictions, including pornography

- www.reclaimsexualhealth.com: an online program designed to help people overcome unwanted sexual behavior

- www.x3pure.com: an online sex and pornography addiction recovery resources site that utilizes online workshops

- www.archkck.org/myhouse: a website created by Sam Meier to educate Catholics on the dangers of pornography

RECOVERY FOR WOMEN

- www.beggarsdaughter.com: a website and blog for Catholic women struggling with pornography addiction

- www.dirtygirlsministries.com: a website and an online community for women struggling with pornography addiction

SUPPORT GROUPS

- Sexaholics Anonymous: www.sa.org

- S-Anon International: www.sanon.org

- Sex Addicts Anonymous: www.saa.org

- Sex and Love Addicts Anonymous: www.slaafws.org

- Celebrate Recovery: www.celebraterecovery.com

APPENDIX: RECOMMENDED RESOURCES

- Co-Addicts in Recovery–COSA: www.cosa-recovery.org
- L.I.F.E. Recovery Groups: www.freedomeveryday.org
- My House Catholic Men's Groups: www.archkck.org/myhouse
- New Life Partners: www.newlifepartners.com
- Recovering Couples Anonymous: www.recovering-couples.org

AUTHENTIC MANHOOD

- www.crossingthegoal.com: a website dedicated to helping men embrace authentic Catholic manhood

- www.familylifecenter.net: the official website for St. Joseph's Covenant Keepers and Family Life Center International

- www.fathersforgood.org: a parenting website sponsored by the Knights of Columbus

- www.focusonthefamily.com: a website that provides Christian resources for being a Godly man, husband, and father

MEN'S MINISTRIES

- Crossing the Goal Workout Groups: www.crossingthegoal.com
  Crossing the Goal Ministries was created to be an outreach ministry to men concerning their spiritual well-being. Workout groups bring Catholic men together to challenge each other to become spiritually fit.

- Knights of Columbus: www.kofc.org
  The Knights of Columbus is an international men's organization dedicated to fraternity, charitable service, promoting Catholic education, and actively defending Catholicism.

- National Fellowship of Catholic Men: www.nfcmusa.org
  The National Fellowship of Catholic Men is an international organization dedicated to encouraging and assisting every Catholic diocese in developing a robust Catholic men's apostolate for the calling, equipping, and development of men to live authentic, masculine, Catholic lives in all spheres of their life.

349

- St. Joseph's Covenant Keepers: www.familylifecenter.net
  St. Joseph's Covenant Keepers is an informal international network of Christian men, under the patronage of St. Joseph, dedicated to strengthening fatherhood and the family.

- That Man is You!:
  www.paradisusdei.org/index.php/programs/tmiy/
  That Man is You! is a national Catholic men's leadership ministry operating throughout the United States and Canada. It seeks to form men who will be leaders capable of transforming themselves, their families, and greater society.

- The King's Men: www.thekingsmen.org
  Under Christ the King's universal call to serve, The King's Men pledge to unite and build up one other to be leaders, protectors, and providers through education, formation, and action.

INTERNET SAFETY

- www.covenanteyes.com: an accountability service for those struggling with internet pornography.

- www.familysafemedia.com: a website that provides resources for protecting your family online

- www.filterreview.com: a website that describes and rates different internet filters

- www.nyfamilylife.org/chastity/truefreedom/: a website sponsored by the Archdiocese of New York that provides resources for overcoming pornography use

- www.isafe.org: a website for internet safety education

- www.moralityinmedia.org: the leading national organization opposing pornography and Indecency through public education and the application of the law

- www.national-coalition.org: a website for the National Coalition for the Protection of Children and Families

HEALTHY SEXUALITY

- www.catholicmodesty.com: a site promoting modesty in dress
- www.tobinstitute.org: website of the Theology of the Body Institute

MARRIAGE

- www.journeytohealingandjoy.com: online resources, support groups, and coaching for women whose husbands are addicted to pornography
- www.maritalhealing.com: the official website of The Institute for Marital Healing
- www.newlifepartners.com: a support group for wives whose husbands are caught in the web of sexual addiction
- www.recovering-couples.org: a support group for couples affected by sexual addiction
- www.sanon.org: a support group for spouses and families of sex addicts

Counselors

A counselor is often the first person that people contact for help with pornography addiction. There are several types of counselors that can help:

- Psychiatrists
- Psychologists
- Therapists
- Social Workers

Ensure the counselor you seek is qualified to treat pornography/sexual addiction. The counselor must be licensed to practice and certified in the diagnosis and treatment of sexual addiction. Counselors are licensed by the states in which they practice. They must have at least a master's degree, pass a state licensing exam, and take annual continuing education courses to maintain their license. This ensures they maintain their skills. There are several independent organizations that certify counselors in the treatment and diagnosis of sexual addiction. They include:

- The American Association for Sex Addiction Therapy Training Program (AASAT) founded by Doug Weiss, PhD

- The American Association of Christian Counselors' Light University Training Program

- The Freedom Begins Here Counselor Training Program founded by Mark Laaser, PhD

- The International Institute for Trauma and Addiction Training Program (IITAP) founded by Patrick Carnes, PhD

For help from a Catholic counselor, contact the following organizations:
- Peter C. Kleponis, PhD
  Comprehensive Counseling Services
  West Conshohocken, PA
  The Integrity Restored Recovery Program
  www.IntegrityRestored.com

- CatholicTherapists.com: a nationwide listing of Catholic therapists. All are licensed and some are certified in the diagnosis and treatment of sexual addiction

- **Coming Soon!** *The Integrity Restored Network*: a nationwide network of Catholic therapists, all of whom are licensed and certified in the diagnosis and treatment of sexual addiction

Films
- *Blessed are the Pure in Heart*: a six-part DVD series on the dignity of the human person and the dangers of pornography, based

on Bishop Robert Finn's 2007 Pastoral Letter of the same title. Produced by the Apostolate for Family Consecration (January 2008)

- *Out of the Darkness:* the incredible story of an ex-porn star's journey from a life in pornography to new life in Christ (2012)

- *Hope Undimmed*: a video presenting the real story about the effects of pornography from producers, consumers, and medical experts. Produced by Paradisus Dei (2010)

- *The Man Talk:* Matthew Fradd lays out a vision for authentic Catholic masculinity and a plan for how to achieve it. Following the examples of some of history's greatest and wisest Christian men, he shows how to build the strengths and practice the habits that will make men true men of God

- *The Porn Trap*: two thirty-minute episodes from the Crossing The Goal series focusing on pornography addiction in men. Produced by EWTN (February 2011)

- *Unfiltered: Equipping Parents for an Ongoing Conversation about Internet Pornography*: Parent workshop kit produced by Covenant Eyes (2013)

- *What's That Purple Building, Daddy?:* a documentary DVD on the dangers of pornography produced by As Written Productions and The King's Men (January 2010)

Training Conferences with
Dr. Peter C. Kleponis

Pornography addiction is an epidemic in America. Millions are affected, and Catholics are not immune. Today, pornography use is one of the most common sins heard in Confession. Pornography addiction is damaging marriages, families, careers and personal lives. There is an urgent need to educate Catholics on the dangers of pornography, how to protect families and how to help those who are addicted.

To meet this urgent need, Dr. Peter Kleponis developed the *Fighting Porn in our Culture . . . and Winning!* conference program. The conference talks cover:

- The Pornography Epidemic in America
- The Path of Pornography Addiction
- The Road to Recovery from Addiction
- Protecting Families from Pornography

Since 2010, Dr. Kleponis has presented over 50 conferences across the United States and internationally to thousands of Catholics. The conferences are excellent for priests, seminarians, religious, Family Life Office staffs, D.R.E.s, youth leaders, teachers, parents and teens.

Several Catholic news sources have published articles about Dr. Kleponis's work, including *Zenit* and *Our Sunday Visitor*. He has also been a guest on EWTN's *Crossing the Goal, Women of Grace,* and *Franciscan University Presents*, as well as numerous Catholic radio programs discussing this issue. You can learn more about Dr. Kleponis's work by logging onto his website:

www.IntegrityRestored.com

Dr. Kleponis has recently published *The Pornography Epidemic: A Catholic Approach*. This book can be purchased at www.WomenofGrace.com

To schedule a *Fighting Porn in Our Culture . . . and Winning!* conference, please contact Dr. Kleponis at 610-397-0960. It is his goal to ensure that all Catholics are trained to effectively deal with this epidemic.